After the Happily Ever After

Funded by the Government of Canada
Financé par la gouvernement du Canada | Canadä

Demeter Press
140 Holland Street West
P. O. Box 13022
Bradford, ON L3Z 2Y5
Tel: (905) 775-9089
Email: info@demeterpress.org
Website: www.demeterpress.org

Demeter Press logo based on the sculpture "Demeter" by Maria-Luise Bodirsky
www.keramik-atelier.bodirsky.de

Printed and Bound in Canada

Front cover artwork: Jessica Ennis

Library and Archives Canada Cataloguing in Publication

Ennis, Linda Rose, 1954-, author
After the happily ever after : empowering women & mothers in relationships / Linda Rose Ennis.

Includes bibliographical references.
ISBN 978-1-77258-128-7 (softcover)

1. Marriage. 2. Marriage--Psychological aspects. 3 Man-woman relationships. 4. Motherhood. 5. Married women. 6. Wives. 7. Mothers. 8. Sex role. 9. Sex discrimination against women--Prevention. I. Title.

HQ734.E565 2017 646.7'82 C2017-905258-6

MIX
Paper from responsible sources
FSC® C004071
FSC www.fsc.org

After the Happily Ever After

Empowering Women and Mothers in Relationships

EDITED BY

Linda Rose Ennis

DEMETER

DEMETER PRESS

To Alan, my best friend and partner in life,
who keeps me believing in the beauty of
the "happily ever after."

Table of Contents

III: MARRIAGE: LOOKING OUT AND FORWARD

Acknowledgements

First and foremost, I thank my publisher and dear friend Andrea O'Reilly for her encouragement and belief in my work.

I am grateful to Demeter Press staff members for their meticulous efforts and hard work in getting this book out to the public in magnificent form. I thank all of the contributors for their thoughtful ideas about the field of marriage.

To my dear family and friends, who have always loved me and encouraged me throughout this lengthy process. For Jessica, whose strength and dedication inspire me. To Jillian, whose unconditional love and insight I cherish, and to Adam, for his consistent interest in my work. Always, to my sweet Nathaniel James, who brings light and sunshine to my world.

With enormous respect and love to my parents, Dina and Wolf Tenenbaum, who really know what being equal partners in a marriage means.

To my loving and caring partner in life, Alan, who is proud of all of my work all of the time. I am humbled by his emotional investment in all that I do and appreciate his unfaltering presence in my life.

After the Happily Ever After

Visiting the Issue Today

LINDA ROSE ENNIS

EVERY FAIRY TALE ENDS the same way: "And they lived happily ever after." But do they really? What happens to the couple after the "happily ever after"? Why do we want to believe in this fantasy when we know that at least half of marriages end in divorce? Slightly more than 43 percent of couples married in 2008 will divorce before their fiftieth anniversary, according to Statistics Canada (Sagan), and between 40 to 50 percent of married couples in the U.S. will divorce ("Marriage and Divorce"). Yet in Western culture, more than 90 percent of people will marry by age fifty ("Marriage and Divorce"). If every woman does not have this happy ending, how can we explain the contradiction of marriage?

Why do we embrace the illusion of the happily ever after, simultaneously with our distrust of marriage, by having our partners sign prenuptial contracts? Is marriage passé and irrelevant or necessary to our security? How does a marriage survive financial decisions, parenting, cultural influences, and political contexts? Does the person who earns more money or has access to more funds, hold the power in the marital relationship or is it an issue of gender differentiation? Who are the participants, other than the couple, that are involved in a marriage? Is there a difference between cohabitation and marriage with regards to living happily ever after? Why would one choose marriage? Do women view marriage differently than their partner? What are the expectations going in and does this have something to do with the outcome? Does happiness have anything to do with marriage? Is the definition of marriage problematic and in need of an update or is the experience, under certain circumstances, an issue? Is it meant for all or are we just doing it wrong? Is there even a "happily ever after" and if so, how do we achieve this state?

To understand the "happily ever after" and have an understanding of what happens after the wedding takes place, I compiled this volume—a collection of twelve chapters that examines the issue theoretically and practically, with a look toward the future of marriage. This book draws on the work of scholars from Canada, the United Sates, Poland, and the United Kingdom, who engage in both quantitative and qualitative methodologies, through psychoanalytic, feminist, sociological, legal, and economic lenses, with a focus on neoliberalism and consumerism. The collection aims to examine the continuing yet controversial institution of marriage today in Western culture, which includes considering it in different contexts and in contrast to different relationships, such as the following: lesbian relationships; teenage marriages; living together versus marriage; the impact of intensive mothering and neoliberalism; the effects of social media; the impact of grandmothering on marriage; and the effects of work on mothering and marriage. Marriage will be explored in terms of gender differentiation in marriage; the professionalization of motherhood; the myth of choice in marriage; and ethnicities, cultural contexts, and class status. It will take into account that "the promotion of gendered marriage norms reinforces the patriarchal family and encourages women to make themselves economically dependent" (Brake 7) and that equal parenting will not exist "unless husband and wife are more truly equal" (Johnson 8).

I became interested in this topic when I was about to marry. The very first thing I did, before looking for a wedding gown and choosing flowers, was write a sociological paper titled "Do You Lose Your Sense of Self in Marriage?" I focused on not losing who you are, as an individual, when you become part of a couple. Throughout my many years of marriage, I have had to monitor these thoughts and reflect upon them.

Two stories come to mind as I venture into this emotionally laden territory, each an impetus for this book on marriage. In the summer of 2014, I met a young bride on a plane. She was going on her honeymoon; I was going to speak at a conference. After I congratulated her, she said dreamily, "When I am older, I would love to renew our vows." Then, she expanded on this wish by adding: "So I can wear my wedding gown again."

This reminded me of my other story, which involved my writing a column for a wedding magazine, several years ago. It was supposed to be a sort of advice column for young couples, specifically brides, to ask questions about their upcoming marriage. In the entire year that I wrote the column, not one person submitted a question about their upcoming marriage. Clearly, the most important thing was to have the most beautiful wedding! It ruins the fantasy and makes it too real by asking questions related to marriage when all you want is beauty, pomp, and circumstance. This disinterested manner related to marriage resonated with my experience of collecting abstracts from potential contributors for this book, which ultimately only included the brave, the most informative, and the invited. As a result, this collection was born for the purpose of examining all that we do not see in marriage. Its aim is to understand what it's all about and how to truly live a life that is an authentic happily ever after.

THE EVOLUTION OF MARRIAGE: MOTIVES AND BELIEFS BEHIND MARRIAGE

The fantasy of the "happily ever after" may be entangled with a fear of marriage or, more likely, an anxiety about divorce. The daunting element about marriage is that it differs from dating, cohabiting, and mothering. Even though just over 50 percent of first cohabiting couples marry, the more recent studies find that when couples are compared by the age, at which they move in together and start taking on the roles associated with marriage, there is no difference in divorce rates between couples that lived together before marriage and those that did not (Kuperberg). The benefits of a close marriage and commitment are related to mental and physical health, which is especially true as one ages (Walton). This is generally not so much the case with cohabitation because of the implied level of commitment in marriage. Nevertheless, some people worry largely about the emotional turmoil that could result from divorce, which may explain why no one likes to talk about it.

Marriage has become more optional and fragile, with more mutual choices to be made, and has become more democratized. The traditional imposing of the husband's will upon his wife has become less prevalent (Coontz 301), although traditional elements still exist within more egalitarian marriages. In this collection, Sarah Bekaert explores such a phenomenon among teenage mothers who desire to marry their baby's father and live as a traditional family unit. In order to work through the traditional elements, the dialogue between partners in a marriage must include the need to close the choice gap inherent in marriage which will entail necessary conversations prior to marriage and having children (O'Brien Hallstein, in volume).

Historically, marriage was closely tied to a financial merging of sorts, which often entailed the importance of in-laws and the substantial material stakes in them. However, "the unprecedented independence of the married couple from their relatives and in-laws have allowed many husbands and wives to construct more satisfying marriages than those of the past" (Coontz 33). It is, though, a more isolating experience without extended family support. Because the extended family has become less important or unavailable due to distance, there is enormous difficulty parenting in the context of an absent supportive family, which may prove to be an extra pressure in marriage. As a result, tension exists to recreate the family unit in marriage, where attachment relationships are duplicated, and family of origin unresolved material is reworked for the purpose of retaining a secure family environment (Johnson and Brassard, in volume). This collection also discusses the changing positive and problematic roles of grandmothers and in-laws (Webb and Norwood; Wilder, in volume). Even though the importance of in-laws today has shifted, their influence is still apparent in family wealth and businesses, which explains the popularity of prenuptial agreements. This collection also asks whether the prenuptial agreement is advisable in all marriages (Gordon and Stokes, in volume).

Social models speak of a contradiction between love and marriage, which requires a reconciliation between "the two competing cultural frames" (Illouz, *Why Love Hurts* 13). Eva Illouz argues the following; "The exercise of imagination has been, in parallel, increasingly solicited toward a form of autotelic desire, a desire that feeds itself and has little capacity to operate the shift from fantasy to daily life" (Illouz, *Why Love Hurts* 237), an aim in itself, but not necessarily routed in reality. As such, the fantasy of love continues to be connected to marriage. In this collection, online talk of marriage in a positive way, but not in person, is addressed, seemingly connected to fantasy rather than reality (Basden Arnold, in volume). Marriage became more fragile when love entered into the equation in the nineteenth century, yet more satisfying, even though "unconscious habits and emotional expectations perpetuated female disadvantage in marriage" (Coontz 311). Such disadvantage is discussed by Solveig Brown in this collection when she shows that the division of labour is the primary source of conflict for many couples. Marrying for love is a relatively new phenomenon, which often obscures the social and economic expectations, which still exist (Maushart 211). To expand upon this thinking, in this collection, Melinda Vandenbeld Giles connects global political economy with ideals of romantic love. "Companionate marriage," with marital ideals characterized by emotional intimacy, companionship and mutual choice has now become more prevalent (Hirsch and Wardlow). This type of marriage includes same-sex marriages, which are considered more egalitarian and less traditional in the gender division of labour (Schulte 166). Several chapters in this volume explore same-sex relationships in comparison to heterosexual marriages.

CAPITALISM AND NEOLIBERALISM IN MARRIAGE AND INTENSIVE MOTHERING

Social class, and how women position themselves financially via work and marriage, is clearly an issue warranting attention in this context. Emotional and economic relationships have "come to define and shape each other" in a way that can be defined as "emotional capitalism" (Illouz, *Cold Intimacies*). As Illouz says, "Fantasies have never been as abundant and multiple in a culture which incessantly engineers them; yet they may have become sterile because they are becoming disconnected from reality, and increasingly organized within the hyperrational world of choice and information about the market" (Illouz, *Cold Intimacies* 114). The culture of capitalism, in the form of the wedding industry, is complicit in promoting this fantasy of love and marriage by offering online dating sites, wedding venues and catering, honeymoon vacations, wedding magazines, and wedding advisors in order to make the dream come true as an entry to marriage, which is not based on fantasy but on reality. Therein lies the split between the wedding and marriage.

Today, neoliberalism has attached commerce to the family. The patriarchal system has had an enormous impact upon mothers' oppression and the perpetuation of the myth that a patriarchal system can only operate at the expense of a matriarchal one. As Vanessa Olerenshaw argues; "The reality is stark: mothers are, in gradual steps, losing the rights, freedom and economic ability to raise their own children, within the patriarchal and capitalist project" (22). The influence of consumerism and neoliberalism, as a way to reduce public expenditure on social services to individualized mothering, also happens in the marriage in the form of "intensive mothering." This philosophy is supported by a type of gender essentialism called the "new momism," which insists "that no woman is truly complete or fulfilled unless she has kids, that women remain the best primary caretakers of children, and that to be a remotely decent mother, a woman has to devote her entire physical, psychological, emotional and intellectual well-being, 24/7, to her children" (Douglas and Michaels 4). Sharon Hays concludes that "intensive mothering" is the dominant ideology of childrearing and that it reflects "a deep cultural ambivalence about the pursuit of self-interest" and helps "to reproduce the existing gender hierarchy" (Hays178) I have suggested that "intensive mothering is neither good nor bad but rather an interplay of self-sacrificial and self-serving mothering practices due to individual and societal expectations" (Ennis 336).

Has society really separated marriage from economics? As Doucet has argued; "Women adjust their lives to accommodate children and need to focus on wider gendered relations" (250). Having children triggers a more traditionalist approach to parenting and subsequently in marriage, and brings back old familial relationships, which are reactivated and worked through in the marriage. The individual needs of women, which may predominate at the beginning of the marriage, become a challenge if she adopts "intensive mothering" in the marriage. Historically, women used to marry for financial gain because they were more dependent on men for security, but now with "intensive mothering," this dependence on the primary breadwinner has resurfaced, which often causes inequity and stress in the marriage. Kathleen Gerson has suggested in her work, as reported by Coontz, that "while most of the women wanted to continue paid employment, the majority of men said that if they could not achieve their egalitarian ideal, they expected their partner to assume primary responsibility for parenting so they could focus on work" (Coontz 6) For women, who have lingered too long on the "mommy track," getting back into work is quite challenging.

MOTHERHOOD, FATHERHOOD, WORK, AND MARRIAGE

Disparity in pay between men and women, which is the price of motherhood, is the single biggest risk for poverty in old age for women (Crittenden). In Crittenden's work, as reported by Coontz, it was estimated that "the typical college-educated woman lost more than $1 million dollars in lifetime earnings and forgone retirement benefits after she opted out" (Coontz 3). Subsequently, low-income women often do not marry for economic reasons because they realize they cannot afford to (Coontz). For those women who do marry, the conflicting message that mothers must be both full-time workers and full-time intensive mothers affects both marriage and the relationship. According to Anne-Marie Slaughter, women spend twice as much time as fathers on childcare (54). She notes that if women want to reach the top, husbands have to stay in the middle ranks, which makes women uncomfortable because of societal influence (27) and makes men anxious about shifting power dynamics (142). Susan Maushart adds that it is the perception of the value of the work, not the actual income, as well as the expectations that play into the working arrangement in marriage and the level of satisfaction. However, she notes that we are a long way from acknowledging that fathers can participate to accepting that he has equal obligation to do so, helping out versus living it (211). Brigid Schulte expands upon this "helping out" quality of many fathers by noting that leisure-time for part-time working mothers is scattered, whereas men have more unbroken leisure time (Frye 28), since stay-at-home women feel guilty and do everything (168). Men often do not do enough. Nevertheless, we aspire to have gender equality, in this often two-tiered system, with job equity and government support, and to establish more "non-gendered parental thinking," (Frye 28) which will hopefully lead to more paternal involvement in the family. The change in expectations within the individual family will be addressed in this collection.

OVERVIEW OF CHAPTERS

To explore marriage "after the happily ever after," this collection examines it through three lenses: thoughts about marriage; living within marriage; and marriage: looking out and forward. The first section discusses theory, thoughts, and speculation about marriage in the hope of better understanding it. The second section examines how marriage looks, from a practical perspective, in various situations, and the last section talks about how marriage may present itself, in the future, if some precautions and strategies were to take place. These chapters have been written by academics from various disciplines, from different parts of the world and at different points in their careers, with a keen interest in this subject and its impact on women's lives and families.

Thoughts about Marriage

The chapters here examine marriage through different theoretical lenses for the purpose of understanding it better, beginning with employing a qualitative, interdisciplinary lens by, theoretically, situating the choice gap of marriage at the intersection of the post-second wave and neoliberal turns and ending with a chapter on how attachment theory can inform the marital relationship and commitment in marriage.

Employing a qualitative and interdisciplinary lens, Lynn O'Brien Hallstein in "But, Didn't I Choose This?" continues and further develops the conversation that Pamela Stone started about contemporary mothers' "choice gap." She details six conversations young women need to have with their future parenting partners and/or their husbands prior to having children to close the choice gap between themselves and their parenting partners and engage in empowered mothering.

In "The Urge to Merge and the Marriage Imperative: The Happily Ever After in Lesbian Relationships," Alys Einion takes a personal-political stance to analyze commonly held stereotypes of lesbian relationships, associated with the "urge to merge," "U-Haul syndrome" and the dominant trope of the co-dependent lesbian relationship, with reference to new possibilities associated with the legalization of same-sex marriage. She analyzes the romanticized view of lesbian relationships using a critical approach, and explores the nature of lesbian relationships, their dynamics and longevity, with reference to research and debate, associated with a sample of social media accounts of lesbian relationship issues and breakdowns. In this context, she relates the history of lesbian relationships to feminism and to heteropatriarchal norms, which she argues, places pressure on women to seek out and conform to normative relationship patterns, but compares this to the desire for mutuality, which can signify a healthy relationship.

Ann Wilder's chapter, "A Sociological Adaptation of the Grandmother Hypothesis: Or, Simply Put, Go Ask Your Grandmother!" is a theoretical analysis of the adaptation of women in metamodern society, and it examines the impact of intergenerational relationships on families. By deconstructing the framework of the grandmother hypothesis, and reframing the concept, using archetypes of motherhood, Wilder explores the importance of grandmothering. She shares examples of supportive grandmothering within the context of metamodern families through the lens of contemporary technology, theories of wisdom, and the integration of narrative constructs.

In the last chapter of this section, "Growing Together or Growing Apart: An Attachment Approach to Understanding Marriage," Audrey Brassard and Sue Johnson describe the adult attachment theory and explain how both partners embark on marriage with their own attachment insecurities, which can then lead them to experience either conflict or harmony, disconnection or intimacy, despair or happiness. Results from a vast body of research are summarized to support how attachment-related anxiety and avoidance can erode relationship and sexual wellbeing, as well as partners' commitment. Some basic concepts of emotionally-focused therapy are also presented to show how partners can foster intimacy and connection within their relationship to prevent loneliness, distance, and separation.

Living within Marriage

In this section, the chapters explore how marriages in both heterosexual and same-sex relationships present themselves, on a practical level, in Western society.

In "After the Baby Carriage: Navigating the Transition to Parenthood," Solveig Brown identifies three areas in which women experience the most stress in their relationship with their spouse or partner after having children: 1) the division of labour; 2) changes in their relationship dynamics; and 3) decreased leisure time. Based on a study of 140 middle-class American mothers, Brown shows that the division of labour is the primary source of conflict for many couples. This chapter shows how heterosexual couples, with children, reproduce or challenge a gendered division of labour. She reveals the diverse ways couples negotiate the division of labour; who is more likely to do what task; and the strategies of those couples who have a more egalitarian division of labour.

In "Sexuality, Intimate, and Parenting Relationships of Women Maintaining Same-Sex Intimate Relationships in Poland," Malgorzata Kot analyzes the parenting relationships of Polish women who maintain an intimate relationship with a female partner while raising a child from a previous, heterosexual relationship. Based on a study conducted among same-sex women couples, Kot's chapter further examines how sexuality is shaped within heteronormative surroundings and how it influences intimate and parenting relationships.

In "Hopefully He Puts the Ring on It: Teenaged Mothers' Voiced Desire for Marriage," Sarah Bekaert explores teenaged pregnancy decision making, in which young mothers demonstrate various effective and creative family-formation models. Moreover, they express a keen desire for marriage to their baby's father and living as a family unit. Bekaert shows how these voiced desires may be a response to the supposed social exclusion of the teenaged parent. The goals for marriage and living in a nuclear family unit actively create a place of inclusion by adhering to social expectations for relationship and family. Unfortunately, as a consequence, celebrating new ways of demonstrating commitment and being a family is stymied.

Lorin Basden Arnold, in her chapter, "Making Marital Face(-book): Husband Posts and Face Management on Facebook," notes the high number of posts that occur each day on Facebook that praise spouses, particularly husbands. In this chapter, she uses qualitative methodology and face management theory to examine a sampling of these posts in an attempt to address how the posts may function for the user. She addresses the potential effects of such posts for both the spousal pair and those who read the posts. She argues that the posts represent an attempt at face maintenance of both writer and spouse; however, they can have unintended consequences that cause them to operate as face threats to writers, spouses, and readers.

In the final chapter of this section, titled "Tending the Privacy Boundary between the Married Couple and the Husband's Mother: Its Impact on Marital Satisfaction and Relationship Solidarity," Kristen M. Norwood and Lynne M. Webb use Petronio's communication boundary management theory as their theoretical base to examine the potentially problematic in-law relationships between a married son, the husband's mother, and her daughter-in-law. A survey of 102 marital dyads reveals a positive association between the husbands' verbally communicated boundary with their mothers and their perception of the mothers' intrusiveness. The authors further suggest a positive association between mothers-in-law and daughters-in-law interpersonal solidarity and the marital satisfaction of both the daughters-in-law and their husbands.

Marriage: Looking Out and Forward

Finally, this section discusses what the future brings for the "happily ever after" in marriage, and what it could look like under particular circumstances.

Marie L. Gordon and Tiffany S. Stokes's chapter, titled "Contracting Out of Legal Protections: How Popular Culture Messaging Clashes With The Lived Realities Of Women Entering into Prenuptial Agreements," provides an analysis of the current prenuptial landscape. It examines the messages directed at young women about prenuptial agreements, the gender dynamics in negotiating these agreements, and the extent to which courts uphold, or refuse to enforce, the terms of prenuptial agreements. They explore the ways in which contractual sanctity and the pressure to enter into prenuptial agreements conflict with the lived reality of women's lives. The authors draw from popular culture sources, such as magazines and wedding sites, academic research, and statistics on women and marriage.

Andrea O'Reilly's chapter, titled "Have Your Cake and Eat It Too: Challenging and Changing Normative Gender Roles through Partnerships," examines the normative wife role and the wifework expected and demanded of women in traditional marriage. It considers how matrifocal family structures, in downplaying the wife role, allow for gender fluidity and equity that make possible true partnerships between men and women in heterosexual relationships. This chapter concludes with a discussion of O'Reilly's relationship with her partner to show how their lived partnership has challenged and changed normative gender roles to make possible Andrea's career success.

In the final chapter in this section, "The Fantasy of Capitalism and Romance: Consuming the Self," Melinda Vandenbeld Giles connects global political economy with ideals of romantic love. Rather than seeing the "happily ever after" as a quaint notion disassociated from global affairs, Vandenbeld Giles argues that we should view "love" as a powerful force within our current era of emotion, finance, and individualized self-gratification. However, if we can alter conceptualizations of love away from fantastical romantic notions and toward, what Vandenbeld Giles identifies as "communal love," there is the potential to create a powerful transformative force to counter the individualistic narcissism of the neoliberal age.

In the epilogue, "Separateness and Connectedness in the Happily Ever After," I use the separation-connection model, which I introduced in previous works, to further understand the "happily ever after." In this context, I suggest the separateness-connectedness model as a parallel to traditionalist and modernist marriages, and I will examine the difficulty of switching tracks from the traditional to the nontraditional forms of marriage. A partnership of two individuals, living together independently in an effective balance of independence and connectedness, will be addressed. This chapter will end with a review of the central issues, highlighted in this collection, with a look toward the future by suggesting what further work is required.

CONCLUSION

This book questions why the fantasy of the "happily ever after" still exists in marriage as a split between the wedding and marriage and whether the two-tiered system of the traditional marriage persists today. It also addresses the role of love and finance in marriage and the interrelationship between the two. These issues are addressed in the context of heterosexual as well as same-sex relationships in different socioeconomic classes, age groups, and countries within Western society. In exploring these matters, I have found several contradictions: the one between the reality and fantasy of marriage; the split between the individual's needs and the couple's; the distinct differences in experience among women, mothers, and working mothers; the polarity between the traditional and the egalitarian marriage; the choice between cohabitating or marrying; and the opposing views of whether to have a prenuptial agreement drawn up or not, thereby setting up the dichotomy between love and financial stability. It becomes increasingly necessary to further explore, challenge, and bridge the different theories that we have in place, to date to reconcile the either-or thinking inherent in marriage. Within this context, there is a need to further understand the role of "intensive mothering" in marriage and its impact on the couple relationship as well as to explore "intensive parenting" and the role of parenting in marriage.

What is left to examine in future is an understanding of the lived experience of all women, including mothers from all classes and different cultures, for the purpose of clarifying the motives for marrying and marriage's dynamics. In addition, the lived reality of men and how they see marriage needs to be explored to fully understand the heterosexual couple in marriage, as well as the experience of marriage for men in same-sex relationships. Furthermore, there is a need to comprehend more fully the role of the nuclear and extended family as it relates to marriage. Finally, it is imperative for us to be clear about the future role of capitalism and neoliberalism as it relates to marriage, the individual, and family relationships. In considering how marriage presents itself today, we can look forward to having a better sense of the "happily ever after," in the hope of empowering women and mothers in nonpatriarchal relationships.

WORKS CITED

Brake, Elizabeth. *Minimizing Marriage: Marriage, Morality and the Law*. Oxford University Press, 2012.

Coontz, Stephanie. *Marriage, a History*. Penguin Books, 2006.

Coontz, Stephanie. "Why Gender Equality Stalled." *The New York Times Sunday Review*, 16 Feb. 2013, www.nytimes.com/2013/02/17/opinion/sunday/why-gender-equality-stalled.html. 25 July 2017.

Crittenden, Ann. *The Price of Motherhood*. Henry Holt & Co, 2001.

Doucet, Andrea. *Do Men Mother?* University of Toronto Press, 2006.

Douglas, Susan, and Meredith Michaels. *The Mommy Myth: The Idealization of Motherhood*. Free Press, 2005.

Ennis, Linda Rose. *Intensive Mothering: The Cultural Contradictions of Modern Motherhood*. Demeter Press, 2014.

Frye, Joanne. "Parental Thinking." *Essential Breakthroughs*. Ed. Fiona Green & Gary Pelletier. Demeter Press, 2015.

Gerson, Kathleen. *The Unfinished Revolution*. Oxford University Press, 2010.

Hays, Sharon. *The Cultural Contradictions of Motherhood*. Yale University Press, 1996.

Hirsch, J. & Wardlow, H. *Modern Loves*. University of Michigan Press, 2006.

Illouz, Eva. *Why Love Hurts*. Polity Press, 2012.
Illouz, Eva. *Cold Intimacies*. Polity Press, 2007.
Johnson, Miriam. *Strong Mothers, Weak Wives*. University of California Press, 1988.
Kuperberg, Arielle. "Does Premarital Cohabitation Raise Your Risk of Divorce?" *Council on Contemporary Families*, 10 Mar. 2014, contemporaryfamilies.org/cohabitation-divorce-brief-report/. Accessed 13 July 2017.
"Marriage and Divorce." *American Psychological Association*, 2016, www.apa.org/topics/divorce/. Accessed 24 July 2017.
Maushart, Susan. *Wifework*. Bloomsbury, 2002.
Olerenshaw, Vanessa. *Liberating Motherhood*. Womancraft Publishing, 2016.
Sagan, Aleksandra. "Marriage, Co-Habitation Contracts Can Be Good Investments." *The Globe and Mail*, 28 Oct. 2016, www.theglobeandmail.com/globe-investor/personal-finance/genymoney/marriage-co-habitation-contracts-can-be-good-investments/article32562573/. Accessed 24 July 2017.
Schulte, Brigid. *Overwhelmed*. HarperCollins Publishers, 2014.
Slaughter, Anne-Marie. *Unfinished Business*. Random House, 2015.
Walton, Alice. "The Marriage Problem; Why Many Are Choosing Cohabitation Instead." *The Atlantic*, 7 Feb. 2012, www.theatlantic.com/health/archive/2012/02/the-marriage-problem-why-many-are-choosing-cohabitation-instead/252505/. Accessed 13 July 2017.

I. Thoughts About Marriage

1.
"But, Didn't I Choose This?"

Laying the Groundwork to Empower Mothers by Closing the Choice Gap between Women and Men before Becoming Mothers and Fathers

LYNN O'BRIEN HALLSTEIN

Finally, recent research suggests that, at least at the outset, young men and women desire and expect an equitable division of household labor and child care responsibilities.
—Erin A Cech (271)

In fact, while respondents in my sample had all discussed their intent *to have children with their partners, almost none had explicitly discussed future parenthood responsibilities and their alignment with work with their partners.*
—Brooke Conroy Bass (370)

GROWING UP IN THE 1960s and 1970s, I would jump rope on the playground with my friends as we sang one of our favourite "happily-ever-after" songs: "First comes love, then comes marriage, then comes a baby in a baby carriage." Indeed, this song was central to the "happily-ever-after" gender story for young women at the time. Of course, as my friends and I jumped rope and sang the song, 1960s and 1970s feminisms were also happening. As a result, by the time I came of age and became a young feminist woman, I refused to believe in and sing this song. Because I took advantage of the educational opportunities that opened up for young women my age as a result of those feminisms, I deferred even thinking about marriage, let alone babies, throughout my twenties. Typical of many of my friends, by my early thirties—after I completed my PhD and while I was in the early years of my first tenure-track job and in a serious romantic relationship with a man who fully believed in the idea of gender equality—I started to think about my intention to have children. As with many women, however, even though I was using birth control, I had, what was for me at that time, the most glorious surprise of my life: an unexpected pregnancy.

Given that it was the late 1990s, I had the education and career that allowed me to support myself on my own, and the fact that my pregnancy occurred in a post-second-wave context where "out-of-wedlock" mothering was beginning to be less stigmatized, I was fully prepared to raise the baby on my own. Ultimately, my partner and I decided that we wanted to raise the baby together and opted to get married prior to my giving birth. So, my post-second-wave version of the "happily-ever-after" song became "First comes feminism, then education, then comes early career, then comes love, then comes pregnancy, then comes marriage, then comes baby in a baby carriage."

Although my husband believed in the idea of gender equality, our post-baby life was not immediately happily ever after and instead was fraught with many challenges, especially in the early years of our parenting together. Once the baby came, like many women, rather than being a co-parent, I was the primary parent to our son. Both popular and academic writers (Crittenden; Hirshman; O'Brien Hallstein and O'Reilly; O'Reilly, *Mother Outlaws*; Warner; Williams; Wolf) confirm that even in the wake of second-wave gains and the accompanying changed beliefs about gender equality, especially for well-educated men and women, women remain primarily responsible for childrearing, childcare, and family-life management. As Linda Hirshman argues, "the assignment of responsibility for the household to women applies in every social class" (11). Ann Crittenden also reveals in *The Price of Motherhood* that women's responsibility for childrearing and care also emerges even if a couple share household labour before the arrival of a child. As she puts it: "Before the arrival of the first child, [professional and educated] couples tend to share the house work fairly equally. But something about a baby encourages the resurgence of traditional gender roles" (25).

Writing in 2015 and reviewing more contemporary research, Brooke Conroy Bass also highlights the following: "Survey data consistently show that while the majority of contemporary couples maintain egalitarian labor arrangements before having children, many tend to shift to more traditional arrangements upon the birth of their first child.... This finding remains even among gender egalitarians" (364). Thus, both in the early days of second-wave feminisms' successes and today, a baby's arrival still encourages the re-emergence of traditional gender roles in heterosexual relationships. Or as Crittenden so aptly says, "once a woman has a baby, the egalitarian office party is over" (88).

Moreover, as with many contemporary post-second-wave beneficiaries—women who took advantage of the large-scale social, educational, and gender changes brought about by second-wave feminisms—I also found myself explaining my primary caregiving role as "my choice," as did my husband, even though I did not feel as if I was choosing anything that I wanted, and both my husband and I worked full time and were invested in our respective professional careers. What I have come to understand is that even though my husband and I desired and expected an equitable division of household labour and childcare responsibilities and we had begun to discuss our intent to have children together prior to my pregnancy, we never explicitly discussed future parenthood responsibilities and work alignment with each other. As a result, we quickly assumed and believed my primary caregiving was "my choice" rather than the result of structures, institutions, and gender roles and assumptions larger than our particular relationship. In short, as with many contemporary mothers, especially well-educated, middle-class, heterosexual ones, I did and sometimes still experience what Pamela Stone describes as a "choice gap" with my husband, which is at the root of much of our unhappily-ever-after parenting struggles.

Stone interviewed contemporary professional mothers who chose to "opt out" of their professional careers and found the following: "While they couch them in the language of choice and privilege, the stories they tell reveal not the expression of choice, but rather the existence of a choice gap, a gap that is a function of a double bind created primarily by the conditions of work in the gilded cages of elite professions" (19). Consequently, in detailing why high-achieving women "opt out" of their professional career in two-career couples, Stone suggests that "The fact that men's careers came first was the underlying and unspoken 'reason' women quit, but men's careers almost always come first; they come first in couples in which women continue working" (78). Thus, whether they opt out or remain working, contemporary mothers struggle to find the energy to "have it all"; in fact, the individual and privatized solution many mothers find themselves "choosing" is the contemporary common-sense solution that continues to make them primarily responsible for caregiving: the neotraditional family structure.

As I have argued elsewhere (*When Neoliberalism)* and Miriam Peskowitz concurs, neotraditional family configurations appear to be new and even progressive because many contemporary, privileged heterosexual families have both an educated and professional mother and father, and are founded on the ideas of gender equity and shared parenting. This family configuration continues to be problematic, however, since the basic foundation of pre-second-wave family roles and responsibilities still hold in the private sphere once children arrive. Mothers continue to be primary caregivers of children in this family type, even when they work and are partnered with men who believe in gender equality and equitable caregiving. In other words, while unencumbered women—women without children and/or childcare responsibilities—have benefited in real and important ways from second-wave feminisms, once women become mothers, especially high-achieving privileged women, most of those women adopt neotraditional family configurations because the intersecting post-second wave and neoliberal foundation of contemporary motherhood combine such that the only common-sense solution to "having it all" is to "choose" the neotraditional family configuration, which, ultimately, further entrenches the choice gap between mothers and fathers.

In this chapter, I continue the conversation that Stone started about contemporary mothers' choice gap. I do so theoretically, at first, by situating this gap at the intersection of the post-second-wave and neoliberal turns. Empowering mothers in their parenting relationships requires that they first understand the mothering context within which mothers both mother and attempt to enact shared parenting. Based on this theoretical grounding, I then detail the six conversations young women need to have with their future parenting partners and/or their husbands[1] prior to having children to lay the foundation to close the choice gap between themselves and their parenting partners and to resist adopting a neotraditional family formation. I also hope that these conversations will help mothers engage in empowered mothering—mothering from a position of agency that values motherwork—rather than hegemonic mothering or patriarchal mothering that devalues and constrains mothers' agency after they become mothers. In short, I hope to encourage a new, more authentic happily-ever-after song: "First comes love, then comes conversation, then comes marriage (or not!), then comes conversation, again, then comes more gender equality in parenting and a baby in a baby carriage."

THE CONTEMPORARY MATERNAL CONTEXT: OR, THE HEADWINDS THAT SHIFT MOTHERS TOWARD RATHER THAN AWAY FROM THE CHOICE GAP

The post-second-wave context that young women find themselves in today is different from the earlier one in which I was raised. Having been born in 1963 and raised squarely within second-wave feminisms as a young girl, by the time I graduated from high school in 1981, I was an early beneficiary of the changes brought about by second-wave feminisms. However, at that time, many young men my age continued to hold pre-second-wave understandings of gender and femininity, most notably the idea that motherhood was women's primary destiny. Fortunately, however, today, many well-educated young men and women now believe in gender equality. Indeed, recent research (Bass; Cech; Gerson; Pedulla and Thébaud; Sevón) confirms that young men and women believe in and assume they will partner in gender-equitable relationships. So, for example, as David Pedulla and Sarah Thébaud reveal, "Our first main finding is that the majority of young men and women in our study, regardless of their education level, prefer an egalitarian relationship structure when that option is available" (132).

Furthermore, many contemporary men also recognize that young women today have educational and career expectations in addition to family aspirations, and as a result, many heterosexual men have different expectations and aspirations in relation to partnership and fatherhood. In fact, a Boston College (BC) study of one thousands professional men titled "The New Dad: Caring Committed and Conflicted" (Harrington et al.) shows the following:

> Young fathers today know that they will have working wives. Their wives are likely to be at least as well if not better educated, just as ambitious as they are, and make more money than they do. More importantly, these men feel that being a father is not about being a hands-off economic provider. It's about paying attention, nurturing, listening, mentoring, coaching, and most of all, being present. It's also about changing diapers, making dinner, doing drop-offs and pick-ups, and housecleaning. (4)

Contemporary American men's belief that it is more likely that they will have working wives is also confirmed by a 2015 Pew Research Center study about working parents:

> Family life is changing, and so, too, is the role mothers and fathers play at work and at home. As more mothers have entered the U.S. workforce in the past several decades, the share of two-parent households in which both parents work full time now stands at 46%, up from 31% in 1970. At the same time, the share with a father who works full time and a mother who doesn't work outside the home has declined considerably; 26% of two-parent households today fit this description, compared with 46% in 1970.

Although young men believe in gender equality and will likely have working wives, men's cultural beliefs are out of sync with the reality of how much fathers actually participate in caregiving; in fact, as Ralph LaRossa first noted in 1998: "the idea that fathers have radically changed—they are now intimately involved in raising their children—qualifies as a folk belief" (379). The BC study, published more recently in 2011, also found that men's aspirations for fatherhood were out of sync with the reality of their actual parenting. As Brad Harrington et al. suggest:

> 65% of the fathers believe that both partners SHOULD provide equal amounts of care while 30% feel that their spouse should provide more care. However, when asked to report on how caregiving IS divided, only 30% of fathers reported that caregiving is divided equally, while 64% reported that their spouse provides more care. This highlights a large and noteworthy gap between aspirations and reality for the majority of fathers in this study. (capitalization in original, 23)

Clearly, this aspirations-reality gap is yet another way that neotraditional family configurations are reinforced while seeming to be progressive. These men say that they are committed to both gender equality with women and to being gender equitable fathers, but they do not practice parenting equality; their wives do far more parenting. In short, a gap exists between what men, such as those in the BC study, say they believe and what they do as fathers.

For many contemporary couples, recognizing this gendered-power imbalance is difficult because the reported desire for gender-equitable marriages and shared parenting are even more intertwined today. As Eija Sevón notes:

> The ideal of gender equality in parenting is linked with the idea that in western countries during the last few decades the role of gender in marriage has become more freely defined and negotiable.... The narrative of shared parenting also supposes features of friendship ties – free choice, equality and balance in reciprocity – that are becoming increasingly attached to the ideal couple relationship. (3)

Because these choice narratives or contemporary ideals are incongruous with the reality of what mothers and fathers do, they hide how gender and power continue to work in neotraditional families. As several scholars argue, the narratives of shared parenting and gender-equitable marriages conceal ongoing gender and power imbalances that continue to structure family life (Gatrell; Pera-Littunen; Sevón; Vuori).

Contemporary Motherhood Today

Although I agree that narratives of choice and shared parenting conceal ongoing gender and power imbalances, I want to nuance the discussion further by making the case that the aspirations-reality and choice gaps that undergird ongoing gender and power imbalances have also become even more intertwined and further entrenched because, as I argue elsewhere (*Bikini-Ready Moms*), contemporary North American motherhood now sits at the epicentre of the post-second-wave and neoliberal turns such that neoliberal principles and sensibilities of individualism, individual responsibility, and choice are now entangled with postfeminist rhetoric of and ideas about reproductive choice and gender equality in ways that, ultimately, make contemporary motherhood and intensive mothering even more demanding for mothers. Equally important, contemporary women who came of age at the centre of the intersection between the neoliberal and post-second-wave turns, as contemporary young women have, employ a kind of maternal agency that integrates both neoliberal and post-second-wave ideas, especially in relation to individualism, choice, and the assumption of privatizing social problems.

One consequence is that many contemporary mothers now believe that family-life struggles and even co-parenting can and should be resolved via their own individual choices in the private sphere. All of which, ironically, is further reinforced by gender-equitable marriages and shared parenting narratives today because these narratives further entrench the erroneous cultural belief that family life is now built on gender equity in both marriages and parenting. Since this flawed belief is now intertwined with neoliberal assumptions of individual choice and personality responsibility, individual mothers are blamed when they have difficulty securing gender equality at home and with their parenting partners. Indeed, if any individual family or parenting partnership is not gender equitable, then, mothers are held responsible because of the bad choices they have made and/or because they have not demanded enough of their parenting partners. In short, rather than blame large-scale social structures, workplace policies and assumptions, and/or fathers, mothers are assumed to have not asserted their post-second-wave maternal agency.

Addressing why many early post-second-wave mothers were apolitical and why they assumed they had to solve any difficulty on their own, Judith Warner has also revealed how these post-second wave and neoliberal connections began to emerge in early post-second-wave mothering: "Good daughters of the Reagan Revolution, we disdained social activism and cultivated our own gardens with a kind of muscle-bound, tightly wound, über-achieving, all-encompassing, never-failing self-control that passed, in the 1980s, for female empowerment" (par. 12). Also raised to be independent and self-sufficient and deferring motherhood for a career as post-second-wave beneficiaries, many mothers integrated second-wave feminist ideas of female independence and self-sufficiency with neoliberal principles in their understanding of motherhood. Again, talking about American mothers, Warner argues that "They've been bred to be independent and self-sufficient. To rely on their own initiative and 'personal responsibility.' To *privatize* their problems" (italicized in original par. 21).

Choice Today

Whereas Warner describes the struggles of early second-wave beneficiaries, more recent scholarship reveals how much more entrenched choice is in both women's and men's understanding of gender equitable marriages and parenting ideals (Bass; Gerson; Pedulla and Thébaud; Webber and Williams; Williams). Indeed, Kathleen Gerson notes that "By defining equality as women's choices or women's right to choose to work or not, men are able to acknowledge women's desire to work while also relying on a second income" (188).

Also exploring young women's identity constructions in the context of competing and changing cultural ideals of womanhood, such as feminist discourses and neoliberal discourses of choice and individualism, Heather A.K. Jacques and H. Lorraine Radtke argue that "Participants privileged individual choice as critical in envisioning their future lives even when endorsing 'traditional' gendered norms and expectations about womanhood" (6). Moreover, Jacques and Radtke also implicitly note how individualized that understanding of choice is:

> In these excerpts, the young women advocated for personal choice and freedom in decision-making. They actively resisted the notion that social pressures, in the form of expectations associated with ideals of womanhood, necessarily shaped their lives and, instead, mounted arguments in favour of individualism, stressing each person's capacity for choice.... In so doing, they positioned themselves, and other women, outside social pressures and placed the onus on individual women to negotiate any contradictions. (450)

As such, young women of this later post-second-wave era have also integrated choice as central to their future as women, mothers, and in terms of any work-life struggles that emerge. Jacques and Radtke conclude the following: "by virtue of positioning themselves as autonomous individuals making free choices, participants held themselves personally accountable for managing any challenges they faced in negotiating contradictions *in their future lives*. Notably, the context in which this was most evident was when they were explicitly talking about combining motherhood and career" (my emphasis, 453).

Equally problematic, women's internalization of the idea that women are now autonomous and freely choosing individuals is also shared by many men. As Stone puts it, "Women's own understanding of their decisions as implementing choice was further reinforced, as we saw earlier, by their husbands, who spoke repeatedly of giving their wives the 'choice' to decide whether or not to quit" (113). Thus, even more so today, both structurally and at the everyday level, then, intersecting neoliberal and post-second wave rationalities have become so entangled that very few "solutions" emerge and/or will emerge when contemporary mothers struggle to find the energy "have it all" and, in fact, the individual and privatized solution many mothers will find themselves "choosing"—and their husbands will support—is the even more common-sense solution: the neotraditional family structure.

As with postfeminism generally—in which key feminist principles are simultaneously acknowledged and refuted—neotraditional family configurations are a postfemininst neoliberal solution that simultaneously acknowledges and integrates key features of second-wave feminist ideas and rhetoric, while also undoing those ideas and undoing state support or function from social provisions for families. The choice gap, then, is also a postfeminist device because post-second-wave women's contemporary relationship to society has fundamentally changed from one of maternal destiny to post-second wave neoliberal maternal choice. The implications of this shift are freeing: unencumbered women's lives are more and more similar to unencumbered men's lives in the public sphere. But they are also problematic: women's encumbered lives in the private sphere continue to be shaped by maternal responsibilities, which are responsibilities that are viewed as women's "free" post-second wave neoliberal maternal choice rather than their "destiny" and, as such, simultaneously conceals ongoing gender-power imbalances in the private sphere and family life.

Contemporary maternal choice then, works as a postfeminist neoliberal rationality because it depoliticizes the second-wave feminist politics of choice by suggesting that the public sphere is no longer sexist; and, if the family is sexist, then, it is a result of women's choice to have and/or to make those sexist arrangements. Thus, the contemporary logic of choice is the following: if family life is problematic because women are not getting enough support at home, women are to blame for their poor choices, not ongoing gender-power structures in both the private and public spheres. Thus, the postfeminist neoliberal focus on individual choice, personal responsibility, and privatization all discourage social solutions for work-life concerns and instead encourage mothers and families to find their own individual solutions in the private sphere.

QUESTIONS TO LAY THE GROUNDWORK FOR EQUALITY AND SHARED PARENTING

Sharing does not come for free; it demands moral commitment, negotiations and the ability of both parties to question gendered narratives and practices.

—Eija Sevón (78)

Far too many divorcing couples fail to understand that a marriage does not just spring into being after the ceremony. Neither the legal nor the religious ceremony makes a

marriage. People do, throughout their lives.
—Judith Wallerstein and Susan Blakeslee (48)

Other scholars and I have begun to argue that it is now time for a mothers' movement to challenge the institutional and structural barriers that mothers face as mothers (Green; Horowitz; O'Reilly, "I Should Have"; Peskowitz; William; O'Brien Hallstein, *Bikini-Ready Moms*). To do so is to push back against the large-scale headwinds that move mothers toward rather than away from neotraditional families. I also believe, however, that participating in the growing mothers' revolution in the public sphere must be accompanied with making real and significant changes in the private sphere and to neotraditional families. As a result, the conversations and questions I suggest next are designed to lay the foundation to resist the prevailing gender-power headwinds that push mothers toward neotraditional families, even when those mothers are partnered with men who genuinely believe in gender equality and shared parenting. These conversations are grounded in two fundamental ideas. The first idea is a very simple point that is often forgotten in families: when children are born, all new parents become encumbered. Second, although it is important that both young men and women now believe in the ideas of gender equality and shared parenting, just believing in those ideas is not enough. Rather, it is now time to move from the ideals of to the doing of shared parenting. In short, given that so many men now believe in both gender-equitable relationships and shared parenting, we no longer need to focus on changing fathers' ideas about family life; rather, we need to ask those fathers to do more of what they say they already believe.

Asking fathers to work on matching their ideas with the realities of family life is one of the most important strategies to resist neotraditional family configurations. Having the right kind of parenting partnerships could be more important for women's long-term success and ability to be both a mother and a professional than structural or institutional changes (Hertz; O'Brien Hallstein, *When Neoliberalism*; O'Brien Hallstein and O'Reilly; O'Reilly, "I Should Have"). Discussing the realities of academic mothers, Andrea O'Reilly argues the following: "if the findings of my interviews are any indication, the type of relationship a woman has with her life partner is a crucial, though largely overlooked, variable, that hugely determines, arguably more so than workplace policies or practices, women's ability to successfully combine an academic career with motherhood" ("I Should Have" 98). Pushing back against inequitable parenting partnerships within our families is crucial to repoliticizing choice today and to getting more satisfying solutions for work-life balance difficulties. Thus, engaging in conversations prior to having children is essential to promote a more authentic "happily ever after" and to resist the ongoing gender-power structures that push mothers toward accepting both the aspiration-reality and choice gaps.

Conversation One: Clarify and Explore What Equality Means in Practice.

I suggest the initial foundational conversation that all couples must have as they explore their intent to have children together is to clarify what equality means both as an idea and in practice. Doing so is important because recent research suggests that many young men and women have different ideas about what gender equality means in the context of family life (Bass; Gerson). In fact, Gerson argues that in the context of future relationships, "Men and women view equality in different ways. Women are eager to find a partner to share caretaking, while men look forward to sharing the financial load" (114). Thus, potential parenting partners must discuss whether an equitable parenting relationship means equal sharing in caregiving or equal sharing in the financial load.

If a potential parenting partner believes equality means equality in terms of sharing caregiving, then, that partner, at least as an idea, is more likely to resist the choice and aspiration-reality gaps. If, however, equality means sharing the financial load, it seems more likely that that partner's idea of equality will reinforce the choice and aspiration-reality gaps, whether intended or not. Gerson further elaborates:

> By defining equality as women's "choice" to add work onto mothering, neotraditionalism allows men to acknowledge

> women's desire for a life beyond the home and also to rely on the financial cushion of a second income. This strategy accepts the end of an era of stay-at-home mothers, but not the disappearance of distinct gender boundaries. Breadwinning men instead define separate spheres of responsibility for fathers and mothers, even if two-earner families are here to stay. (188)

Future mothers must understand that they might have a different understanding of what equality means than future fathers, especially in the context of childrearing and childcare. For each parent, then, does equality mean shared caregiving? Or, alternatively, does it mean sharing the financial load of caring for children? The answers to these two questions will push a couple down two different paths. Shared caregiving is less likely to lead to neotraditional family configurations, whereas sharing the financial load is more likely to reinforce the separate spheres ideology that entrenches and reinforces neotraditional family configurations.

Conversation Two: Anticipate What It Takes to Share the Everyday Tasks or "Doing" of Shared Parenting.

The "doing" or practices of everyday shared parenting require much anticipatory thinking and planning to realize. Both young men and women must anticipate their future family life prior to becoming parents together. Recent research has shown that young men in particular avoid this anticipatory planning surrounding parenthood (Bass; Cech; Harrington et al.; Gerson), which can reproduce future inequality in families. Moreover, even when young men and women do have future family plans, they do not put those shared parenting ideas into practice; they hope everything will just "work out" when children arrive.

In some ways, of course, deferring to think about parenting makes sense because the norm today is for men and women to postpone having children until they are in their late twenties and early thirties, especially well-educated, middle-class men and women who want to focus on establishing themselves in their careers first. However, as Erin Cech notes about the college-age interviewees with whom she spoke:

> Interviews indicate that most students with family plans articulate a *temporal disjuncture* between their early occupational choices and their family plans. Career plans are something to be worried about during college, while family formation is perceived as a consideration for a distinct, later life stage. A Stanford woman explains that she will think about accommodating caregiving considerations 'maybe later on down the road' when the "time comes," but "right now, I don't even think about it so it doesn't really concern me." (emphasis in original, 281)

This temporal disjuncture suggests that many young men and women believe that it will all just "work out," somehow. For women especially, this is a problematic belief—even I might suggest another postfeminist "folk belief."

Equally worrisome is that some contemporary fathers do not even prioritize the "doing" of parenting as part of their understanding of being good fathers. In fact, in a chart titled "Six Aspects of Being a Good Father" from the BC study, Harrington et al. reveal six characteristics of good fathering and how the fathers they interviewed prioritize those characteristics. Each aspect was rated on a five-point scale and in order of importance. The findings are as follows: provide love and emotional support (4.7/5); be involved and present in your child's life (4.6/5); be a good teacher, guide, and coach (4.5/5); provide discipline (4/5); provide financial security (4/5); do your part in the day-to-day childcare tasks (3.9/5) (13).

Three key findings of this data relate to conversation two. First, these fathers report that they strive for gender equality in their home life. Second, they aspire to be emotionally supportive and present in their children's lives and place providing financial security lower. Clearly, this is evidence of a different kind of post-second-wave fathering than these men probably received from their own fathers, in which providing financial security was the hallmark. Third, and problematic however, is that these men rank "do your part in the day-to-day childcare tasks" as the least important characteristic of good fathering. Thus, even though 65 percent of these men believe both partners should provide equal amounts of care, this belief is contradicted by the importance these men place on the actual "doing" of daily fathering. A gap exists between what these men believe and what they do, which fuels the mothers' ongoing primary responsibility for childrearing and family-life management.

Clearly, as I have shown here, if parenting partners are not actively and reflectively thinking about the "doing" of parenting both before and after they become parenting partners, then, the solution that most couples will strive toward is neotraditional family configurations. As a result, potential parenting partners must ask explicit questions to probe how each partner intends to do their part in day-to-day childcare tasks. Such questions may include the following examples. What will you do to ensure that you participate in the every-day tasks of childcare? If you believe being a good father means sharing in the work of family life, what accommodations will you make to actually do that work? What will you be willing to change in your daily life to share in the daily tasks of caregiving?

Conversation Three: How Hard Shared Parenting Is, Especially When Children Are Young

Couples also must discuss the great amount of time and care young children need, which makes it even more difficult for true shared parenting at every stage of children's lives. As a result, whoever is the primary caregiver of children, especially of young children, will need to devote substantial time to caregiving. Such intensive caregiving will make it difficult for caregivers to participate in the public sphere as if they were unencumbered by family responsibilities. Some women and feminists, understandably, are afraid to have this conversation. They believe that to acknowledge caregiving requires much energy and time will encourage both the resurgence of the maternity-as-women's-destiny thesis and give professional institutions "ammunition" to penalize women for their difficulty meeting ideal worker standards. These worries are reasonable. If we, however, continue to decouple femininity and maternal choice by redefining maternal desire and maternal agency within the context of empowered mothering, while also reframing how and what the contemporary conversations are about, we can acknowledge that caregiving does require much time and attention without necessarily further entrenching maternal choice or further reinforcing professional barriers against mothers in professional institutions.

Equality-minded partners must reframe how they understand the fact that the care of young children requires much of any caregiver. Indeed, childcare does require much time and is a biological fact. As Petra Buskins argues, "Infancy and early childhood *are* periods of high emotional and physical dependency and, moreover, this is not a pure invention of patriarchal science.... *The problem is not the fact of this requirement but rather that meeting this need has come to rest exclusively, and in isolation, on the shoulders of biological mothers*" (emphasis in original, qtd. in O'Reilly, *Mother Outlaws* 11). As such, O'Reilly argues that intensive mothering "becomes oppressive not because children have needs, but because we, as a culture, dictate that only the biological mother is capable of fulfilling them; that children's needs must always come before those of the mother; and, that children's needs must be responded to around the clock and with extensive time, money, and energy" (11). What needs to be reframed, then, is the solution to the fact rather than the fact itself. In other words, if we acknowledge the fact that children do require time and attention, while also, simultaneously, making clear that the real problem is the fact that the responsibility for that care is exclusively assigned to women within the context of an intensive mothering ideology that has intensified rather than decreased, then, not only would we insist on reframing the conversation to address the real problem, we would also lay the groundwork for planning for this fact prior to having children rather than as a result of having children, while also resisting the resurgence of the previous iron-clad connection between femininity and motherhood.

Couples need to explore these facts together and clarify how shared parenting will unfold in light of the needs of children at each stage of their development. Because children become less dependent as they age, parents can revisit these conversations at each major stage of their parenting together. One consequence of this is that partners may "take turns" being the primary parent. In other words, rather than shared parenting at each and every stage, shared parenting can unfold across the life span of the children and across the parenting partnership. Thus, in order to reframe the facts of childrearing and to challenge placing the onus of responsibility exclusively on the shoulders of biological mothers, potential parenting partners need to ask of one another the following questions. How do you imagine we will manage the caregiving of our children? How can we continue to strive for shared parenting in light of the needs of our children, especially during infancy? And is it possible to take turns being the primary parent at different stages of our children's development?

Conversation Four: Shift from Maternal Choices to Parental Choices When "It Just Isn't Working."

Because of the choice and aspiration-reality gaps, "when it just isn't working"—when juggling work, home, and children is hard and challenging—the only problem-solving questions asked to solve the difficulty of "juggling it all" revolve around a woman's maternal choices. Should she have a career and have primary responsibility for childcare and household labor? Should she quit work and be home full time to meet her ongoing private sphere responsibilities? Should she interrupt her career for some length of time to focus on her family responsibilities and then try to return to work when the children are older?

Rather than have the problem solving revolve around questions about mothers' choices, we need to insist on shifting the ground to parental questions that ask men to enact what they say they believe and that make the social pressures of maternal choices more visible and explicit. It is now time to re-politicize choice both within the mothers' movement and within our own families to make the ongoing gender and power imbalances there more visible and explicit. To do so, parenting partners must insist on asking and answering the following questions. How can each of us have a career and actually do our part in childcare and household labour? Can we each make career changes to accommodate family life? Is it possible to take turns prioritizing career over family, at least when the children are young and have so many needs? When there is any resistance to this shift in grounding, women must be clear that these are the kinds of questions that must be addressed by anyone who believes in more equitable family partnerships.

Conversation Five: What Is Your Fallback Plan?

Another "tricky" planning conversation that must occur prior to becoming parents together is about "fallback plans." Gerson's recent research suggests that young men and women already understand that the ideals of shared parenting and equitable relationships are ideals and, as such, are what Gerson calls "Plan A." Given that many young men and women understand that Plan A may be difficult to enact fully, many young women and men have what Gerson calls Plan B, which is the "fallback plan." Both Gerson's and Pedulla and Thébaud's recent research reveals that men's and women's fallback plans are quite different, and I would argue also further push women toward the choice gap and neotraditional families.

Of course, part of the reason why men and women have different fallback plans, as I described earlier, is because they do not have the same understanding of equality. And, a result, they perceive different obstacles to equality. As Gerson notes:

> Perceiving different obstacles, men form different fallback strategies. Uneasy about the price equality might exact, seven out of ten men look to modified traditionalism, in which they retain the position of a family's main breadwinner while also granting their partner the right, and need, to work. If equality proves impossible or just too costly, these men seek to preserve some distinct gender divisions that most women resist. (159)

This means then, as Gerson also shows, that rather than imitate one another's fallback plans, men's and women's fallback plans are at odds with one another and, ultimately, further reinforce neotraditional family configurations. Therefore, men and women end up employing fallback plans that are gender differentiated: men report preferring a more traditional arrangement, and women report preferring an arrangement that allows them to be financially autonomous. As such, crucial questions that young women must ask of their potential partner include the following. What is your fallback plan? And if that fallback plan supports a choice gap and a neotraditional family formation, how are you willing to resist that, given your belief in gender equity and shared parenting? What must we both change to make sure we have the same fallback plan?

These questions will undoubtedly be challenging to these young men. Even so, if men really do believe in shared parenting, then, they also must do the hard work to ensure shared parenting. As Eija Sevón points out, "Sharing does not come for free; it demands moral commitment, negotiations and the ability of both parties to question gendered narratives and practices" (78). Thus, at this post-second-wave juncture, it is time for equality-minded men to put their ideals into their everyday practices within their families.

Conversation Six: What Do Children Need to Be Healthy and Well Cared for As They Grow Up?

The final planning conversation revolves around what children need to grow up healthy. Although gender equity and shared parenting are now the norms, many people still remain convinced that children fare better when at least one parent is devoted to their care. Indeed, the idea that children do better with their mothers, especially when young, is still a persistent belief today and is reinforced by principles two and three of the "new momism": "that women remain the best primary caretakers of children, and that to be a remotely decent mother, a woman has to devote her entire physical, psychological, emotional, and intellectual being, 24/7, to her children" (Douglas and Michaels 4). And in order to enact the belief that children do better when one parent is devoted to their care and to adhere to the new momism, many men and women reach different conclusions for how to guarantee that their children are being raised by at least one parent.

The belief that children fare better when at least one parent is devoted to the care of children, unfortunately, means that gender equality plays out in an intriguing way. As Gerson notes, "With few exceptions, neotraditional men do not believe mothers are inherently more qualified than fathers to care for children; but they do believe parents are inherently more qualified than other caregivers" (171). Even though many fathers now believe they are equally qualified to parent, this does not mean, as I have shown here, that men are choosing to be the primary, devoted parent; women continue to be the primary parent. Thus, these beliefs need to be explored, even interrogated, by potential parenting partners. And if both partners believe that parents are more qualified than other caregivers to raise their children, potential parenting partners must also explore explicitly what that means for each parent in practice. How will both of us enact this belief that children are better off with their parents? How will we share in this responsibility together? What will each of us do to make this happen? Is it possible for us to take turns being the primary devoted-to-our-children parent? If these questions are not explored, as I have argued throughout, the only conversations that will emerge to guarantee children have at least one devoted parent are questions that focus only on women's maternal choices rather than parental choices.

CONCLUSION

Although these conversations may result in potential parents not becoming parents together, these conversations must occur to lay the groundwork to empower mothers by closing the choice gap between mothers and fathers. If not, as early second-wave beneficiaries like me have revealed and experienced, "happily ever after," either in marriages or shared parenting, will not "just work out" just because both partners believe in gender-equitable partnerships and shared parenting. Rather, shared-parented marriages and/or partnerships take work to enact and actually practice. At this post-second-wave moment, then, I believe young men and women have no choice but to have these conversations because, as Judith Wallerstein and Susan Blakeslee remind us: "Far too many divorcing couples fail to understand that a marriage does not just spring into being after the ceremony. Neither the legal nor the religious ceremony makes a marriage. People do, throughout their lives" (48). Thus, my hope for contemporary young men and women is that they have the kinds of conversations I suggest here (and I wish I had understood were necessary prior to having children) in order to lay a foundation that pushes them more toward gender-equitable relationships and shared-parenting practices rather than toward the choice and aspiration-reality gaps that prop up neotraditional family configurations.

ENDNOTE

[1]Because I am interested in challenging gender imbalances between mothers and fathers, I focus primarily on heterosexual relationships in this chapter. This does not mean, however, that I do not think that the conversations I propose would also be helpful for all kinds of parenting partnerships nor do I do so to devalue or make invisible other kinds of families. Rather, my intention is to explore how gender-power imbalances continue to work in mother-father family configurations.

WORKS CITED

Bass, Brooke Conroy. "Preparing for Parenthood? Gender, Aspirations, and the Reproduction of Labor Market Inequality." *Gender & Society* vol. 29, no. 3, 2015, pp. 362-85.

Cech, Erin A. "Mechanism or Myth? Family Plans and the Reproduction of Occupational Gender Segregation." *Gender & Society*, vol. 30, no. 2, 2016, pp. 265-88.

Crittenden, Ann. *The Price of Motherhood: Why the Most Important Job the World is Still the Least Valued.* Henry Holt and Company, 2001.

Douglas, Susan J., and Michaels, Meredith. *The Mommy Myth: The Idealization of Motherhood and How It Has Undermined Women.* Free Press, 2004.

Gatrell, Caroline. "Whose Child is it Anyway? The Negotiation of Paternal Entitlements within Marriage." *The Sociological Review*, vol. 55, no. 2, 2007, 352-72.

Gerson, Kathleen. *The Unfinished Revolution.* Oxford University Press, 2010.

Green, Fiona. "Empowered Mothering." *Encyclopedia of Motherhood Volume One*, edited by Andrea O'Reilly, Sage, 2010, pp. 347-48.

Harrington, Brad, Fred Van Deusen, Beth Humberd. "The New Dad: Caring Committed and Conflicted." Boston: Boston College Center for Work & Family, 2011.

Hertz, Rosanna. "Book Review: The Contemporary Myth of Choice." *American Academy of Political and Social Science*, vol. 596, 2004, pp. 232-44.

Hirshman, Linda R. *Get to Work: A Manifesto for Women of the World.* Viking, 2006.

Horowitz, Erika. "Resistance as a Site of Empowerment: The Journey away from Maternal Sacrifice." *Mother Outlaws: Theories and Practices of Empowered Mothering*, edited by Andrea O'Reilly, Women's Press, 2004, pp. 43-58.

Jacques, Heather AK, and H. Lorraine Radtke. "Constrained by Choice: Young Women Negotiate the Discourses of Marriage and Motherhood." *Feminism & Psychology*, vol. 22, no. 4, 2012, pp. 443-61.

LaRossa, Ralph. "The Culture and Conduct of Fatherhood." *Families in the U.S.: Kinship and Domestic Politics,* edited by Karen Hansen and Anita Garey, Temple University Press, 1998, pp. 377-85.

O'Brien Hallstein, Lynn. *Bikini-Ready Moms: Celebrity Profiles, Motherhood, and the Body.* SUNY Press, 2015.

O'Brien Hallstein, Lynn. "When Neoliberalism Intersects with Post-Second Wave Mothering: Reinforcing Neotraditional American Family Configurations and Exacerbating the Post-second Wave Crisis in Femininity." *Mothering in the Age of Neoliberalism*, edited by Melinda Vandenbeld Giles, Demeter Press, 2014, pp. 297-314.

O'Brien Hallstein, Lynn. *White Feminists and Contemporary Maternity: Purging Matrophobia.* Palgrave MacMillan, 2010.

O'Brien Hallstein, D. Lynn, and Andrea O'Reilly. "Academic Motherhood in a Post-Second Wave Context." *Contemporary Motherhood in a Post- Second Wave Context: Challenges, Strategies, and Possibilities*, edited by D. Lynn O'Brien Hallstein and Andrea O'Reilly, Demeter Press, 2012, pp. 1-48.

O'Reilly, Andrea, editor. *Mother Outlaws: Theories and Practices of Empowered Mothering.* Women's Press, 2004. Print.

O'Reilly, Andrea. "I Should Have Married Another Man; I Couldn't Do What I Do Without Him: Intimate Heterosexual Partnerships and their Impact on Mothers' Success in Academe." *Contemporary Motherhood in a Post- Second Wave Context: Challenges, Strategies, and Possibilities*, edited by D. Lynn O'Brien Hallstein and Andrea O'Reilly, Demeter Press, 2012, 197-213.

Pedulla, David S. and Sarah Thébaud. "Can We Finish the Revolution? Gender, Work-Family Ideals, and Institutional Constraint." *American Sociological Review*, vol. 80, no. 1 2015, pp. 116-39.

Pera-Littunen, Satu. "Gender Equality or Primacy of the Mother? Ambivalent Descriptions of Good Parents." *Journal of Marriage and Family*, vol. 69, no. 2, 2007, pp. 341-51.

Pew Research Center. "Raising Kids and Running a Household: How Working Parents Share the Load." *Pew Research Center*, 2015, www.pewsocialtrends.org/2015/11/04/raising-kids-and-running-a-household-how-working-parents-share-the-load/. Accessed 12 July 2017.

Peskowitz, Miriam. *The Truth Behind the Mommy Wars: Who Decides what Makes a Good Mother?* Seal Press, 2005.

Sevón, Eija. 'My Life Has Changed, but His Life Hasn't': Making Sense of the Gendering of Parenthood during the Transition to Motherhood." *Feminism & Psychology*, vol. 22, no. 1, 2011, pp. 60-80.

Stone, Pamela. *Opting Out?: Why Women Really Quit Careers and Head Home*. University of California Press, 2007.

Vuori, Janna. "Men's Choices and Masculine Duties: Fathers in Expert Discussions." *Men and Masculinities,* vol. 12, no. 1, 2009, pp. 45-72.

Wallerstein, Judith and Susan Blakeslee. "Happily Ever After." *Networker,* Nov-Dec. 1995, 47-51, 59.

Warner, Judith. "Mommy Madness (excerpted from *Perfect Madness*): What Happened when the Girls Who Had It All Became Mothers? A New Book Explores why this Generation Feels so Insane." *thedailybeast.com*, 21 Feb. 2012, www.thedailybeast.com/newsweek/2005/02/21/mommy-madness.print.html. Accessed 11 July 2012.

Webber, Gretchen, and Christine Williams. "Mothers in 'Good' and 'Bad' Part-time Jobs: Different Problems, Same Results." *Gender & Society*, vol. 22, 2008, pp. 752-77.

Williams, Joan. *Unbending Gender: Why Family and Work Conflict and What to Do About It.* Oxford University Press, 2000.

Wolf, Naomi. *Misconceptions: Truth, Lies, and the Unexpected on the Journey to Motherhood.* Anchor Books, 2003.

2.
The Urge to Merge and the Marriage Imperative

The Happily Ever After in Lesbian Relationships

ALYS EINION

ONCE UPON A TIME always ends with happily ever after, at least in the stories. The stories that we consume, day after day, each time we switch on the television, go to the cinema, open up Facebook, each moment of each day, women are surrounded by stories that place relationships and relationship permanence as the truest and highest ideal of womanhood, second only to motherhood, which is viewed as one of the prime motivations for finding and securing a partner. Having grown up with the inevitable heteropatriarchal discourses of what Adrienne Rich has defined as "compulsory heterosexuality," I internalized the ideals of the dominant culture's model of dyadic, committed, and monogamous relationships, sanctioned by law and society through marriage. Within the current sociopolitical context, these issues, and their attached problems, have shifted focus and shape, such that the "normativity" I was denied through legal and social recognition of my relationship, though available, has become questionable in its desirability.

This chapter examines the stereotypes of lesbian relationships—associated with the "urge to merge," "U-Haul syndrome" and other tropes of lesbian relationships (to be defined below)—and takes into account the changes in UK law and the law in other nations that have made same-sex marriage possible. Considering the typical romanticized view of the lesbian relationship, I critically examine the nature of the "happily ever after" as a potentially false ideal, which does not account for the lived reality of lesbian partnership. The aim is to explore questions relating to the mainstreaming of lesbian relationships and families, and the pros and cons of wider social acceptance within the frameworks of heteropatriarchal models of relationship validation.

Marriage between individuals of the same sex has recently been legalized in the USA and the UK, and as a feminist and lesbian, I feel strongly that the significance of this achievement, and its connection to deeply-held and internalized ideals of marital bliss, has not yet been fully critiqued. I speak from a unique position, as I have been "married" three times, each time in a somewhat deviant manner. The nature of that deviance lies in the nature of the relationships and their transgression of the accepted and traditional norms of marriage. My first marriage was to a gay man, who knew I was a lesbian. Our relationship was loving and was based on a deep mutuality of belief and spirituality, but our marriage was at once transgressive and redemptive. Through marriage, he repaired his relationship with his natural father, whereas marriage for me represented an oppositional act—a defiance of the mandates laid down by domineering parents. Had they, and his friends, not been so violently opposed to our marriage, I might never have married him, but marriage also represented to me a form of escape. Early experiences on the lesbian scene left me disillusioned and almost desperate because nowhere did I see signs of what I had been socialized to perceive as healthy, normative relationships. Instead, I was faced with the almost inescapable array of evidence that maybe the straights were right, that homosexuality was primarily, maybe exclusively, about sex (Atkins), and I wanted more. Atkins describes the "internalised self-hatred that comes with closeting" (5), and it was this that drove me both into and out the other side of my first attempt at the happily ever after.

My second marriage was a civil partnership to my son's co-mother. The very day that it was announced that civil partnerships would come into law, I proposed, and she accepted. We attended the register office to register our union the very first day that it was possible, and our marriage took place on the very first day it was legal to do so. The forms had not even arrived at the register office, and the lovely registrar had to handwrite our certificate. The staff members were so gentle and loving, seeming to be truly delighted to celebrate our wedding with us. When we emerged from the ceremony, the crowd of people waiting for the next wedding (between a man and a woman) spontaneously burst into applause as we exited the building. It was one of the happiest days of my life. I felt that I was gaining equality and recognition for my partner, who was now legally the stepmother and co-parent of our child, and was also transgressing the unequal power relations of heteronormative marriage, rewriting the marriage script, as it were, to express true equality. Seven years later, we separated, despite all our best efforts, as we had, stereotypically, grown apart.

My third marriage was a headlong rush into commitment and the happily ever after, and it took place only nine months after we first met. There is no need to discuss how that came out. As a lesbian, understanding how relationships work and the forces that influence them has become a central feature of my quest for both intellectual understanding and personal happiness, but I approach this discussion from a bidirectional lens, as insider and as critic.

The central proposition of this chapter is that lesbian relationships have been subject to social forces, which define both their scope and their indexes of desire, and that these forces support the stereotypes of lesbian relationships (Van Eeden-Moorefield et al.). The childhood fantasies of the perfect other, the divine state of coupledom, beginning with the romantic courtship and culminating, always, in the big wedding—all of these ideals are as entrenched in the psyches of the lesbian nation as they are in the wider population. Unless we have been brought up in a separatist community—entirely unaffected by the larger world of media and politics, in conditions where heteropatriarchy holds no sway—and have never attended a mainstream school or read a mainstream children's book, these are the shared ideals of personhood. We are all taught, somehow, that to be alone is a negative state and that to be in a relationship with a significant other is to be successful. Some are more powerfully subject to this rhetoric than others. And in the lesbian dyad, it might be that the drive for togetherness is doubled simply because there are *two* women, socialized into feminized concepts of romance, love and marriage. To quote from my favourite film *Claire of the Moon*, "Instead of one pining for the white picket fence, you got two."

The history of lesbian relationships is associated with the history of feminism, especially radical feminism and, prior to that, with the cultural construct of deviance and all the angst that must come from identifying as deviant. But this deviance is also a form of empowering agency, a means by which women can reject the mandates of heterosexuality, which so powerfully limit the value, identity, and expression of self for most women. However, lesbians in the current context, especially in the UK, experience a changed social landscape in which there is both overt mainstreaming of their identity, which removes their status as radical and different, and a commercialization of that identity in line with every other social norm of womanhood, including marriage and motherhood. Even the forms of marriage that I embraced, twice, no longer exist. There is no longer a special form of legal union for the lesbians and gays. We can now all get married, divorced, and widowed. We have arrived. We occupy that elusive and sanctified status of normal.

What of the persistent tropes of the lesbian relationship that exist outside the heteronormative boundaries of marriage? Have they disappeared or become eroded by our being catapulted headfirst into social acceptability? Did they even exist in the first place? The stereotype of the lesbian relationship arc is well known within the lesbian community. The predisposition of the lesbian relationship is that it begins with a rapid commitment to a monogamous relationship, typically involving cohabitation (Gordon). This has been linked to potential explanations, including double the amount of oxytocin, the hormone, which promotes intimate relationships (Diamond). Oxytocin, which promotes maternal infant bonding and ensures extended maternal nurturing of the dependent child, is a hormone that powerfully affects the brain and nervous system and has been shown to promote human sociality (Carter). It is linked to feelings of safety (Carter). Women naturally produce a significant amount of oxytocin, and whilst this may seem a risky proposition, it could be argued that there may be a biological predisposition to engage in greater intimacy and yearn for partnering when two women get together. But this is simply a theory derived from my own background in reproductive health and a question I would like to raise for future consideration. I would not argue that we are biologically determined and fully believe in the liberty we all possess to craft and create our own life scripts. I simply wish to question why the tropes of lesbian relationships, and in particular, that headlong dash into commitment, continue. The precipitous nature of lesbian relationships can also be linked to the ways in which women are socialized to believe that being in a committed relationship is a marker of personal and social success.

Following on from this, there is the "urge to merge," known as lesbian twinning or fusion, within which two women in a relationship achieve such a degree of mutual interdependence that their identities (and appearances) seem to blend together. There is no longer Sara and Louise, two women who exist separately, but Sara-and-Louise, a unit, with blurred lines between where each individual ends and the other begins. They become seen and known as that unit, occupying space within lesbian social contexts as a kind of metamorph, even when they are not in physical proximity. In literary studies this has been characterized as "lesbian symmetry," defined by Melissa Solomon as "the symmetrical correspondence of size, shape, beauty, proportion, form or feeling allegedly visible or operative between, and in turn supposedly the result of, the corresponding bodies of lesbians" (356). It is viewed by some, particularly in psychology, as problematic, as it involves an "intense anxiety over any desire for separateness or autonomy within the relationship" (Krestan and Bepko 277). This appears to be an unconscious process and may be linked to efforts of both women to set and define the nature and "define the rules of their relationship within the context of a larger system in which no rules relating to them exist" (Krestan and Bepko 277).

This "fusion" appears to be a common phenomenon in popular discourse, and some authors have linked it to the nature of lesbian relationships under oppressive social systems (Frost and Eliason). If, for example, a social system is unequally gendered and affords more power to males than females, as is typical of many cultures globally, then a degree of intimacy and fusion develops in lesbian relationships, as both partners unite as women, to survive or fight against that oppression, or to develop a deeper sense of mutuality because of a sense of shared experience and knowledge unavailable to outsiders. Psychologists also explain that the kinds of cultural messages that dominate certain social systems can provide strong and sometimes difficult to negotiate messages about the nature of relationships and the expected behaviours required for relationship maintenance (Szymanski et al.). Thus, internalized and external heterosexism and sexism can affect women's relationships (Szymanski et al.). The lesbian relationship may be positively or negatively affected by this situation, although the experience of negative social conditions can have an overall negative effect (Einion).

However, not all relationships display this degree of fusion. A degree of similarity may exist because in finding a partner who is of the same gender and sexual orientation, the woman is actually looking for "self" in the other, so there is a predisposition to commonality. Other authors have identified that although this degree of intimate fusion can contain some pathological dimensions, such close coupling is not in essence problematic but may simply be a function of a healthy relationship in which mutuality and shared behaviours strengthen the bond and promote longevity (Ackbar and Senn). Salma Ackbar and Charlene Senn argue that preconceptions about lesbian relationships may lead to an unnecessary pathologizing of what could be viewed as a potentially supportive and satisfying degree of closeness. Their research shows that women who score higher on closeness scales experience greater relationship satisfaction, but also that fusion (which they describe also as intrusiveness) was not associated with relationship satisfaction (Ackbar and Senn). Another interesting finding from this research is that attachment style and age were correlated with fusion, as older women showed less signs of fusion (Ackbar and Senn). This is clearly a complex issue, but it is evident that the negative stereotypes attached to the concept of fusion need to be challenged. Other research also suggests that this can be viewed as normal closeness, and suggests that it is clinicians who measure this closeness against heterosexual norms and view it as pathological (Spencer and Brown).

Finally, the third phase of the relationship arc is lesbian "bed-death": a state of commonality that appears to involve a desexualization of the relationship, despite its continuing intimacy and co-dependence. Studies in the 1980s showed this to be a common feature of the lesbian dyad: lesbian couples experienced less frequent sexual activity than male-male couples or heterosexual couples

(Nichols). To understand this, it is necessary to understand some of the proposed theories of women's sexuality and lesbian sexuality. For example, one assertion is that women tend to experience sex within close, committed, and generally longer-term relationships and that lesbians experience higher relationship quality than men, as they identify sexual behaviour not necessarily as being associated with orgasm but with other activities such as kissing and hugging (Treger et al). Suzanne Johnson argues that we need to understand cultural paradigms in order to make sense of women's intimate relationships, particularly those concerning femininity and the social construction of gender which occurs from a young age. Therefore, I would argue that a cultural paradigm that associates femininity with a lack of sexual aggression or with sexual passivity, when doubled in a lesbian relationship, could lead to an eventual lack of sexual activity. Other research has associated bed-death with female gender, hormonal factors, reduced sexual initiative, and the existence of a symbiotic relationship (Van Rosmalen-Nooijens et al.). Suzanne Lazenza argues against the use of the term "lesbian bed-death." She suggests it overgeneralizes the sexual experience of lesbians and, thus, does not allow for an appreciation of the complexity of sex between women. However, a study by Jacqueline Cohen and Sandra Byers also shows that sexual satisfaction is not necessarily associated with genital sexual activity in relationships between sexual minority women.

This is not the only manifestation of lesbian relationships, which have also embraced nonbinary gender, nonmonogamy, and other manifestations of relationship, but these three features are certainly commonly held stereotypes of how lesbians create relationships.

Little concrete evidence exists of how and why these phenomena have become the signifiers of lesbian relationships, but some authors speculate about how these tropes have developed and persisted. Certainly, lesbian stereotypes aside, there is now an argument that the emergence of queer theory, and greater understanding of sexual identity fluidity, and nonbinary gender identity has resulted in a dilution of these norms, But for some women, the adherence and belonging to lesbian-feminist and radical lesbian identities, communities, and politics is a key part of meaning making in the quest for and expression of self (Shugar). Similarly, engaging in the standard form of lesbian relationships is a culturally constructed phenomenon, which serves to give the lesbian dyad both a sense of identity and ingress into lesbian community space through validation of the adherence to the expectations of that community. It begs the question, however, now that lesbianism has been mainstreamed, of whether such communities will change in their nature or whether they will even cease to exist if their prime function is "as a source from which we publicly confront challenges to our sexuality, general well-being, even our existence" (Shugar 12). Some argue that the intensity of the lesbian urge to merge derives from the need to draw strength from each other in the face of external oppression from negative social institutions. With the advent of legal relationship equality (as an option), there is, therefore, an argument that the conditions within which such relationships have typically developed have changed, and this may change the nature of such relationships. However, Laura Gold suggests a strong argument exists for a strengths-based approach to valuing lesbian relationships for their unique qualities.

The "urge to merge" and "U-Haul syndrome," (when lesbians move in with each other very early on in their relationship) and, to some extent, "lesbian bed-death" may simply be a product of the ways in which women connect to each other in deeper and more intense ways, as the history of romantic friendship shows (Nichols 363). Women connect more emotionally and do not need to us sex to form a connection (Gordon). Peplau et al. in their research in the 1970s show that women-only relationships feature two dominant values: dyadic attachment and personal autonomy ("Loving Women"). The research associated these with personal characteristics—such as greater romanticism being associated with greater dyadic attachment and involvement in feminism and higher levels of education being associated with greater levels of personal autonomy (Peplau et al. "Loving Women"). It appears that women value and gain great benefits from relationships that involve close connection, social mutuality and support, intimacy, and confidence (Liang et al.). These relationships involve

> mutual engagement (as defined by perceived mutual involvement, commitment, and attunement to the relationship),

> authenticity (the process of acquiring knowledge of self and the other and feeling free to be genuine in the context of the relationship), empowerment/zest (the experience of feeling personally strengthened, encouraged, and inspired to take action), and the ability to deal with difference or conflict. (Liang et al. 26)

Although not everyone wants to fit in, or is capable of it, "to fit the norm, one must often erase the complexity of one's histories and desires" (Atkins 5). The threat of the loss of lesbian distinctiveness is very real. Lesbian relationships no longer take place in secret, in private, or within lesbian communities. They take place in the larger social world where, regardless of any persistent personal or even community homophobia, we cannot be discriminated against. What then is there left to fight for? Whereas once such relationships were placed under significant strain because of a lack of ability to be "out," to experience social recognition, validation, and support (Caron and Ulin), now in the UK, we can undergo the same rites of passage as anyone else, and experience the same social recognition. However, I would argue that this valorization is not universal and that the negative stereotypes of lesbian relationships—particularly the external and mass-media association of same-sex relationships with sex or seeing them as less real than those between men and women— continues to affect women as they negotiate the unknown country of legitimacy, marriage, and divorce. From the failure of colleagues to cope with discussions of wedding preparations, to families refusing to attend weddings, to friends and colleagues failing to recognize the significance of a relationship breakdown or to feel real compassion for a woman going through a lesbian divorce, the creation of laws and legal systems has not yet changed the internalized values and cognitive models with which people personally and privately categorize us. We have fought against being "denied, shut out" (Reid 199), and legally in the UK, we are no longer excluded but socially we continue to be. For lesbian parents, for example, the parental politics at the school gate each morning, the behaviours of the other mums in playgroup, the sanctions they can place on their children playing with our children—all still allow for the exclusion of lesbians from mainstream social spaces.

All relationships take place within "a complex social context" that affects the quality of those relationships (Caron and Ulin 413). As Peplau et al. show, research historically cites high levels of satisfaction within lesbian relationships ("Satisfaction in Lesbian Relationships"). But a scan of a random selection of lesbian-defined groups within social media shows a high level of relationship turnover and, within this space, continuing evidence of at least one phenomenon—"U-Haul syndrome." I analyzed five lesbian-identified UK groups on the most popular social media site, looking at posts over a one-year period, and found narrative tropes among the posts of relationship breakdowns followed by swift reformations within new configurations. These groups—which range in age and self-defined identity, as set out by their group definitions of purpose—contain a range of posts relating to women's experiences of relationships and a worrying trend to cite past lovers as abusive or to pathologize prior relationships or partners. For example, in one UK closed group for a particular age group (forty plus), the appearance of posts about narcissists and consequent discussions of the power play between narcissists and their partners suggest, anecdotally, that there are unhealthy power dynamics within many dyadic connections cited by these women. However, this is pure speculation and could be an artefact of the medium. Women in relationships with high satisfaction and positive power dynamics, for example, may simply not engage in such groups, which are often a source of social support for single women or women who feel socially isolated. Social media offers any woman with Internet access the potential to access this particular form of social support and to experience its pitfalls as well. The public nature of many relationships, which form and disintegrate so publicly, provide potential evidence of a high degree of impermanence and continuing issues relating to the power transactions that signify lesbian connections. To view one member of a once-happy couple criticizing her ex-lover online, posting photographs and negative comments that for people in the know, have little or no truth, shows that the urge to merge too often seems to result in the subsuming of one woman into another's reality, with negative consequences in many cases.

But this is all anecdotal, and constitutes a personal and critical reflection on the wider experience of trying to understand the nature of both lesbian relationships and inclusion and exclusion. Such behaviours occur in real life as well, and there appears to be a kind of brutal reality in which lesbian women place high value on the ability to find and keep a lover regardless of personal consequences, including potential loss of self and dilution of sexual desire (Gordon). Even outside the world of heteronormativity, women are still subject to the same kinds of forces, including the idea that a successful woman is one who has secured a partner and managed to maintain a long-term relationship (Gordon). Similarly, the nature of lesbian community is not all woman-loving positivity. Lesbian communities are just as successful at marginalizing those who do not fit in as any others (Hird and Germon; Gordon).

However anecdotal and biased the representation of relationships may be on the Internet, and however incestuous and exclusive lesbian communities can sometimes be, this reflection on such relationships echoes research which has historically demonstrated that a significant number of intimate connections between women show an imbalance of power, which in turn is associated with relationship problems and a lack of satisfaction (Caldwell and Peplau).Questions remain about the future evolution of the lesbian dyad and its place in wider social contexts in the face of marriage equality. In her critical yet personal essay exploring the process of getting married, Catherine Reid states that this act "links us with every heterosexual union that has ever preceded us" (198). This connection is a a double-edged sword, a legacy of both positive and negative models that which must be carefully assimilated into a new kind of construct, that of lesbian marriage. I would argue that having a legal union frees lesbians to pursue their individual interests and retain autonomy, for example perhaps because they are no longer expending energy fighting to establish the validity of their relationship or defend its legitimacy. The research by Stephen Haas and Laura Stafford seems to show that in general, lesbian couples show similar relationship maintenance behaviours to heterosexual married couples, but there are some differences, particularly in relation to working on the relationship through meta-relational communication. Will social legitimacy within marriage reduce the "urge to merge" and align these relationships differently, and therefore allow for greater autonomy? However, it could be argued that this is a generalization and that the degree of equality will depend on the individuals within the relationship and their personal histories and personalities. Personal experience on the part of the author, however, would suggest that lesbians do seem to spend a lot of time thinking and talking about their relationships.

Lesbians have always engaged in this kind of union, regardless of legal recognition, and have always created new ways of being that are unique to lesbian partnership (Nichols). The advent of legal protection and marriage equality raises questions about how much our distinctiveness, which has perhaps been the key defining feature of the all-female dyad, will become subsumed into the commercialized, socially sanctioned definition of happily ever after. Lesbians are now subject to the same targeted marketing about 'the wedding' and the associated commercialization of this life event. Wedding shows and sales events are now targeted at same-sex couples. The UK's most popular lesbian publication, *Diva Magazine*, features sanitized and highly polished versions of the lesbian marriage ideal and is heavily supported by advertising about weddings, which firmly entrenches mainstream ideals of marriage within lesbian culture. We are now as free as any other woman to dream of the ideal wedding day, destination, or dress. Thus, lesbians are also subject to the powerful forces of marketing that highlight the wedding as the goal, not the relationship; the big day now becomes the focus, not the happily ever after.

It is yet to be seen how much this will affect stereotypes of lesbian relationships. Will they change? Or will they become more evident and reinforced? Now that lesbians can marry, will they hurtle headlong into legal union as quickly as they have moved in with each other historically? Will the role of spouse affect identity and fusion? I cannot answer these questions. I can only suggest that future research and debate should continue to focus on the significance of relationships for lesbians as women, as distinctive from others and as distinctive from heterosexual women. According to Judith Jordan (13), "for women, especially, connection with others is central to psychological well-being." Searching for a sense of mutuality, and in particular relational mutuality, is the hallmark of the lesbian happily ever after because those relationships are between women (Jordan). This mutuality is more critical in lesbian relationships because, as discussed previously, there appears to be a desire for and manifestation of greater levels of equality and closeness, resulting in positive benefits for the relationship (Ackbar and Senn). However, we have yet to see how this will be affected by legal marriage.

I believe that marriage equality has brought about vast improvements in the lives of lesbian-defined women, but it comes with a price. "In the comfort of knowing we *belong*, we risk forgetting what happens on the margins and in the dramas that defined us, and which continue to shape all other minority groups" (emphasis in original, Reid 204). We are formed by the powerful forces of struggle and resistance that historically shaped our very identities. Marriage itself is viewed by many feminists as a state of inequality. Will lesbians change the very nature of marriage by making it about true mutuality rather than the contract of possession of one woman by one man that it has typically signified as a historical, legal, and religious construct? Or will it result in continued power plays between women who have internalized gendered power relationships and place expectations on the wife to perform a traditional role? I can only hope that the former will be true and that lesbians continue to be at the forefront of changing social forces that liberate women to become everything they wish to become and through this, change the world for our daughters, sisters, mothers, and grandmothers through creating and living a different relationship ideal. It may not always be happily ever after, but it will certainly involve personal happiness and the ability to live and love as we see fit.

WORKS CITED

Ackbar, Salma, and Charlene Yvette Senn. "What's the Confusion about fusion? Differentiating Positive and Negative Closeness in Lesbian Relationships." *Journal of Marital and Family Therapy*, vol. 36, 2010, pp. 416-30.

Atkins, Dawn. "Introduction: Lebian Sex Scandals." *Journal of Lesbian Studies*, vol. 3, no. 3, 1999, pp. 1-9.

Caldwell, Mayta A, and Anne Letitia Peplau. "The Balance of Power in Lesbian Relationships." *Sex Roles*, vol. 10, no. 7/8,1984, pp. 27-39.

Caron, Sandra L, and Marjorie Ulin. "Closeting and the Quality of Lesbian Relationships." *Families in Society*, vol.78, no. 4, 1997, pp. 413-19.

Carter, Sue. "Oxytocin Pathways and the Evolution of Human Behavior." *Annual Review of Psychology*, vol. 65, 2014, pp. 17-39.

Cohen, Jacqueline N., and Sandra Byers. "Beyond Lesbian Bed Death: Enhancing Our Understanding of the Sexuality of Sexual-Minority Women in Relationships." *The Journal of Sex Research*, vol. 51, no. 8, 2014, pp. 893-903.

Diamond, Lisa. "The Evolution of Plasticity in Female-Female Desire." *Journal of Psychology and Human Sexuality*, vol. 18, no. 4, 2007, pp. 245-74.

Einion, Alys. "Lesbian Families, Sons, and Mothering: Parenting Outside the Boundaries." *Essential Breakthroughs: Conversations about Men, Mothers and Mothering*, edited by Fiona Joy Green and Gary Lee Pelletier, Demeter Press, 2015, pp. 90-109.

Frost, David M., and Michele J. Eliason. "Challenging the Assumption of Fusion in Female Same-Sex Relationships." *Psychology of Women Quarterly*, vol. 38, no. 1, 2014, pp. 65-74.

Gold, Laura. "A Critical Analysis of Fusion in Lesbian Relationships." *Canadian Social Work Review*, vol. 20, no. 2, 2003, pp. 259-71.

Gordon, Liahna E. "Bringing the U-Haul: Embracing and Resisting Sexual Stereotypes in a Lesbian Community." *Sexualities*, vol. 9, no, 2, 2006, pp. 171-92.

Haas, Stephen M., and Laura Stafford. "Maintenance Behaviours in Same-Sex and Marital Relationships: A Matched Sample Comparison." *The Journal of Family Communication*, vol. 5, no. 1, 2005, pp. 43-60.

Hird, Myra J., and Jenz Germon. "Women on the Edge of a Dyke-otomy: Confronting Subjectivity." *Journal of Lesbian Studies*, vol. 3, no, 3, 1999, pp. 103-11.

Johnson, Suzanne. "From Cultural Scripting to Autonomy: Influences on Lesbian Identity." *Transactional Analysis Journal*, vol. 34, no. 2, 2004, pp. 170-79.

Jordan, Judith V. "Traditional Development: Therapeutic Implications of Empathy and Shame." *Women's Growth in Diversity*, edited by Judith Jordan, The Guildford Press, 1997, pp. 2.

Krestan, Jo-Ann, and Claudia Bepko. "The Problem of Fusion in Lesbian Relationships." *Family Process*, vol. 19., 1980, pp. 277-89.

Lazenza, Suzanne. "Beyond 'Lesbian Bed Death': the Passion and Play in Lesbian Relationships." *Journal of Lesbian Studies*, vol. 6, no. 1, 2002, pp. 111-20.

Liang, Belle, et al. "The Relational Health Indices: A Study of Women's Relationships." *Psychology of Women Quarterly*, vol. 26, no. 1, 2002, pp. 25-35.

Nichols, Margaret. "Lesbian Sexuality/Female Sexuality: Rethinking 'Lesbian Bed Death.'" *Sexual and Relationship Therapy*, vol. 19, no. 4, 2004, pp. 363-71.

Peplau, Letitia Anne, et al. "Satisfaction in Lesbian Relationships." *Journal of Homosexuality*, vol. 8, no. 2, 1982, pp. 23-35.

Peplau, Letitia Anne, et al. "Loving women: Attachment and Autonomy in Lesbian Relationships." *Journal of Social Issues*, vol. 34, no. 3, 1978, pp. 7-27.

Reid, Catherine. "Getting Hitched v. the Trashing of Marriage." *The Massachusetts Review*, vol. 46, no. 2, 2005, pp. 197-209.

Rich, Adrienne. "Compulsory Heterosexuality and Lesbian Existence." *Signs: Journal of Women in Culture and Society*, vol. 5, no. 4, 1980, 631-66.

Shugar, Dana R. "To(o) Queer or Not? Queer Theory, Lesbian Community and the Functions of Sexual Identities." *Journal of Lesbian Studies*, vol. 3, no. 3, 1999, pp. 11-19.

Solomon, Melissa. "'The Queen's Twin': Sarah Orne Jewett and Lesbian Symmetry." *Nineteenth-Century Literature*, vol. 60, no. 3, 2005, pp. 355-74.

Spencer, Bernadette, and Jac Brown. "Fusion or Internalized Homophobia? A Pilot Study of Bowen's Differentiation of Self Hypothesis with Lesbian Couples." *Family Process*, vol. 46, no. 2, 2007, pp. 257-68.

Szymanksi, Dawn M., et al. "Sexual Minority Women's Relationship Quality: Examining the Roles of Multiple Oppressions and Silencing the Self." *Psychology of Sexual Orientation and Gender Diversity*, vol. 3, no. 1, 2016, pp. 1-10.

Treger, Stanislav, et al. "Women's Sexuality in Close Relationships." *The Essential Handbook of Women's Sexuality*, edited by Donna-Marie Castaneda, Praeger, 2013, pp. 47-70.

Van Eeden-Moorefield, Brad, et al. "Same-Sex Relationships and Dissolution the Connection between Heteronormativity and Homonormativity." *Family Relations*, vol. 60, 2011, pp. 562-71.

Van Rosmalen-Nooijens, Karin, et al. "Bed Death and Other Lesbian Sexual Problems Unraveled: a Qualitative Study of the Sexual Health of Lesbian Women Involved in a Relationship." *Women and Health*, vol. 48, no. 3, 2008, pp. 339-62.

3.
A Sociological Adaptation of the Grandmother Hypothesis

Or, Simply Put, Go Ask Your Grandmother!

ANN REED WILDER

TYPICALLY, OLDER GENERATIONS in society begin to lose support as their economic productivity and physical capabilities start to decline. Depending on the cultural attitudes, family functioning, and resources available, older adults often become isolated and sometimes ostracized in communities. The "grandmother hypothesis" was developed from theoretically questioning why women live so much longer past the age of fertility in societies worldwide. If older adults tend to lose support as they age, why is it that women continue to live so much longer past their reproductive capacity? What is it that sustains women later in life? The adaptation of roles for women in society is directly linked to the ability to procreate (Strassman and Garrard 3). Fertility is marked by the onset and cessation of menses, which typically declines for women in most cultures on average during their forties.

The impact of menopause upon the lifespan development of women is a profound developmental milestone often associated with old age and the "wise woman" or crone archetype. This stage of a woman's development serves as a time when thoughts deepen and take on a more existential and spiritual meaning. Moreover, the process of aging and its limitations of the physical body become more pronounced; it also becomes more psychologically important for women to remain mentally active and to engage in the mentoring of younger generations (Ray 111). The grandmother hypothesis asserts that the significance of life span development for women goes well past menopause and that women typically live longer than men because of the connection to family and the importance grandmothering has for families and the subsequent generations. This chapter explores the relationship between the grandmother hypothesis and the myth of the happily ever after in marriage for women and intergenerational relations within families.

Women live well beyond their time of procreation in life, which challenges the question of role and purpose for women in society from a sexist or patriarchal belief system wherein women are determined worthy based on their ability to reproduce. The grandmother hypothesis is a modern construct with basic concepts that have evolved from evolutionary choices related to finding a mate, procreating, tending to hearth and home, and the beginning of menopause into more complex decision making for women. Conceptually, this hypothesis has evolved in such a way to include more complex metamodern choices, such as the tension of choosing a career over parenthood and working or handling the sandwich generation stress of parenting and elder caregiving with aging parents. Metamodernity is a term for the era that sociologists and humanists are beginning to reference since the closing of postmodernism in the late twentieth century. Metamodernity is defined by global crisis, rapid exchange of information, and human expressions of desire for widespread change.

The early part of the twenty-first century has seen multiple global crises that have impacted on the environmental climate and population demographics in profound ways (Vermeulen and Van den Akker 56). The multitude of global crises in contemporary society is linked to the reality that women sustain health and economic productivity well into the years of postmenopause (Hawkes & Coxworth 1). How does having all of these options and choices affect the adaptation of women and the relationships they have with their daughters in the twenty-first century? What are some of the critical windows of adaptation that can help lay the groundwork for a life rooted in the reality of choice, struggle, and balance, versus one fueled by fairy tale notions of the happily ever after painted into picturesque landscapes with princes, storks, and picket fences? How can intergenerational connections with grandmothers strengthen the bonds that help sustain traditional family ties and assist with the positive adaptation for women in society? How does the involvement of a grandmother in a woman's life help for the better and the worse in a marital fairy tale?

Women who are faced with the many choices of young adulthood amid the tensions of metamodern society may want to also consult with their grandmothers and talk about what kinds of life choices make the most sense in a world full of rapidly increasing options. After all, it is the generations that come before who are considered to be the wisdom keepers and seasoned elders in family and society. Wisdom tells us that asking your grandmother important questions about life is a smart thing to do. Still today, it is considered common practice for some research methodologists to encourage students to review their research hypothesis with their own grandmothers to see if the topic and questions make sense (Lavery). Grandmothers help to maintain the collective narrative for individuals and families, uphold meaningful traditions, and stitch together the gaps found in metamodern society, which can be done in ways that both enhance and impede the growth of the next generation for a woman and her family. Grandmothers can help to integrate the mythical archetypes of marriage and motherhood that is transmitted through intergenerational wisdom, or can perpetuate the fairy tale myths that keep women stuck in toxic patterns of relating that can originate within a family of origin.

Taking time to pass down the wisdom of mothers to daughters and granddaughters is critical in how women knit together their life stories and perceive the significance of family traditions (e.g., wearing your grandmothers dress for a special occasion, getting married in your mother's wedding gown, attending a college where family are alumni, and making choices in parenting practices). Much like traditions, fairy tales are cultural stories passed down in society, generation after generation, with archetypes that continue to ring bells of universal truth inside the human psyche. The myth of the happily ever after for women in mate selection is often linked to gender roles and expectations for career and social status, which involves living out life happily together with a sense of satisfaction. This fairy tale ideal can be dangerous for women who become psychologically attached to the role of submission and enraptured with the need for adoration— two aspects of womanhood that can drastically change later in life.

Examples of female archetypes, representing the role of grandmothering and wisdom found in fairy tales and sacred texts include the Crone Goddess and Sophia, the goddess of wisdom. These archetypes represent the late life aspect of motherhood that no longer has reproductive capacity, is a keeper of wisdom, a healer, and is available to share her knowledge with the world around her. Drawing from the model of the grandmother hypothesis and theories of wisdom, this analysis will further address unique angles created from the questions that have been posed. Through this analysis, I place emphasis on the ability of women to reconstruct stories that pass down wisdom and tell the truth about their lives through intergenerational support and family bonding. The ability to reconstruct these personal narratives becomes necessary for women to psychologically transform the myth of the happily ever after into a well-integrated and balanced psyche complete with the strength necessary to confidently navigate a rapidly changing world.

GRANDMOTHER HYPOTHESIS

The grandmother hypothesis came into cultural awareness in the later part of the twentieth century when several anthropologists began debating the purpose of grandmothering in postmodern society. Debates ensued over a concept that had no empirical data to support its relevance. These questions about the societal roles of women in late adulthood have since led to an abundance of academic research related to evolution in both human and primate communities. Research since then has found that human grandmothering is a critical factor in determining the longevity of the human species and is now accepted as a critical part of a lifespan and of family development (Hawkes 129). Initially, much of the controversy related to this hypothesis was over the reproductive capability of women and how the purpose of women in society changes at the time of menopause when reproduction is no longer possible. Life span development beyond menopause is now seen as a critical aspect of healthy aging related to longevity and quality of life for older women who have an obvious purpose in the evolution of the human family beyond that of reproduction.

Grandmothers investing in the needs of family members has played an important part in the evolution of menopause over time and is believed to lengthen the postmenopausal lifespan. This hypothesis emphasizes the relationship of maternal grandmothers with their children, which tends to be related to geographical proximity and opportunity for interaction with family members (Strassman 2). In most cultures, it is more common to see mothers of mothers, as opposed to mothers of fathers, actively engaged and leading families in grandmothering. Maternal grandmothers are often seen as having more importance to the next generation of family development than mothers of fathers or grandfathers. Proponents of the grandmother hypothesis tend to devalue the role of males beyond wage earning and mating, and highlight the role that women play in childrearing as part of the extended family empire (Hum Nat 203). Based on this societal observation, the relationship a woman has with her own mother becomes significant in how she chooses to play out the fairy tale myth in her own marriage and reproductive decision making.

It seems now, more than ever, that the phenomenon of grandmothering has become exceedingly important in the role of support and nurturance for women who are of childbearing age. Research on age and reproductive capacity reveals that entry into grandmothering is becoming less predictable because of advanced maternal age and changes in women's fertility trends over the last several decades (Silverstein and Marenco 495). What does this mean for women today, who are caught in the mire of juggling career, childrearing, and family responsibilities? More specifically, over the last four decades, the number of children in the U.S. being raised by grandparent-head of households has dramatically increased in all cultural and socioeconomic categories. Economic challenges in the U.S. brought on by unemployment and the housing crisis associated with the "great recession" has played a part in this increased phenomenon of grandparent-head of households now referred to as "grand families" (Goyer).

Grandparenting is culturally bound and encompasses a variety of unique experiences. The meaning of grandparenting is considered to be fluid and changes over time depending on the unique passages in and out of developmental life stages. In the early 2000s,

6.3 percent of all children in the U.S. were being raised by their grandparents, and this number continues to rise (Goodman and Silverstein 676). More recent population studies indicate that as of 2010, 7 percent of all children (one in every fourteen) are raised by grandparents (U.S. Census Bureau). Sociologists and population demographers agree that this rise is because of the increased longevity of women.

Unique to the human species, reproduction stops in the middle of life for women. Despite patriarchal attitudes that imply a woman's worth is hinged upon her ability to procreate, studies prove that women are more likely to remain engaged with their families over time and help with the growth and development of their children's children. How can intergenerational connections strengthen the bonds that help sustain traditional family ties and help women adapt? These intergenerational connections have a positive secondary gain by providing protective barriers for women and children, therefore, improving quality of life and lengthening the human lifespan. The importance of the grandmother's role in the lives of her grandchildren can be defined, understood, and attributed to the criterion of choice. These choices are often economically based and may or may not have a positive influence upon the psychological development of women who are emerging into motherhood.

The involvement from grandmothers—who are in a custodial relationship involving guardianship (engaged with children and absent parent) versus a cooperative co-parenting relationship (engaged with children and present parent)—contributes to a decrease in stress and increase in coping within the family. The health of a grandparent, history of the first generation parenting experience, and the economic condition of the family positively affect the development of intergenerational relationships in families (Goodman and Silverstein 687). This supports the notion that when parents have had a positive and enriching history with their family growing up, they are more likely to reach out and engage with their own parents for support in parenting the next generation. However, there are times when a crisis in the happily ever after—such as divorce, military deployment, or death of a spouse—may unexpectedly catapult a family into intergenerational parenting and create tension in relationships, as in when past hurts have been unresolved.

Results of contemporary health research indicate that the increase in length of human survivorship addresses the meaning of the elusive concept of the development of metamodern society from both the biological and behavioural aspect of human evolution. The increased longevity of human life allows for more investment of older adults in their children's families, which creates an evolutionary advantage (Caspari and Lee). The grandmother hypothesis also stresses that longer lives improve the fitness of older women in family and society, who are more likely to be positively invested in the wellbeing of their reproductive age daughters and grand-daughters (Caspari and Lee). This advantage can be seen through a decrease in financial and time constraints, as the grandmother becomes an extra adult to provide care, feeding, transportation, supervision, and advocacy for the next generation of children in a family. Grandmothers can drive children to extracurricular events when parents are working and be a second set of eyes when there are issues related to health care or education. They can also take on leadership in the family and advocate for the needs of their grandchildren in complicated scenarios (e.g., schools, healthcare systems, or competitive sports) (Davis).

Grandmothers are an important part of family strength and survival now, since they help to protect the intergenerational value base of a family. The simplicity of being able to explain something complex to your grandmother can serve as a litmus test of meaningfulness and relatability (Lavery). Transgenerational relationships that act across multiple generations become important for the development of society by increasing the value placed upon in older populations. These relationships can uphold traditions and pass down wisdom and specialized knowledge (Caspari and Lee). This becomes a feminist concern because of how the rights of women are affected by the labour market and laws pertaining to birth control and reproductive rights. Whether the political position of a grandmother as elder female in the family is more liberal or conservative, without the intergenerational transmission of wisdom and knowledge, young women with children are more at risk of falling into the crevices of social-structural lag. This includes the restriction of gender roles and increased competition in metamodern society that is characterized by wide sweeping change, crisis and global chaos. Grandmothers can help create a safety net for the complex trapeze artistry of new motherhood in metamodern society.

WOMEN AND ADAPTATION

Many sociologists assert that people of all ages face problems in accepting change, determining core values, adjusting attitudes, developing social behaviours, and interacting with social networks at some time across their lifespan. Technology has helped to create more scaffolding for young mothers by promoting online parenting resources, mom support systems, and information sharing with friends and family. Grandmothers who live far away can stay connected through social media, photo sharing, live-video streaming, or video conferencing, which makes it more beneficial for children who cannot interact in person with their grandmothers more often. All of these struggles are seen as significant to adaptation, which can be defined as the ability to adjust to the environment in a way that allows for optimal functioning so that an individual is capable of meeting their own basic human needs (Blackburn and Dulmus 94).

Learning to adapt and "go with the flow" of the natural world is critical for surviving and thriving in any environment. Significant life changes—such as marriage, childbearing, and grandparenting—cause individuals to modify their core values and attitudes toward the world around them. This, in turn, triggers a cycle of change, modification, and adaptation at a core level that continues as part of the developmental aging process. These core values and attitudes are what psychologically carry women through the inevitable changes in life and serve as navigational rudders for optimal development in later adulthood. Grandmothering is an example of one such major life change that many women go through later in life, often affecting not only the individual member but subsequent generations of an entire family.

Human relations deepen in older age, which affects the emotional regulation and exclusivity of social networks, as noted in socioemotional selectivity theory (Blackburn and Dulmus 69). This phenomenon can allow for grandmothers to be less reactive and more able to comprehend reasons behind actions, of which overextended parents may not recognize because of hectic family lifestyles in a fast-paced, highly automated society. A sharing of experience, strength, and hope from grandmothers to mothers and children helps to strengthen the lessons learned and can possibly reduce the negative impact of personal mistakes in order to make life easier for the next generation, which challenges the influence of fairy tale realities for women.

How does having all the options found in a metamodern society affect the adaptation of women and the relationships that they have with their daughters and granddaughters in the twenty-first century? This situation can be considered within the framework of social-structural lag, which affects many aspects of older adulthood. Structural lag refers to the phenomenon that occurs when a society moves and changes in one direction without the compensation or modification necessary for the corresponding and related aspects that serve to maintain homeostasis. The term social-structural lag was first identified as a concept by sociologist, Matilda Wiley, referencing how behaviour and attitude interact with opportunities in society in such a way that mutually shapes one another (Peine and Neven 130). Contemporary examples include extended retirement age, postretirement employment opportunity, individual role definition, gender identity, and family constellation. These examples each have corresponding results that challenge systems and societies in maintaining structural homeostasis (e.g., an economic example is age of retirement and opportunity for employment). When this imbalance happens, there is a structural lag in the ability of society to meet the changing needs of older adults (Peine and Neven 137).

Advancements in equal opportunity have demanded that women take on multiple roles in both family and society, which further challenges the gender roles and expectations associated with the fairy tale myth of the happily ever after. This is primarily evident in the economic and career choices that women make, in addition to marriage and childbearing. Educational and vocational advancement has created both opportunity and stress for women, who are seeking work-life balance between vocation and family. The ability to appraise for and adapt to stress has become necessary for women in the era of metamodern society. This stress has much to do with the onset of the information revolution and the subsequent technology invented to enhance the transfer of personal information, which has created an unprecedented acceleration in data and human information exchange generating more societal pressure and competition.

Being able to share pictures of events, accomplishments, and milestones at a moment's notice has become a popular trend in social networking, contributing even further to societal competition, individual angst, and pressure from juggling career and family life for women in a world that never stops talking. The implication is that the myth of fairy tale marriages with utopic happy endings is being deconstructed and reclassified based on modern societal interpretations. Grandmothers can help narrate the telling of stories and therefore engage directly in the process of accepting and believing a myth or fairy tale reality for the next generation of women in a family.

The involvement of grandmothers provides stress buffers for mothers and grandchildren. This can be seen in kinship care arrangements where grandmothers share financial burdens with mothers and children (Barnet et al. 636). Grandmothering is often seen as an investment in a child's health for higher income families and as a means of survival in low-income families, where kinship care is the norm (Silverstein and Marenco 497). When family relations are positive, the physical presence of grandmothers can help reduce the impact of negative parenting. Patterns of negative parenting can be described as an ineffective or abusive means of relating between parent and child. When families are functional and mothering role models are strong, grandmothers can provide a positive buffer for parental stress in childrearing, which can help reduce the chances of children acting out or developing a reactive temperament (Barnet et al. 637). When families are more dysfunctional and weak with ambivalent or collapsed mothers, both grandmothers and grandfathers can become negative influences that perpetuate toxic patterns of interrelating.

Women are now expected to work and maintain contact with their children through technological means in a society demanding more from women, which is why positive support from grandmothers becomes critical in filling the gaps of care needed for optimal child and family development. Being able to assess for new opportunities arising from drastic ecological change is critical for women in order to have a positive impact on human adaptation in later adulthood and support the transference of wisdom from older to younger generations. Because of an increase in life expectancy and healthy aging, grandmothering is an opportunity for families that is shifting dramatically as the baby-boom generation continues to reach older adulthood, turning sixty-five in a massive population demographic. Grandmothers help build cognitive bridges and create emotional adhesive to fill the physical gaps of the social-structural lag beyond a simplistic emphasis on reproduction. This makes grand mothers an important link in the evolutionary chain of metamodern society.

WISDOM THEORY

"Wisdom" is an elusive concept which is difficult to define. The concept dates back as far as human civilization, yet the scientific study of wisdom only began in the 1970s (Jeste et al. 9). Wisdom is typically associated with old age; however, all elderly people do not necessarily possess wisdom. A universally accepted view does not exist on the relationship between wisdom and age and researchers disagree on how wisdom actually relates to the biological process of aging (Sternberg 20). Philosophers, theologians, sociologists, and psychologists have attempted to describe and define this term since the sixth century BCE. Conceptually, wisdom is identified as having cognitive, reflective, and affective domains (Ardelt, "Are Older Adults" 202). Successful aging involves optimal adult development in later adulthood that acknowledges an integral relationship between the individual and the development of wisdom. By looking at these concepts, gerontologists can better understand aging from a positive and holistic perspective as it relates to the overall function of life identity and healthy aging.

There is interplay between the striving for optimal success and the chronic incompleteness of metamodern life that often occurs in later adulthood. This striving is thought to exist until death, even for older adults that have high levels of health, income, and life satisfaction. The Germanic term "*sehnsucht*" addresses the meaning of yearning and life longing that equates to a feeling of desire and need to fill the chronic incompleteness that exists in an older person's life (Blackburn and Dulmus 117). These concepts are, however, elusive as they relate to wisdom and life yearnings, encompassing several points related to lifespan development in later adulthood. Finding ways that adults can mentor and contribute to the next generation, not only to their families but also to society at large, begins to take on more importance. These experiences can be both positively shared in families through storytelling and actual parental engagement, allowing individuals to create more positive relationships with their children and grandchildren.

In fast paced societies where the process of aging is often devalued, the wisdom of older adults may prove to be even more valuable during such times of historically rapid technological, environmental, and social change (Ardelt, "Are Older Adults"204). The ability to face the challenges of a complex and rapidly changing world include emotional intelligence, social competence, and self-regulation. Consensus within wisdom research agrees that empathy and compassion for others are necessary components of wisdom (Sternberg 2). The Berlin Wisdom Model explores how cognition, personality, and lifespan development theories fit within this paradigm: "Five criteria are considered to be an important part of this wisdom model: 1) factual knowledge about human nature and life course, 2) procedural knowledge about dealing with life's problems, 3) life span contextualism and how the context of life changes over time, 4) value relativism and tolerance, and 5) knowledge about handling uncertainty" (Blackburn and Dulmus 123). Other models look at the interplay between life experiences, life skills, a willingness to learn, soft skill human interaction ability, and altruism as components for measuring wisdom (Greene and Brown 293).

In older adulthood, reflecting on one's life journey can lead to a desire to engage in generative behaviours—such as mentoring, leadership, and work—necessary to develop a positive legacy that will be left behind for others, all of which are associated with the development of wisdom (Parisi et al. 872). Focusing on wisdom and life longings creates an infusion of positivity into the understanding of later adulthood. Wisdom-related knowledge is linked to positive development and interests in self-actualization or helping others grow, which is often directly connected with older adults and family (Ardelt, "Antecedents and Effects" 381). The ability to successfully integrate life experiences directly relates to the quality of life and biopsychosocial health later in life. This is a significant topic in the field of aging because of the relationship of lifespan development and the psychological integration of life experiences when using a holistic approach. An example of this is seen in reminiscence and the engagement of personal life storytelling, which can help women to integrate their personal relationship history through the shedding of the fairy tale myths often associated with youthful perspectives on marriage.

Wisdom and life longing are significant topics in the field of aging that affect the quality of life, lifespan development, and psychological integration of life experiences. Life longings affect directionality in life and the management of loss and things unattained. This concept, paired with desire and yearning, has been researched and identified as part of a person' self-conception and is not considered to be something fleeting or passing in later adulthood. In fact, cognitive theorists typically characterize later adulthood as a time for integrating and solidifying one's self-concepion, which sometimes happens through a deepening of interpersonal relationships, spiritual quests, or "bucket list" type experiences. These experiences can take the form of travel to beloved areas, doing an activity that someone has always dreamed of, learning a new skill, or meeting a specific person they have always wanted to know more about before they die. Life longings are usually more about a "personal utopia of life," as it relates to the integration of desire, opportunity, and life experience, which creates opportunity for myth busting and the rupturing of fairy tale realities.

Cognitive and emotional struggles are common later in life. Obtaining a better understanding of the development and application of wisdom is significant, as it relates to the emotional struggle of life yearnings and interpersonal integration, and can serve to shed light on the evolution of marriage, childbearing, parenting, and the structural adaptation of family for the aging population. Individuals very often make choices around marriage and childbearing based upon their own experiences in life, including the choice to marry before starting a career or perhaps waiting until later in life after obtaining education and career experience. Taking time to reflect upon the personal narratives in life can help women as grandmothers to reconstruct narratives rooted in truth and resiliency. This can provide a more optimistic and productive time ahead for future generations who will not fall prey to the fairy tale myth of an unrealistic happily ever after.

The ability to successfully integrate life experiences relates to the quality of life and biopsychosocial health of older adults. A direct and positive correlation exists between the level of wisdom that an individual carries within her and an ability to maintain a satisfactory quality of life necessary to support the next generation of family members. Ecological aging principles address the broader social and environmental components affecting quality of life and promoting healthy aging for older adults (Greene and Brown 3). Some progressive societies, for example, integrate intergenerational programming in the same setting with children, such as having a daycare in an older adult care facility or a volunteer grandparent brigade in a primary age school. Here, elements of health and sustainability become the focus by emphasizing strengths as opposed to encouraging a deficit-based outlook (Harris et al. 199). This viewpoint implies and supports a need for harmony and balance between human beings and the natural world in order to improve both individual and intergenerational functioning for families and society.

CONSTRUCTING NARRATIVE

Narrative work is an important technique for life integration. Older adults will often spontaneously tell their life stories as part of a natural process of coping within the context of their existing environment. The narration and development of life stories relate to cognition, information processing, and emotional regulation (Ray, "The Search for Meaning" 132). Through repetition of detail in the telling of a life story, there is a cognitive aspect involving memory and linkage of past, present, and future events. Information processing is an integral part as well as linking the context of the story and present situation. A focus is often the emotional processing of subjective goals within the retelling of a life story. Personal narrative has been found to provide a window into emotional regulation. With every telling of a story, an emotional connection is made to the perceived loss and goal attainment in life. Grief can be resolved through the telling of a story and scripts of life events can be rewritten in ways that accentuate positive experiences. This process can enhance healing, not only for the individual but also for families and subsequent generations (Ray "The Search for Meaning" 135). The repeating of life stories and personal narratives becomes a significant part of family attachment and, in some cases, has been found to be predictive of one's behaviour in future generations (Pinkola Estes 190).

There has been a recent resurgence of interest in narrative therapies with older adults, especially on the topic of improved health outcomes. Life story narratives help integrate past, present and future and therefore supporting improved mood. Studies have shown that when people engage in reminiscing about positive events, positive emotional and behavioural outcomes are increased. Some of the emerging ideas that incorporate narrative techniques can be found in the development of life story narrative groups as a form of qualitative research designed to support enrichment and the cultivation of meaning later in life (Ray "The Search for Meaning" 132). This approach does not focus on behaviour as much as it focuses on the feeling and depth of meaning. Narrativity allows an individual to leave behind the wounds of the past, to explore the context of the present, and to set goals for the future in ways that are positive and enriching. When women live through the next generation of mothering, they can face their own challenges of being ambivalent, collapsed, motherless, or strong, and they can step into the role of grandmother as they continue to enrich their children and grandchildren (Pinkola Estes 178).

Humans live their lives and experiences therein, less in terms of facts and more in terms of stories (Randall 35). Learning never ceases. As individuals grow older, developing an ability to tell and retell life stories can be a transformative process allowing individuals and families to transcend human experience. When the stories within families are based on the fairytale mythology of the happily ever after, dysfunctionality is often perpetuated into subsequent generations. Grandmothering can help to rewrite life stories for daughters and granddaughters by allowing for future generations to transcend fixed narratives that can sometimes keep individuals stuck inside of time realities defined by traditional structures.

Personal narrative reconstruction can become healing. This happens when negative experiences are rewritten into positives, and experiences of trauma and human suffering are integrated and reframed into that of learning (Randall 33). This process is intrinsically linked to the development of wisdom and the knowledge a person has been able to integrate within themselves over a lifetime. Aging takes women through the transitory experiences of present time into that of future reality and gives them the opportunity to retext and represent personal narratives, which helps in rupturing any residue remaining from fairy tale realities. Mothers have the capacity to help their daughters recreate new realities through their relationships with one another and to transmit wisdom, as a part of these relationships, from one generation to the next (Randall and Kenyon 334). Grandmothering offers a special opportunity to make positive changes for the next generation of a family.

CONCLUSION

Having an acceptance of self and being in harmony with family, society, and the natural process of aging are all strengths of the ecological perspective. Extending beyond the years of procreation, women in society contribute extensively to the wellbeing of subsequent generations; so much so, that this has an evolutionary impact on how women can adapt to and shape the future for their own families. Calling back to the image of the Crone and the archetype of the wise woman Sophia, there are many things about growing old that are not considered to be attractive or beautiful. For women, it is important to put these images into a developmental context in order to come to grips with the myth of the happily ever after and the limitations of fairy tale realities. It is within this context that the stages of female development can be explained and the importance of intergenerational ties, supported by the grandmother hypothesis, can help women to grow beyond the limitations of fairy tale mythology and live fully in nurturing and holistic partnerships (Ray, "Toward the Croning" 110).

Wisdom and compassion are aesthetic components that very much relate to an intuitive understanding inherent within the grandmother hypothesis. Grandmothering is one way for women to make connections and share in positive growth for the next generation. When biological grandmothering is not possible due to proximity or dysfunctionality, alternatives can be found that still enhance the role of women beyond reproduction in metamodern society. Programs exist in some communities that help match adoptive and foster grandparents with adults and children to generate connectedness and develop supportive community. This is important because intergenerational connectedness has been shown to have a positive influence on quality of life and is significant to the survival of the human species because of the extended lifespan of women that far exceeds their ability to procreate.

Theologian Jean Chittister has studied and written about the concept of wisdom from a faith perspective, and encourages humans to continue to grow until the moment of death. She wants them to stay in close contact with their grandchildren and to engage in discussion with them about things that are important in their lives (Fox 18). Although older adults in society help to strengthen the intergenerational fabric in society, grandmothers find a unique place in the circle of life, as wisdom keepers who help retain history and support the healthy maintenance and growth of families.

Many conditions exist in contemporary globalized economies that contribute to the migration of populations around the world which in turn impacts the proximity of grandmothers to their offspring. Sociopolitical conditions related to violence in the Middle East and Eastern Europe, along with climate change and global economic disparities, has created a push-pull tension for many families affecting their ability to remain closely intact. A recent study notes that when chimpanzees are observed in protective captivity, offspring that experience nurturance and support from grandmother chimps fare better and have longer life expectancies than those who do not (Hawkes and Foxworthy 298). This is an example from the primate world on the beneficial aspects of grandmothering for subsequent generations when a species is able to remain intact that can also be reflected upon for human females whose lifespans typically far exceed the years of reproductive capability.

Climate change related food and water insecurities have caused many individuals and families to migrate in recent history. This demographic trend has greatly affected the geographical proximity of individuals and families in several cultures worldwide. Despite the migration of individuals because of social issues—such as technology, economic opportunity, globalization, and climate change—there is still the need for intergenerational connectedness in families. This connectedness manifests itself through the transmission of wisdom handed down by grandmothers to protect future generations and sustain harmony in family relations. When there is a willingness to learn from the experience of elders in a society, such as that of grandmothers, wisdom can be developed and passed on to future generations creating a whole new understanding of what it means to live a happy life. This, in turn, supports the need for grandmothers to serve as a positive adaptation for women within a rapidly changing metamodern society to assist in the deconstruction of myth and fairy tale realities by helping to promote intergenerational strength and resiliency.

WORKS CITED

Ardelt, Monika. "Antecedents and Effects of Wisdom in Old Age: A Longitudinal Perspective on Aging Well." *Research on Aging*, vol. 22, no.4, 2000, pp. 360-94.

Ardelt, Monika. "Are Older Adults Wiser Than College Students? A Comparison of Two Age Cohorts." *Journal of Adult Development*, vol. 17, no. 4, 2009, pp. 193-207.

Barnet, Scaramella, et al. "Grandmother Involvement as a Protective Factor for Early Childhood Social Adjustment." *Journal of Family Psychology*, vol. 24, no. 5, 2010, pp. 635-45.

Blackburn, James A., and Catherine N. Dulmus. *Handbook of Gerontology: Evidenced-Based Approaches to Theory, Practice and Policy.* John Wiley and Sons, Inc. 2007.

Caspari, R., and Sang-Hee Lee. "Older Age Becomes Common Late in Human Evolution." *PNAS*, vol. 101, no. 30, 2004, 10895-900.

Davis, Joan. Personal interview. 16 June 2016.

Fox, Thomas C. "Joan Chittister Speaks of Wisdom, Graceful Aging." *National Catholic Reporter*, vol. 45, no. 2. 2008.

Goodman, Catherine and Merril Silverstein. "Grandmothers Raising Grandchildren: FamilyStructure and Well-Being in Culturally Diverse Families." *The Gerontologist*, vol. 42, no. 5, 2002, 676–89.

Goyer, Amy. "More Grandparents Raising Grandkids." *AARP: Real Possibilities*, 20 Dec. 2010, www.aarp.org/relationships/grandparenting/info-12-2010/more_grandparents.html. Accessed 17 July 2017.

Green, Jeffrey A., and Scott C. Brown. "The Wisdom Development Scale: Further Validity Investigations." *International Journal of Aging and Human Development*, vol. 68, no. 4, 2009, pp. 289-320.

Harris, N. et al. "Ecological Aging: The Settings Approach in Aged Living and Care Accommodation." *Eco Health*, vol. 5, no. 2, 2008, pp. 196-204.

Hawkes, K. and J. Coxworth, "Grandmothers and the Evolution of Human Longevity: A Review of Findings and Future Directions." *Evolutionary Anthropology*, vol. 22, no. 6, 2013, 294-302.

Hawkes, Kristen. "The Grandmother Effect." *Nature* vol. 428, 2004, pp. 128-9.

Jeste, Dillip, et al. "Expert Consensus on Characteristics of Wisdom: A Delphi Method Study." *The Gerontologist, vol.* 50, no. 5, 2010, 668-80.

Lavery, Michelle. "Explain It to Your Grandmother." *Inside Higher Education*, 12 Oct. 2014, www.insidehighered.com/blogs/gradhacker/explain-it-your-grandmother. Accessed 17 July 2017.

Parisi, Jeane, et al. "Can the Wisdom of Aging Be Activated and Make a Difference Socially?" *Educational Gerontology*, vol. 35, no. 10, 2009, pp. 867-79.

Peine, Alexander, and Louis Neven. "Social-Structural Lag Revisted." *Gerotechnology*, vol. 10, no. 3, 2011, pp. 129-39.

Pinkola Estes, Clarissa. *Women Who Run with the Wolves*. Random House Publishing Group, Inc. 1995.

Randall, William L. "Transcending Our Stories: A Narrative Perspective on Spirituality Later in Life." *Critical Social Work*, vol. 10, no. 1, 2009, pp. 31-46.

Randall, William, and Gary Kenyon. "Time, Story and Wisdom: Emerging Themes in Narrative Gerontology." *Canadian Journal on Aging*, vol. 23, no. 4, 2004, pp. 333-46.

Ray, Ruth E. "Toward the Croning of Feminist Gerontology." *Journal of Aging Studies*, vol. 18, no. 1, 2004, pp. 109-21.

Ray, Ruth E. "The Search for Meaning in Old Age: Narrative, Narrative Process, Narrativity." *The Gerontologist*, vol. 42, no. 1, 2002, 131-6.

Silverstein, Merril, and Anne Marenco. "How Americans Enact the Grandparent Role across the Family Life Course." *Journal of Family Issues*, vol. 22, no. 4, 2001, pp. 493-522.

Sternberg, Robert. "Older but Not Wiser? The Relationship between Age and Wisdom." *Ageing International*, vol. 30, no. 1, 2005, 5-26.

Strassman, Beverly, and Wendy Garrard. "Alternatives to the Grandmother Hypothesis. A Meta-Analysis of the Association between Grandparental and Grandchild Survival in Patrilineal Populations." *Human Nature*, vol. 22, no. 1-2, 2011, pp. 201-22.

United States Census Bureau. "General Demographic Characteristics; Head of Household." *American Fact* Finder, 2010, factfinder.census.gov/faces/nav/jsf/pages/community_facts.x.html. Accessed 17 July 2017.

Vermeulen, Timotheus, and Robin Van den Akker. "Utopia, Sort of: A Case Study in Metamodernism." *Studia Neophilologica*, vol. 87, sup. 1, 2016, pp. 55-67.

4.
Growing Together or Growing Apart

An Attachment Approach to Understanding Marriage

AUDREY BRASSARD AND SUE JOHNSON

MOST PEOPLE WHO GET MARRIED expect to live "happily ever after." In contrast with this popular belief about this postmarriage state of bliss, when partners get married, their journey continues, and marriage is definitely not going to be an ideal, a peaceful, and an uneventful adventure. Although marriage comes with great moments of happiness, meaning, and connection, it cannot always be total bliss, laughter, and fun. Research consistently shows that most couples experience a decrease in relationship satisfaction with time (e.g., Karney and Bradbury; Mitnick et al.), especially after the wedding and when children are born. Some believe that routine and conflict are mainly responsible for such disillusion and distance, but many other factors are important to consider as well.

For many couple therapists, growing together or growing apart is likely to be a matter of the couple's ability to maintain intimacy, emotional and sexual connection, respect, and admiration. However, not all marriages are born equal in that matter. Partners come from different backgrounds, and their past experiences are likely to influence how they will feel, think, and behave with each other, which will, in turn, affect their relationship happiness and, ultimately, the stability of their marriage. In their model of marital quality and stability—called the vulnerability-stress-adaptation model (VSA)—Benjamin Karney and Thomas Bradbury have reviewed more than one hundred studies on the long-term predictors of marital outcomes ("The Longitudinal Course"). They have proposed that the factors responsible for the partner's happiness and commitment could be organized in three large categories: stressful events, enduring vulnerabilities, and adaptive processes. Stressful events include any event—whether positive (e.g., birth of a child) or negative (e.g., health issues, job loss)—that can add additional strain to the partners or the relationship. Enduring vulnerabilities include personal characteristics and past experiences that each partner brings to the relationship, such as personality traits, parental divorce, past traumatic experiences, or self-esteem. Adaptive processes can be described as all strategies that the partners may use to deal with their stressors and vulnerabilities to maintain their relationship. According to Karney and Bradbury, the interaction of each partner's stressors, vulnerabilities, and adaptive processes would explain the couples' variability in their levels of relationship satisfaction and stability over time.

In this chapter, we focus on an important factor that affects all three categories of factors—attachment security—as it represents one of the most documented predictors of marital quality and stability over the last thirty years (Feeney; Mikulincer and Shaver, *Attachment in Adulthood*). Attachment security between partners is influenced by each person's past relationship experience and is, thus, a vulnerability factor. It also affects how stressful events are perceived and responded to and the processes that partners will habitually use to deal with differences, conflict, and moments of emotional disconnection.

We aim to highlight the theoretical, clinical, and research evidence supporting the crucial role of romantic attachment in committed relationships.

We first present an overview of the developmental process of attachment and the principles of attachment theory, as well as how each principle translates into relationship processes that structure the quality of a couple's bond and its long-term viability. We then follow with a summary of several studies that support the role played by attachment in various aspects of romantic relationships. Finally, we describe basic concepts of an attachment-based couple therapy to illustrate how partners can learn to foster intimacy and connection within their relationship and prevent loneliness, distance, and separation.

BRIEF PRESENTATION OF ATTACHMENT THEORY

Attachment theory is based on the pioneering work of John Bowlby and Mary Ainsworth on the infant's attachment to their primary caregiver. Bowlby has posited that an infant's reliance on (and emotional bond with) its mother is the result of a fundamental, instinctual behavioural system aimed at survival. In times of need or in the presence of threats, the basic human survival strategy to obtain reassurance, protection, or soothing comfort is to seek proximity with a significant caregiver that is an attachment figure (i.e., the mother, the father, or another significant person in the child's life). During infancy, attachment security is developed, when the attachment figure, typically the mother, provides sensitive and consistent care to the child's needs and bids for affection and proximity. The child can then learn, through repeated nurturing experiences, to regulate his or her emotions constructively and shape mental models that she or he is worthy of love (positive model of the self) and can confidently get support from others in times of need (positive model of other).

However, for a number of reasons, attachment figures may not be consistently available and sensitive, which can negatively affect the child's regulation strategies and models of self and other. Specifically, attachment-related anxiety tends to arise when attachment figures do not respond consistently to the child's needs. When the child is not heard, she or he learns to scream louder to get attention and care from the attachment figure and to be more and more vigilant for lack of accessibility and responsiveness, the signs of secure attachment, from others. Such strategies—which often translate into demanding, complaining, or critical responses in adults—are termed anxious preoccupied attachment; they are a chronic hyperactivation of the attachment system. In contrast, attachment-related avoidance and a corresponding negative model of other can arise when the attachment figure is cold and distant, overvalues autonomy and invulnerability, or becomes abusive. By being repeatedly dismissed or punished in times of need, a child gradually learns that it is useless to turn to others for help and that it is better to minimize distress and feelings of need, to maintain distance from others, and to rely only on oneself. This chronic deactivating strategy is termed "avoidant attachment" (Mikulincer and Shaver, *Attachment in Adulthood*). These early representations of the world (self and other) and the associated affect regulation strategies will consistently influence how the child—then the adolescent and the adult—will perceive him or herself (as lovable or not) and others (as reliable or not) through a number of beliefs (e.g., I should not depend on others) and the chronic use of ways of engaging others to deal with insecurity and distress (proximity seeking, hyperactivation or hypoactivation of the attachment system). According to Bowlby, our need to form attachment with significant others remains a, if not *the,* primary motivation for human behaviour from the cradle to the grave. Emotional isolation is seen as traumatizing for human beings and attachment insecurity has, indeed, been shown to be a risk factor for relationship distress and most kinds of mental health problems in adulthood (Mikulincer and Shaver, *Attachment in Adulthood*).

According to the adult attachment theory and science (e.g., Hazan and Zeifman, "Sex"), in adulthood one's romantic partner becomes a key attachment figure. This perspective lays out key principles that allow us to understand adult romantic bonds. First, this partner is a primary target for proximity seeking, especially at times of uncertainty and stress, and serves as a safe haven in times of need (i.e., reliably providing protection, comfort, support, and relief, when one is distressed). Second, this partner serves as a secure base, which allows the individual to confidently explore and pursue nonattachment goals in a safe environment (e.g., work, leisure, personal projects) and to take interpersonal risks in relationships. Secure dependency leads to the ability to be independent, perhaps because attachment figures are internalized as mental models and offer an ongoing source of strength and support. Third, this partner's real or expected disappearance evokes separation distress (i.e., people react with intense distress to actual or potential unwanted separations from (or loss of) an attachment figure). This distress typically unfolds in a process of angry protest and complaint, which if there is no soothing response, morphs into attempts to shut down attachment emotions and depression or withdrawal. From an attachment standpoint, this distress is the main trigger for chronic, relationship-defining conflicts in a romantic relationship and shapes the repetitive demand-withdraw dance that is typical of most distressed couples (Johnson, *Love Sense*). The key factor in relationship distress is then a recurring lack of perceived emotional connection that primes conflict and distancing in love relationships. Fourth, it is emotional accessibility, responsiveness, and engagement that define secure connection in adult love relationships. Evidence shows that such secure connection fosters not only relationship satisfaction but such qualities as empathy for others, the ability to formulate and assert one's needs and seek support effectively, and more ability to deal with anger constructively and repair the relationship (Mikulincer and Shaver, *Attachment in Adulthood*). Fifth, the above principles are normative, but in terms of individual differences, attachment orientations can be categorized as secure, anxious (hyperactivated), and avoidant (hypoactivated); these styles are discussed in more detail below. Attachment is linked to the experience and expression of other aspects of a romantic relationship; for example, secure partners are more attuned and responsive caregivers, whereas avoidant partners report more interest in sensation in sexual encounters rather than interest in closeness or affection.

Real attachment relationships may take one to two years to develop fully through three stages 1) the "pre-attachment" phase, in which the romantic relationship usually begins with flirtation, affiliation, or uncommitted sexual involvement; 2) the "attachment-in-the-making" phase, which involves increased selectivity and commitment; and 3) the "clear-cut-attachment" phase, which is often formalized through marriage, engagement, or cohabitation (Hazan and Zeifman, "Pair Bonds").

Many studies have demonstrated that early attachment security (or insecurity) largely determines the adult's romantic attachment style or insecurity, unless a major event (i.e., trauma, maternal depression, therapy) occurs (Fraley and Brumbaugh; Pinquart et al). Although several approaches exist to describe the individual differences in attachment (Ravitz et al. for a review), authors have generally conceptualized adult or romantic attachment in two main ways: attachment styles (i.e., three or four categories) and attachment insecurity dimensions (i.e., continuum). For the sake of this chapter's brevity, we decided to describe the four attachment styles conceptualized by Kim Bartholomew ("Avoidance," "Adult") and the two attachment insecurity dimensions of Kelly Brennan et al., both of which are shown in Figure One.

Attachment-related anxiety is defined as a strong desire for closeness and protection, intense worries about partner availability and one's own value to the partner, and use of hyperactivating strategies (e.g., hypervigilance to the partner's signs of rejection or unavailability, excessive proximity seeking, and reassurance demands) to deal with insecurity and distress. In contrast, attachment-related avoidance is defined by discomfort with closeness and depending on relationship partners, by preference for emotional distance and self-reliance, and use of deactivating strategies (e.g., denial or minimization of distress, emotional suppression, inhibition of proximity-seeking behaviours) to deal with insecurity and distress (Mikulincer and Shaver, *Attachment in Adulthood*).

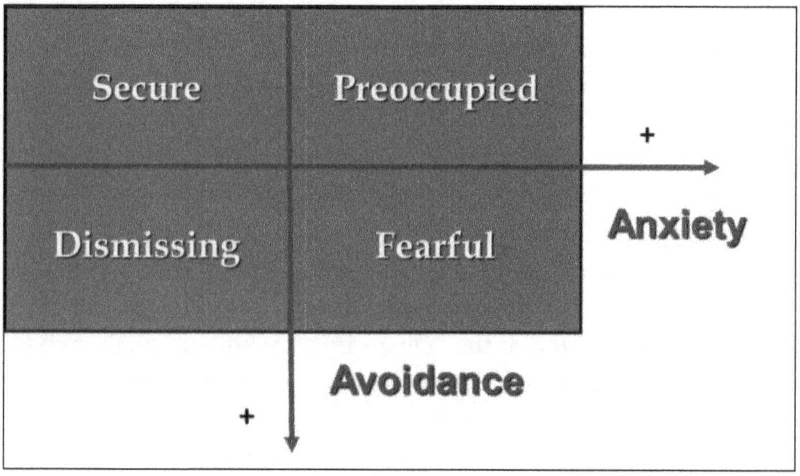

Figure One: Model of Romantic Attachment Combining the Four styles (Bartholomew, "Avoidance," "Adult") and Two Dimensions (Brennan et al.).

Attachment security or secure attachment style can be seen either as the adult positive models of the self and other (Bartholomew, "Avoidance") or as the lower end of the two continuums of attachment-related anxiety and avoidance (Brennan et al.). Secure individuals represent 50 to 60 percent of the general population. They tend to have good self-esteem and to perceive themselves as worthy of love. In relationships, they expect positive responses and comfort from their partners in times of need, and they are comfortable with closeness, interdependence, and commitment. Many studies have repeatedly showed that these individuals are happier in life and in their marriages (see Feeney for a review). They are also more resilient and better at regulating their emotions, their security acting as a protective factor for psychological distress (Mikulincer and Shaver, *Attachment in Adulthood*).

Dismissing attachment style (15 to 20 percent of the general population) is characterized by a generally positive model of the self (low anxiety) and a negative model of other or high attachment-related avoidance. The dismissing individuals tend to have doubts about their partner's ability to fulfill their needs, which leads them to maintain a certain degree of emotional distance from others, to hide their vulnerability, and to refuse to depend on their partner. They are more comfortable with "distant" relationships, characterized by high levels of autonomy and low levels of emotional disclosure. They have learned to rely solely on themselves and to minimize the importance of relationships to protect themselves from potential injuries in relationships. By never seeking help or support from their partner, they tend to confirm their perception that the other is not going to be there for them. As with the anxious style, the limited way in which avoidants engage with partners, sets up experiences that repeatedly confirm their avoidant beliefs.

Preoccupied anxious attachment style (20 to 25 percent of the general population) is characterized by a positive model of other (low avoidance) and a negative model of the self or high levels of attachment-related anxiety. The preoccupied individuals have perpetual doubts about their self-worth and lovability, which leads them to chronically fear rejection and to constantly seek support, love, and reassurance from their romantic partners. They also demonstrate emotional instability, jealousy, and dependency to deal with their constant fear of abandonment. They tend, however, to annoy or alienate their partners by being overly demanding, needy, and almost impossible to please, which can eventually confirm their fear that the partner is going to leave.

Fearful avoidant attachment style (10 to 15 percent of the general population) is characterized by negative models of self and other, or high levels of attachment-related anxiety and avoidance. Fearful individuals both feel unlovable and doubtful of the other's reliability, availability, and trustworthiness. They wish to establish intimate relationships, but they fear both the pain of rejection and the discomfort of closeness, so they tend to flip between anxiously demanding connection and then fleeing from connection. These fears can often be explained by a history of trauma, neglect, or instability in their family of origin. They have learned that an attachment figure can even be dangerous, which justifies their ambivalent stance towards relationships.

The above principles offer a new, rich and empirically supported map to the territory of adult romantic bonds, which have previously been defined in terms of sentiment or sexuality in ways that have emphasized their mystery and apparent random unpredictability.

GROWING TOGETHER OR GROWING APART: THE ROLE OF ATTACHMENT

As stated above, attachment security has been consistently related to a higher perception of relationship satisfaction or marital quality, whereas attachment insecurity (anxiety, avoidance) is consistently related to poorer relationship functioning (Feeney). For many years now, researchers and couple therapists have sought to identify the mechanisms through which attachment security (or insecurity) could lead to either a happy marriage filled with connection and love or an unhappy marriage filled with distance, anger, loneliness, or pain.

Phillip Shaver and his colleagues first suggested in 1988 that the attachment system's interaction with two other systems—the caregiving system and the sexual system—explains much of the functioning of a romantic relationship. These systems, and their associations with the attachment system, will be described consecutively.

ATTACHMENT AND CAREGIVING

According to attachment theory, the activation of one partner's attachment system during dangerous or stressful events triggers care-seeking behaviors. The other partner's caregiving system is then activated by perceptions of his or her mate's distress (Bowlby). This systemic process depends on each partner's perceptions of the other's need for support, willingness to accept and benefit from support, and when occupying the caregiver's role, ability to provide sensitive support and perceive it as necessary and useful. Both partners have attachment-related representations that guide their reactions to stressors and to their partner's signs of distress (Collins and Feeney, "A Safe"). When partners are secure, the roles of careseeker and caregiver are easily exchanged between partners, which is a normal feature of couple interdependence. Their ability to be there for each other, in times of need, can foster connection between partners and deepen the feelings that they are special, loved, and cared for. Attachment insecurities, however, are likely to interfere with this process.

Attachment-related anxiety. Individuals who fear abandonment are more likely to perceive that their partners are not available and responsive enough, partly because their needs for support are nearly impossible to meet (Bachman and Bippus; Davila and Kashy; Kane et al.). It is worth mentioning, however, that anxious individuals tend to infer negative intentions from their partner's behaviour and to get upset as a result, especially when they are also avoidant (i.e., fearful attachment style, [Collins and Feeney, "Working"]). As for caregiving, although anxiously attached individuals see themselves as supporting their partner, the support they provide tends to be ineffective (Feeney and Collins, "Predictors") or less frequent than in more secure individuals (Davila and Kashy; Karantzas et al.). This is because anxious individuals are too preoccupied with their own attachment needs and emotions and often have insufficient cognitive and emotional resources to understand and respond sensitively to their partner's needs (Collins et al.; Mikulincer and Shaver, *Attachment in Adulthood*).

Attachment-related avoidance. Attachment-related avoidance is related to perceiving relatively little or negative support from partners, including overprovision of support and less positive support (Bachman and Bippus; Brock and Lawrence; Kane et al.). This is consistent with their negative model of the other (as not available for them in times of need) and can be explained by the avoidant individuals' tendency to minimize their self-disclosure of distress or to express their need for support in an indirect way. A recent study has even showed that in order to react positively to the support they received (i.e., decreased distress and distance), avoidant individuals needed their partners to provide high levels of sensitive and adjusted support (Girme et al.), which suggests that they need an especially caring partner to overcome their negative model of other. More avoidant individuals also have a lower propensity to provide care. When the partner seeks their help, they usually minimize the partner's needs, feel irritated, or withdraw from the partner (Bachman and Bippus; Collins et al.; Simpson et al.). They appear to lack both the skills and the motivation to provide sensitive care (Feeney and Collins, "Predictors").

ATTACHMENT AND SEXUALITY

A growing body of research has also documented the links between the attachment and the sexual systems (Birnbaum, "On the Convergence"). The sexual system includes motives or goals to engage in sexual interactions (e.g., express love, stress relief, pleasure, and procreation) as well as emotions, thoughts, and behaviours in the sexual domain. Attachment and sexuality have a lot in common, such as proximity, touch, and feelings of connection between partners. Indeed, sexual interactions are a particularly efficient way to meet attachment needs, including proximity, intimacy, connection, and reassurance (Davis et al.). Sexual interactions also help foster attachment bonds in the beginning of the relationship and contribute to the quality of established romantic relationships (Birnbaum, "Bound"; Hazan and Zeifman, "Sex"; Johnson and Zuccarini). Secure individuals' positive models (of self and other) allow them to develop and maintain a comfortable and secure environment during sexual activities and be free of worries that interfere with enjoyable sexual intercourse. They display openness, respect, assertiveness, which contribute to their higher sexual satisfaction, positive emotions, pleasure, and sexual intimacy (Birnbaum, et al., "When Sex"; Dewitte, 2012). Attachment insecurities, however, have been related to lower sexual satisfaction, more sexual difficulties (e.g., erectile dysfunction and sexual pain), and lower sexual assertiveness and self-esteem (Birnbaum, "Attachment"; Brassard et al., "Romantic"; Brassard et al., "Attachment"; Butzer and Campbell; Leclerc et al.).

Attachment-related anxiety. More specifically, Dewitte has suggested that anxiously attached individuals seek proximity and intimacy through sexuality, which they often equate with love. They see sexuality as a way to keep their partner close and be reassured that they are loved (Birnbaum et al., "Desire"; Dewitte). Any negative sexual interaction is likely to be perceived as a threat to their relationship, since they consider sex as a relationship barometer (Birnbaum et al., "When Sex"). Studies have shown that anxious women are more likely to engage in sexual intercourse with their partner to please him or make sure he does not leave them (Tracy et al.). They are also more likely to engage in extradyadic sex to fill their need for intimacy or to boost their self-esteem (Allen and Baucom; Bogaert and Sadava; Frias et al). In committed relationships, our study shows that anxiously attached male partners reported sexually pressuring their partner, which was confirmed by their female partners (Brassard et al., "Attachment"). However, when both partners in the couple were highly anxious, they reported a higher frequency of sexual intercourse than other pairings of attachment.

Attachment-related avoidance. Because partners who are highly avoidant prefer to maintain an emotional distance with their partners, they tend to engage in sexual behaviors for nonrelational motives, such as stress reduction (Schachner and Shaver). Our work has shown that committed individuals that were high in attachment-related avoidance tend to avoid sexual encounters with their partner and fantasize less about their partner than more secure individuals (Brassard et al., "Attachment"). They are less comfortable with display of affection (Hazan and Zeifman, "Sex"), favour solitary sexuality (e.g., masturbation) and are more likely to report engaging in extradyadic sex for reasons such as autonomy (Allen and Baucom; Frias et al.). When both partners are avoidant, they report the lowest sexual frequency and the highest prevalence of sexual difficulties of all couple pairings (Brassard et al., "Attachment").

ATTACHMENT AND COMMITMENT

Securely attached individuals experience higher degrees of couple commitment than insecure individuals—either anxious or avoidant (Pistole et al.; Simpson, 1990). Although anxiously attached individuals express a strong desire for commitment in their relationships (Mikulincer and Erev), they have difficulties maintaining their commitment. In fact, they see themselves as highly investing in their relationship (Etcheverry et al.), but they also perceive greater costs in their relationship (Pistole et al.). Our recent work looked at commitment from three different modes: optimal commitment, over-commitment, and under-commitment. Our results revealed that highly anxiously attached individuals are not optimally committed: they have a hard time reconciling the negative and positive aspects of their relationships and they lack perseverance when difficulties arise (Brassard et al., "A New Perspective"). Our results also highlight the ambivalent nature of anxiously-attached individuals, who are more likely to simultaneously feel overcommitted (i.e., sacrificing other aspects of their life for the relationship and compulsively wanting to be with the partner) and undercommitted (being overwhelmed with the couple's difficulties and thinking about leaving the relationship).

Partners who are more avoidant tend to fear commitment and dependency. They invest less, perceive fewer rewards from the relationship, and feel that they are sacrificing more than what they are really giving (Brassard et al., "A New Perspective"; Etcheverry et al.; Gere et al.). Their aversion toward commitment is related to their expectation that all relationships are eventually going to fail, so they are less willing to put in the effort a relationship needs when facing difficulties (Birnie et al.).

THE NOT HAPPY EVER AFTER

Attachment security and insecurity also directly affect the everyday interactions between romantic partners. Conflict, aggression, distance, disconnection, or despair is often the norm. Why does marriage hurt so much when partners were supposed to live happily ever after?

Attachment and conflict. All couples experience conflicts, unless partners make a lot of effort to avoid them. Conflicts are necessary to establish a couple's intimacy and cohesion, and to set out rules to follow when adverse events occur. Many studies have shown how a secure attachment style protects both the individual and couples when it comes to conflict management, which does not mean that secure partners do not encounter conflicts (Mikulincer and Shaver, *Attachment in Adulthood*). Secure individuals have more resources to handle conflicts when they happen. They are more emotionally stable and are more confident in their ability to deal with the issues. They have better skills to compromise and consider their partner's point of view, while not making negative attributions about their partner's behaviours or intentions.

Insecure individuals, whether anxious or avoidant, show poorer communication skills and negative conflict strategies (Feeney). Therefore, conflict is more likely to lead them to hurt each other during negative interactions or to create distance, disconnection, and loneliness when both partners are retreating from engaging in perceived insolvable problems. Research has shown that both anxious and avoidant partners perceive higher levels of conflict in their relationship (Brassard, "Attachment, Conflict") in part because they tend to experience disagreements as potential threats to the relationship. For anxiously attached individuals, conflict tends to quickly trigger fears about potential rejection and abandonment, which usually leads to overwhelming negative emotions and relationship-damaging behaviours (e.g., critics, complaint). In contrast, avoidantly attached individuals tend to perceive conflict as a threat to their independence; they feel pressured to self-disclose and engage in intimate conversations (which they dislike and wish to avoid), leading them to stonewall or withdraw (Pietromonaco et al.). In the long run, chronic patterns of anxious and critical demanding, followed by avoidant withdrawal or patterns of mutual withdrawal seen when demanding partners become exhausted, not only create helplessness and emotional isolation but also prevent repair attempts and effectively undermine positive bonding experiences of accessibility and responsiveness (Johnson, *Love Sense*).

Attachment and intimate partner violence. There is also growing evidence showing that insecure attachment, especially anxiety, is a risk factor for perpetrating violent behaviours toward a romantic partner. Anxiously attached partners would use physical or psychological aggression as a reaction to potential threats to the relationship in an inadequate and dysfunctional attempt to keep the partner from leaving them (Bartholomew and Allison). Indeed, studies conducted on men have shown that the more anxious they were, the more likely they were to perpetrate physical and psychological aggressions toward their female partners (Mikulincer and Shaver, *Human Aggression*). In some studies, this pattern was explained by the men's use of the "man demands-woman withdraws" pattern of communication (Fournier et al.), their greater difficulty to regulate their anger (Brassard et al., "Childhood"; Lafontaine and Lussier), and their difficulty to understand their partner's point of view or emotions (Péloquin et al.). Avoidantly attached individuals would, on the contrary, use violent behaviours (psychological aggression, contempt, and lack of respect) as a way to remove themselves from unpleasant situations and to keep a certain distance with their partner, especially when the partner insists on talking about intimate topics (Fournier et al.). They, too, display less empathy for their partners (Péloquin et al.,) and some difficulties regulating their anger (Brassard et al., "Childhood").

WHAT EMOTIONALLY FOCUSED THERAPY CAN BRING TO MARRIAGE

The map of relationships, presented above, not only offers a guide to the phenomenology of love but is specific enough to guide intervention. What we truly understand, we can shape. Emotionally focused couple therapy (EFT) is an approach to changing distressed relationships, which is solidly based on attachment concepts and research and developed alongside the study of adult attachment (Johnson, *The Practice*). As such, it is the only form of couple intervention that is based on a clear, tested model of romantic relationships, what goes wrong in these relationships, and what is needed to heal these relationships. EFT represents, at present, the gold standard for empirical validation in the field of couple therapy (see www.iceeft.com for a list of all research studies). It has obtained large effect sizes and positive follow-up results in a number of studies. There are also many studies of effective change that support attachment and the general EFT theory of change, as well as studies with different relationally distressed populations—for example, depressed partners and partners facing posttraumatic stress disorder (see Brassard and Johnson for a review; Wiebe and Johnson). A relationship education model based on EFT has also been recently tested with excellent results (Kennedy et al.).

A recent study (Burgess-Moser et al.) has found that twenty sessions of EFT were able to improve relationship satisfaction as well as relationship-specific attachment security in both anxious and avoidant distressed partners. This fits with Bowlby's formulation of attachment models as being able to be "revised" by new positive bonding experiences and with recent research that shows attachment models can, indeed, change over the lifespan. Since more secure attachment is associated with almost every indicator of mental health, this is promising, not just for the field of relationship intervention but for using relational interventions to create growth and address problems in individual partners. Using a brain scan methodology (Johnson et al., "Soothing"), our study also has shown that in contrast to pretherapy scans, at the end of EFT, the brains of female partners, who held their partner's hands, responded to the threat of electric shock with a calm lack of arousal and reported the shocks as less painful than before therapy. This did not occur in the brain scan when the female partners were left alone or when a stranger held their hand. This study supports the premises of attachment theory and also the conceptualization and interventions used in EFT.

EFT assumes that negative self-sustaining interactions patterns—such as one partner becoming critical ("You never talk to me. And you didn't do the chores again. Guess what I need doesn't matter to you") and the other defending and stonewalling ("There you go again. I can't talk to you. You are angry all time. I have to go back to work now")—prime attachment fears of rejection and abandonment, and constantly undermine safe, open connection between partners. Emotional signals are the music of this attachment dance, and insecure partners, in distressed relationships, are experts at sending signals that prime all the other's attachment insecurities and elicit default insecure strategies, such as dismissal or aggressive demands for contact. In this drama, the negative expectations and perceptual biases, negative engagement strategies, and ways of regulating emotion become constricted. They, then, generate more and more disconnection and reactivity. Both partners are in, what Bowlby terms, "emotional starvation." Any problem or difference between partners results in this dysfunctional anxiety producing cycle. The solution is then to deescalate this negative cycle (in stage one of EFT) and restore emotional balance and a secure base, from which to gradually guide partners into potent moments of accessibility and responsiveness, which build a positive cycle of more secure emotional connection (in stage two of EFT). Specific corrective bonding experiences—where softer emotions, such as fear and sadness and attachment needs and longings, are discovered, distilled and disclosed to a partner in a way that elicits responsive caring—consistently predict success at the end of EFT and positive follow up (Greenman and Johnson).

Briefly, how does EFT operationalize an attachment orientation to relationship repair that results in more secure and more emotionally balanced partners? First, the therapist is an emotionally present surrogate attachment figure for both partners. She constantly helps regulate difficult emotions with interventions, such as attuned empathic reflection, and creates a safe validating environment and guides gradual risk-taking as partners stumble into new emotional territory. Second, Bowlby constantly points to the power of emotion in relationships, and EFT frames this emotion in attachment terms, which views reactive anger as a coping secondary response to the fear of abandonment, emotional numbing, or avoidance as reflecting the loss, helplessness, and hurt that comes with perceived rejection. Bowlby highlights the despair underneath the surface when human beings cannot move an attachment figure into accepting responsiveness. The EFT therapist, thus, with reflection and repetitive normalization moves partners into this level of affect. The therapist is first accepting of a client's surface emotion, since once we understand the attachment drama every emotional response is clear and "reasonable," but then moves him or her into a deeper, more core emotional state. Attachment theory also stresses that interactions with loved ones regulate and shape our emotional responses, and these emotions then prime our associated cognitive models of self and other. Third, attachment sets out the pathway to health for self and relational system, which the EFT therapists constantly follow, moving partners into more accessible, responsive, and engaged interactions, which offer corrective emotional experiences of connection (see Johnson, *The Practice* for further discussion of these elements).

Although EFT tends to intensify across sessions of therapy, moving into deeper emotions and shaping more potent corrective interactions, in all sessions, the therapist repeats a basic set of steps or processes. In the clinical literature, this is called the EFT tango, since the tango is an improvised dance typified by coordinated moves, which are structured by emotional music. This can be described in the following terms: the therapist focuses on present processes, both within and between emotional and interactional processes, and describes them simply in a way that captures each partner's experiences; then this experience is deepened. For example, anger is deepened into a sense of threat and lonely desperation and distilled. This new emotional music is used to create a new dance with more connection, when the therapist guides evocative disclosure of this emotion to the other partner. The therapist then helps each partner process this new interaction and frame it in attachment terms, helping each person respond constructively to the disclosure of sadness, shame, or various forms of attachment fears. Finally, the therapist reflects this whole process in a way that frames the partners as competent and able to deal with emotions and interactions and able to take risks with each other in a way that generates connection.

So, William pursues his wife constantly for sex and affection, vigilantly pointing out any lapse in attentiveness and flipping between anger and confused anxiety, whereas his wife, Linda, who is clinically depressed and has been married to William for thirty years intones that she is numb and wishes to have her own bedroom. She believes that she will never be enough for him, and he sees her retreat as proof that she has never loved him. The therapist first reflects this interactive process of push and retreat between the couple, which leaves both of them in lonely despair and seeing the other as the enemy. The therapist also reflects on the underlying process in which William is triggered into a cascade of loss and fear, body tension, thoughts of being irrelevant and unloved, and aggressive demanding. Second, the therapist supports William to tune into this experience and pinpoint his terror that his wife has never loved or needed him and he is not enough for her. Third, the therapist helps him disclose these emotions in a way that does not threaten his wife. Fourth, the therapist helps William reflect on his new "move" and helps him integrate this way of inviting his wife close as well as helping her "see" the fragility and need under her husband's aggression. Fourth, the therapist reflects this whole process, pointing out that Linda does respond and move closer, when William opens up in this way, and William is then calmer and able to create a moment of connection with his wife. If all goes well, these kinds of continuous, small, corrective moments of connection culminate in more intense bonding moments that predict change in EFT studies. William and Linda can now formulate, tolerate, and coherently own and express their attachment fears, including the models of self and other, which are up and running in these interactions, and ask for their needs to be met in a manner that pulls the other close. William can ask for reassurance as to his worth and take in his wife's comfort, for example, and Linda can own how overwhelmed she is by his perceived criticism and ask to be seen, accepted, and comforted. This kind of corrective bonding experience is a shift in terms of affect regulation, perceptual frame and cognitive meaning making, and behavioural response. It is a shift that opens the door to secure connection and takes on an existential level of significance in people's lives in that they feel, sometimes, for the first time, accepted and cared for and that others can be a safe haven and secure base for them.

CONCLUSION

Adult attachment science has exploded in the last two decades (Johnson, *Love Sense*; Mikulincer and Shaver, *Attachment in Adulthood*). It offers a map to love and loving that empowers clinical intervention. As such, it heralds a new era of on-target effective intervention in couple and family therapy and allows us to understand emotion, both constructive functional and more dysfunctional, in a new way. It allows us to see mankind as a social bonding animal, and this has profound implications for all psychotherapy. For partners envisioning marriage, as well as for newlyweds or long-standing husbands and wives, understanding each partner's attachment insecurities and needs can help them prevent, understand, or even change their way of interacting with each other. Together (or with the help of a therapist), they can learn to deeply understand, support, and comfort each other in a way that fosters connection or "growing closer together" rather than hurting each other, feeling lonely, or "growing apart."

WORKS CITED

Ainsworth, Mary S., et al. *Patterns of Attachment: A Psychological Study of the Strange Situation*. Lawrence Erlbaum, 1978.

Allen, Elizabeth S., and Donal H. Baucom. "Adult Attachment and Patterns of Extradyadic Involvement." *Family Process*, vol. 43, no. 4, Dec. 2004, pp. 467-87.

Bachman, Guy Foster, and Amy M. Bippus. "Evaluations of Supportive Messages Provided by Friends and Romantic Partners: An Attachment Theory Approach." *Communication Reports*, vol. 18, no. 2, Oct. 2005, pp. 85-94.

Bartholomew, Kim. "Avoidance of Intimacy: An Attachment Perspective." *Journal of Social and Personal Relationships*, vol. 7, no. 2, May 1990, pp. 147-78.

Bartholomew, Kim. "Adult Attachment Processes: Individual and Couple Perspectives." *British Journal of Medical Psychology*, vol. 70, no. 3, Sept. 1997, pp. 249-63.

Bartholomew, Kim, and Colleen J. Allison. "An Attachment Perspective on Abusive Dynamics in Intimate Relationships." *Dynamics of Romantic Love*, edited by Mario Mikulincer and Gail Goodman, Guilford Press, 2006, pp. 102-27.

Birnbaum, Gurit E. "Attachment Orientations, Sexual Functioning, and Relationship Satisfaction in a Community Sample of Women." *Journal of Social and Personal Relationships*, vol. 24, no. 1, Feb. 2007, pp. 21-35.

Birnbaum, Gurit E. "Bound to Interact: The Divergent Goals and Complex Interplay of Attachment and Sex Within Romantic

Relationships." *Journal of Social and Personal Relationships*, vol. 27, no. 2, Mar. 2010, pp. 245-52.

Birnbaum, Gurit E. "On the Convergence of Sexual Urges and Emotional Bonds: The Interplay of the Sexual and Attachment Systems during Relationship Development." *Attachment Theory and Research: New Directions and Emerging Themes*, edited by Jeffry A. Simpson, Steven W. Rholes, Guilford Press, 2015, pp. 170-94.

Birnbaum, Gurit E., et al. "When Sex Is More Than Just Sex: Attachment Orientations, Sexual Experience, and Relationship Quality." *Journal of Personality and Social Psychology,* vol. 91, no. 5, Nov. 2006, pp. 929-43.

Birnbaum, Gurit E., et al. "Desire under Attack: Attachment Orientations and the Effects of Relationship Threat on Sexual Motivations." *Journal of Social and Personal Relationships,* vol. 28, no. 4, Jun 2011, pp. 448-68.

Birnie, Carolyn, et al. "Attachment Avoidance and Commitment Aversion: A Script for Relationship Failure." *Personal Relationships*, vol. 16, no. 1, March 2009, pp. 79-97.

Bogaert, Anthony F., and Stan Sadava. "Adult Attachment and Sexual Behavior." *Personal Relationships*, vol. 9, no. 2, June 2002, pp. 191-204.

Bowlby, John. *Attachment and Loss: Vol I. Attachment.* 2nd ed. Basic Books, 1982.

Brassard, Audrey, et al. "A New Perspective on the Associations between Romantic Attachment and Couple Commitment Using the Multimodal Couple Commitment Model." 2017, manuscript in review.

Brassard, Audrey, et al. "Attachment, Conflict, and Couple Satisfaction: Test of a Dyadic Model." *Family Relations,* vol. 58, no. 5, Dec. 2009, pp. 634-46.

Brassard, Audrey, et al. "Attachment Insecurities and Women's Sexual Function and Satisfaction: The Mediating Roles of Sexual Self-Esteem, Sexual Anxiety, and Sexual Assertiveness." *Journal of Sex Research,* vol. 52, no. 1, Jan. 2015, pp. 110-19.

Brassard, Audrey, et al. "Attachment, Sexual Experience, and Sexual Pressure in Romantic Relationships: A Dyadic Approach." *Personal Relationships,* vol.14, no. 3, Sep 2007, pp. 475-94.

Brassard, Audrey, et al. "Childhood Sexual Abuse and Intimate Partner Violence in a Clinical Sample of Men: The Mediating Roles of Adult Attachment and Anger Management." *Journal of Aggression, Maltreatment, and Trauma,* vol. 23, no. 7, Aug. 2014, pp. 683-704.

Brassard, Audrey, et al. "Romantic Attachment Predicting Sexual Satisfaction in Couples Seeking Marital Therapy." *Journal of Sex and Marital Therapy*, vol. 38, no. 3, May 2012, pp. 245-62.

Brassard, Audrey, and Sue M. Johnson. "Couple and Family Therapy: An Attachment Perspective." *Handbook of Attachment.* 3rd ed. Edited by Jude Cassidy and Phillip R. Shaver, Guilford Press, 2016, pp. 743-61.

Brennan, Kelly A. et al. "Self-Report Measurement of Adult Attachment: An Integrative Overview." *Attachment Theory and Close Relationships*, edited by Jeffry A. Simpson and Steven Rholes, Guilford Press, 1998, pp. 46-76.

Brock, Rebecca L, and Erika Lawrence. "Intrapersonal, Interpersonal, and Contextual Risk Factors for Overprovision of Partner Support in Marriage." *Journal of Family Psychology*, vol. 28, no 1, Feb. 2014, pp. 54-64.

Butzer, Bethany, and Campbell, Lorne. "Adult Attachment, Sexual Satisfaction, and Relationship Satisfaction: A Study of Married Couples." *Personal Relationships,* vol. 15. no. 1, Mar. 2008, pp. 141-54.

Burgess-Moser, M. "Changes in Relationship-Specific Romantic Attachment in Emotionally Focused Couple Therapy." *Journal of Marital and Family Therapy*, vol. 42, pp. 23-45.

Collins, Nancy L., and Brooke C. Feeney. "A Safe Haven: An Attachment Theory Perspective on Support Seeking and Caregiving in Intimate Relationships." *Journal of Personality and Social Psychology*, vol. 78, no 6, Jun. 2000, pp. 1053-73.

Collins, Nancy L., and Feeney, Brooke C. "Working Models of Attachment Shape Perceptions of Social Support: Evidence from Experimental and Observational Studies." *Journal of Personality and Social Psychology*, vol. 87, no. 3, Sept. 2004, pp. 363-83.

Collins, Nancy L., et al. "Responding to Need in Intimate Relationships: Normative Processes and Individual Differences." *Dynamics of Romantic Love: Attachment, Caregiving, and Sex,* edited by Mario Mikulincer and Gail S. Goodman, Guilford Press, 2016, pp. 149-89.

Davila, Joanne, and Deborah A. Kashy. "Secure Base Processes in Couples: Daily Associations between Support Experiences and Attachment Security." *Journal of Family Psychology*, vol. 23, no. 1, Feb., 2009, pp. 76-88. doi: http://dx.doi.org/10.1037/a0014353

Davis, Deborah, et al. "Attachment Style and Subjective Motivations for Sex." *Personality and Social Psychology Bulletin*, vol. 30, no. 8, Aug. 2004, pp. 1076-90.

Dewitte, Marieke. "Different Perspectives on the Sex-Attachment Link: Towards an Emotion-Motivational Account." *Journal of Sex Research*, vol. 49, no. 2-3, Mar. 2012, pp. 105-24. doi: http://dx.doi.org/10.1080/00224499.2011.576351

Etcheverry, Paul E., et al. "Attachment and the Investment Model: Predictors of Relationship Commitment, Maintenance, and Persistence." *Personal Relationships*, vol. 20, no. 3, Sept. 2013, pp. 546-67.

Feeney, Judith. "Adult Romantic Attachment: Developments in the Study of Couple Relationships." *Handbook of Attachment: Theory, Research, and Clinical Applications*, 2nd. edited by Jude Cassidy and Phillip R. Shaver, Guilford Press, 2016, pp. 456-81.

Feeney, Brooke C., and Nancy L. Collins. "Predictors of Caregiving in Adult Intimate Relationships: An Attachment Theoretical Perspective." *Journal of Personality and Social Psychology*, vol. 80, no 6, Jun 2001, pp. 972-94.

Fournier, Benoit, et al. "Attachment and Intimate Partner Violence: The Demand-Withdraw Communication Pattern and Relationship Satisfaction as Mediators." *Journal of Interpersonal Violence*, vol. 26, no. 10, July 2011, pp. 1982–2003.

Fraley, R. Chris, and Claudia Chloe Brumbaugh. "A Dynamical Systems Approach to Conceptualizing and Studying Stability and Change in Attachment Security." *Adult Attachment: Theory, Research, and Clinical Implications*, edited by W. Steven Rholes and Jeffry Simpson, Guilford Press, 2004, pp. 86-132.

Frias, Maria Theresa, et al. "Childhood Sexual Abuse and Attachment Insecurities as Predictors of Women's Own and Perceived-Partner Extradyadic Involvement." *Child Abuse &*

Neglect, vol. 38, no. 9, Sept. 2014, pp. 1450-58.

Gere, Judith, et al. "The Independent Contributions of Social Reward and Threat Perceptions to Romantic Commitment." *Journal of Personality and Social Psychology*, vol. 105, no 6, Dec. 2013, 961-77.

Girme, Yuthika U., et al. "All or Nothing": Attachment Avoidance and the Curvilinear Effects of Partner Support." *Journal of Personality and Social Psychology*, vol. 108, no 3, Mar. 2015, pp. 450-75.

Greenman, Paul, and Sue M. Johnson. "Process Research on EFT for Couples: Linking Theory to Practice." *Family Process*, vol. 52, no 1, Mar. 2013, pp. 46-51.

Hazan, Cindy, and Zeifman, Debra. "Sex and the Psychological Tether." *Attachment Processes in Adulthood*, edited by Kim Bartholomew and Daniel Perlman, Jessica Kingsley, 1994, pp. 151-78.

Hazan, Cindy, and Zeifman, Debra. "Pair Bonds as Attachments: Evaluating the Evidence." *Handbook of Attachment: Theory, Research, and Clinical Applications*, edited by Jude Cassidy and Phillip R. Shaver, Guilford Press, 1999, pp. 336-54.

Johnson, Sue M. *Love Sense: The Revolutionary New Science of Romantic Relationships*. Little Brown, 2013.

Johnson, Sue M., et al. "Soothing the Threatened Brain: Leveraging Contact Comfort with Emotionally Focused Therapy." *PLoS ONE*, vol. 8, no. 11, 2013, pp. 1-10.

Johnson, Sue M. *The Practice of Emotionally Focused Couple Therapy: Creating Connection*. 2nd ed. Brunner-Routledge, 2004.

Johnson, Sue, and Dino Zuccarini. "EFT for Sexual Issues: An Integrated Model of Couple and Sex Therapy." *The Emotionally Focused Casebook: New Directions in Treating Couples,* edited by James L. Furrow et al., Routledge, 2011, pp. 219-46.

Kane, Heidi S., et al. "Feeling Supported and Feeling Satisfied: How one Partner's Attachment Style Predicts the Other Partner's Relationship Experiences." *Journal of Social and Personal Relationships*, vol. 24, no. 4, Aug 2007, pp. 535-55.

Karantzas, Gery C., et al. "Towards an Integrative Attachment-Based Model of Relationship Functioning." *British Journal of Psychology*, vol. 105, no. 3, Aug. 2014, pp. 413-34.

Karney, Benjamin R., and Thomas Bradbury. "The Longitudinal Course of Marital Quality and Stability: A Review of Theory, Methods, and Research" *Psychological Bulletin*, vol. 118, no 1, Jul 1995, pp. 3-34.

Kennedy, N.W. et al. "Conversations for Connection: An Outcome Assessment of the Hold Me Tight Relationship Education Program for Couples." 2017, (manuscript in review).

Lafontaine, Marie-France, and Yvan Lussier. "Does Anger towards the Partner Mediate and Moderate the Link between Attachment and Intimate Violence." *Journal of Family Violence,* vol. 20, no. 6, Dec. 2005, pp. 349–61.

Leclerc, Bianca, et al. "Attachment, Sexual Assertiveness, and Sexual Outcomes in Women with Provoked Vestibulodynia and their Partners: A Mediation Model." *Archives of Sexual Behavior,* vol. 44, no. 6, Aug. 2015, pp. 1561-72.

Mikulincer, Mario, and Irit Erev. "Attachment Style and the Structure of Romantic Love." *British Journal of Social Psychology,* vol. 30, no 4, Dec. 1991, pp. 273-91.

Mikulincer, Mario, and Phillip R. Shaver. *Human Aggression and Violence: Causes, Manifestations, and Consequences*. American Psychological Association, 2011.

Mikulincer, Mario and Phillip R. Shaver. *Attachment in Adulthood: Structure, Dynamics, and Change.* Guilford Press, 2016.

Mitnick, Danielle M., et al. "Changes in Relationship Satisfaction across the Transition to Parenthood: A Meta-Analysis." *Journal of Family Psychology*, vol. 23, no 6, Dec. 2009, pp. 848-52.

Péloquin, Katherine, et al. "A Dyadic Approach to the Study of Romantic Attachment, Dyadic Empathy, and Psychological Aggression." *Journal of Social and Personal Relationships*, vol. 28, no. 7, Nov. 2011, pp. 915-42.

Pietromonaco, Paula R., et al. "Conflict in Adult Close Relationships: An Attachment Perspective." *Adult Attachment: Theory, Research, and Clinical Implications,* edited by W. Steven Rholes and Jeffry A. Simpson, Guilford Press, 2004, pp. 267-99.

Pinquart, Martin, et al. "Meta-Analytic Evidence for Stability in Attachment from Infancy to Early Adulthood." *Attachment & Human Development,* vol. 15, no 2, Mar. 2013, pp. 189-218.

Pistole, M. Carole, et al. "Love Relationships: Attachment Style and the Investment Model." *Journal of Mental Health Counseling*, vol. 17, no 2, Apr. 1995, pp. 199-209.

Ravitz, Paula, et al. "Adult Attachment Measures: A 25-Year Review." *Journal of Psychosomatic Research*, vol. 69, no 4, Oct. 2010, pp. 419-32.

Schachner, Dory A., and Phillip R. Shaver. "Attachment Dimensions and Sexual Motives." *Personal Relationships*, vol. 11, no 2, Jun. 2004, pp. 179-95.

Shaver, Phillip R., et al. "Love as Attachment: The Integration of Three Behavioral Systems." *The Anatomy of Love,* edited by Robert J. Sternberg and Michael L. Barnes, Yale University Press, 1988, pp. 68-98.

Simpson. Jeffry. A. "Influence of Attachment Styles on Romantic Relationships." *Journal of Personality and Social Psychology*, vol. 59, no 5, Nov. 1990, pp. 971-80.

Simpson, Jeffry A., et al. "Working Models of Attachment, Support Giving, and Support Seeking in a Stressful Situation." *Personality and Social Psychology Bulletin*, vol. 28, no 5, May 2002, pp. 598-608.

Tracy, Jessica L., et al. "Attachment Styles and Adolescent Sexuality." *Adolescent Romantic Relations and Sexual Behavior: Theory, Research, and Practical Implications*, edited by Paul Florsheim, Lawrence Erlbaum Associates, 2003, pp. 137-59.

Wiebe, Stephanie A., and Susan M. Johnson. "A Review of the Research in Emotionally Focused Therapy for Couples." *Family Process*, vol. 55, no 3, Apr. 2016, pp. 390-407.

II. Living With Marriage

5.
After the Baby Carriage

Navigating the Transition to Parenthood

SOLVEIG BROWN

LAUREN SMILED BROADLY as she talked about the carefree years early in her marriage when she worked, went to the club, and hung out with her husband and friends in the evenings. "It was easy, and the whole focus was on your career and yourself. You could do whatever you want," Lauren exclaimed.[1] Women often laughed as they reminisced about the "freedom" and "fun" of their "life before kids," in which they had ample time to spend with their husband or partner and friends, just hanging out, or doing things they enjoyed—eating out, going to movies and concerts, hiking, camping, and travelling. Women observed that once they had children, their life changed dramatically, and most felt they did not have realistic expectations about what being a parent would be like or how the daily responsibilities of parenting would affect their relationship with their spouse or partner.

Marital satisfaction frequently declines after the birth or adoption of a child, in part, because most people do not have accurate expectations of what parenting will entail (Lawrence et. al.; Shapiro et al.). Additionally, new parents are often sleep deprived as they experience a steep learning curve of caring for a baby, an increased domestic workload, extra expenditures, and significantly less leisure time. Both partners must also figure out how to incorporate their new role as a parent into their primary relationship, friendships, extended family, and their workplace, amid traditional and changing cultural expectations for mothers and fathers.

During 2007 and 2008 and 2014 and 2015, I conducted interviews and focus groups, and gathered survey data, from 140 middle-class mothers living in the Minneapolis and St. Paul metropolitan in order to elicit women's thoughts, feelings, and experiences related to their role as a mother.[2] In this chapter, I identify three areas in which women experienced the most stress in their relationship with their spouse or partner after having children: 1) the division of labour; 2) changes in their relationship dynamics; and 3) decreased leisure time. I also highlight the strategies couples used to focus on their primary relationship after they had children. My hope is that the stories of these women's challenges and successes in navigating their transition to parenthood will offer a realistic portrayal of the ways in which parenting can potentially create conflict in a relationship, and can serve as a guide to help other couples successfully navigate the transition to parenthood.

THE DIVISION OF LABOUR

Married heterosexual couples without children tend to have a stable division of labour over time. However, when a couple has a child, a shift in the division of labour occurs that increases wives' domestic labour to approximately two-thirds of the household responsibility while their market labour decreases; whereas, husbands' domestic labour decreases, and their market labour remains constant (Sanchez and Thomson). Women always discussed the division of labour in the interviews and focus groups I conducted, even when I did not specifically ask about it. Many women vented or joked about their respective division of labour. The belief that individual men had lower standards of cleanliness or were unaware, either intentionally or unintentionally, of the work that running a household and raising children entails was a recurring theme in several women's stories. Conversely, some women spoke highly of their partner's domestic and childcare contributions. Yet, for a fair number of women, the division of labour was a primary source of ongoing stress and conflict that put strain on their relationship.

There were several interesting trends in how couples navigate the division of labour. 1) Heterosexual couples with similar gender attitudes about household and childcare labour (whether traditional, egalitarian, or somewhere in between) were less likely to have conflict over the division of labour. 2) Couples employed diverse strategies for negotiating domestic and childcare labour—ranging from no discussion to daily discussion, from calm conversations to arguments, and from detailed chore lists to each person doing what she or he liked best. 3) For some women, there was a tendency to state that their household division of labour "fell" into place "naturally." Invoking a "natural" division of labour was usually associated with traditional gender roles. 4) Women expressed a wide breadth of feelings about their respective division of labour, which fell on a spectrum of being completely satisfied (regardless of the level of equality in some cases) to feeling angry, disappointed, and frustrated by the inequality of their domestic and childcare roles. 5) Over half of the women in this study reported that they "always" or "usually" did over two-thirds of the household and childcare labour, which is consistent with other studies. However, a quarter of the women reported a more equitable division of labour.

When there is conflict over the division of labour in heterosexual relationships, the female partner is the one who usually feels the most discontent (Kluwer). This is not surprising, considering that women often end up doing the bulk of domestic work. In 1989, *The Second Shift* revealed that most mothers also did the majority of household labour (Hochschild). I was curious whether this was still the case, so I asked eighty women to complete a comprehensive questionnaire that included a list of thirty-three household and childcare responsibilities (Brown). More than half of the women reported "always" or "usually" doing the following twenty-three tasks:

Buying clothes for the children (93 percent)
Scheduling playdates (91 percent)
Keeping the family calendar (89 percent)
Choosing extra activities/classes (86 percent)
Buying presents for child to bring to birthday parties (85 percent)
Making lunch for children (82 percent)
Buying presents for extended family members (78 percent)
Getting dinner ready for family (77 percent)
Scheduling babysitter (77 percent)

Doing the grocery shopping (75 percent)
Doing the laundry (73 percent)
Making daycare or preschool arrangements (73 percent)
Cleaning the bathroom (70 percent)
Taking care of sick child (70 percent)
Picking up stuff around the house (66 percent)
Vacuuming (65 percent)
Getting up with the child in the night (64 percent)
Driving child to activities (63 percent)
Preparing breakfast for the children (62 percent)
Picking child up from daycare or preschool (55 percent)
Bringing child to daycare or preschool (52 percent)
Changing diapers or used to changing diapers (52 percent)

This is a dramatic difference from the two tasks more than half of the women reported that their husband or partner "always" or "usually" did—mowing the lawn (83 percent) and taking out the garbage (52 percent). Additionally, 75 percent of the women noted that their husband or partner worked more hours outside the home. The tasks the fell to fathers were primarily one that have been traditionally associated with men. The responsibilities most often equally shared by couples included the following: disciplining a child, putting a child to bed, playing with children, deciding who does what job around the house, and managing the household finances.

An unequal division of labour was the number one issue that caused conflict in the postpartum relationships of the women I interviewed. Several women felt disappointed when their relationship dynamic mirrored traditional gendered expectations. "We fought about the division of labour for a good long time," confided Robin. "I wasn't working so I was the one who got up in the middle of the night, and I was the one who did all of the laundry, the dishes, the cleaning, the vacuuming, everything. Everything!" Robin and her husband Jeff sought counselling because Robin was beginning to feel "like the servant." Counselling helped Robin and Jeff untangle traditional gendered relationship patterns that felt oppressive to Robin. Lauren and her husband Brian went to counselling after their third child was born. During counseling, they agreed that

Brian would contribute more to household labour and childcare and that they would start having a regular date night. They came up with a schedule in which Brian did the dishes three nights a week and put the kids to bed most nights. Lauren thought these little things were enough to help her feel as if they were partners. She also noted that before she and her husband started having a regular date night, her role as a wife had been eclipsed by her other responsibilities. Taking time to go out together gave Lauren and her husband a chance to talk, reconnect, and have fun doing things they enjoyed together. Ashley was ready to divorce her husband because she was doing everything around the house while also working three jobs and going to school. Her husband did not want a divorce and began to do more housework and childcare. "Now we actually have a partnership, and it's really nice," commented Ashley. Julia was dissatisfied with the division of labour when she was married to her spouse; however their divorce agreement mandates their specific responsibilities, and now she is very satisfied with their respective roles.

Many women who did not seek counselling or threaten to divorce their husband had varying levels of chronic frustration with their respective division of labour. "I can't help but keep a chart in my head of how much I'm doing compared to my husband, and it seems very uneven lately," remarked Fiona. One full-time working mother exclaimed, "My husband does nothing. I do it all!" The division of labour was a "constant struggle" for Kelly and her husband. "We've discussed it many times, but we have different opinions about workloads," commented Kelly. "I feel I do 90 percent of the housework, but he feels we're evenly split. Given that I am working from the moment I wake to the moment I go to bed, I can't understand how he can make that claim when he watches two-plus hours of TV per day." Kelly, who worked longer hours and made more money than her husband did, felt that their household work had become more gender-divided over time. Kelly's story also illustrates that women in heterosexual couples who make more money than their husband usually contribute equal or more household labour than their husband, even if the husband is unemployed. However, the reverse does not hold true in that men in heterosexual couples who make more money than their wife contribute significantly less to household labour (Davis et. al.; Diefenbach).

A traditional gendered division of labour is a deeply embedded cultural construct, and married, heterosexual couples tend to move toward conventional gender roles after the birth or adoption of a child, often times contrary to the couple's expectations prior to having a child (Arendell; Walzer). Images of heteronormative parenting with women in charge of domestic work and childcare and men as breadwinners still dominate popular cultural representations of parenting. Women hypothesized that one of the reasons it may be challenging for men to be equal contributors to domestic work and childcare was because they did not have a model for equal participation. Many women noted that their husband was the first in their family to break with traditional gendered norms, and some saw their husband getting pushback for his domestic contributions from family members and co-workers. Some women also got pushback from their family and friends for having high expectations for their husband's participation in housework and childcare.

Kelly felt that her husband did not take into account all the things he did not see. "I'm constantly filling out forms, providing clothes for daycare, and making sure our daughter has everything she needs." Another woman who expressed similar concerns as Kelly noted that her husband felt they were equally divided because his "internal list" of everything that needed to be done was significantly shorter than her "internal list." Women identified several time-consuming "invisible" tasks that they were responsible for: doing the Target and grocery store runs; filling out permission slips and paperwork; scheduling appointments and play dates; signing kids up for lessons and activities; and coordinating carpools. The "invisible" household and childcare tasks that women were more likely to do, even in the most egalitarian relationships, often related to consumerism, child socialization, and facilitating kinship or friendship ties. It is difficult to assess whether women are more likely to do these jobs because there is a deeply engrained gendered component to them within the confines of traditional heteronormative marriage and family structure, or because they give women control over family spending, child socialization, and the family calendar.

EGALITARIAN RELATIONSHIPS

About a quarter of the women in this study who were in a heterosexual relationship reported sharing twenty-three tasks equally with their spouse or partner. These women felt they had an egalitarian relationship and were satisfied with their division of labour. Couples who had egalitarian heterosexual relationships had three things in common. 1) Both partners were committed to intentionally organizing paid work, housework, and childcare responsibilities in a nongendered way. 2) The male partner had primary responsibility for childcare at some point. 3) Every woman made a conscious decision to let their partner do housework and childcare in his own way, letting go of wanting to control how their partner did things (Brown).

Tara and her husband Rob worked together parenting their children and managing their household. "We define equal in a very different way than before we were actually doing it," observed Tara. "It isn't half and half; it is doing different things and being equally engaged in our kids' lives." Tara was proud of the fact that when the children woke up in the middle of the night, it was completely random whom they called for. Rob was able to take a six-week paternity leave after Tara returned to work. Rob's sole responsibility for childcare during this time helped them establish their equal parenting roles. Most companies in the United States do not have paternity leave policies equitable with maternity leave policies, which institutionalizes a gendered expectation that women should be the primary caretaker for children, which in turn feeds into unequal relationship patterns in the home. Men in Norway, Sweden, and Canada were reluctant to take paternity leave for decades; however, once these countries offered "nontransferable and well-paid leave for fathers" over eighty percent of men took advantage of these leave policies (Doucet 328). The rationale for these policies was to intentionally "disrupt a deeply rooted pattern and social norm of women as primary care-giving experts and men as main breadwinners" (Doucet 328). Even if a male partner could not take an extended paternity leave, couples where the father had regular sole responsibility for some aspect of childcare were more likely to have egalitarian caretaking roles.

In practical terms, both partners "learn" to parent, and the fact that women are more likely to take a longer parental leave than their male partner gives women more time and opportunities to develop their parenting skills at a faster rate than their male partners. This often sets up the dynamic of women as the "expert" parent and facilitates women's greater control over parenting and housework, which aligns with traditional gender norms. Letting go of wanting to control how their spouse or partner did things was especially important for women who were attempting to create egalitarian relationships. "I'm not OCD about the cleaning shit anymore," exclaimed Ashley, who was ready to divorce her husband for not pulling his weight. "My husband does all the laundry now. When I was in charge of laundry, the towels had to be just so in my linen closet, and there was a hand space between every hanger in my closet. I let that all that go, and now I don't care how the towels are stacked." When Rachel vented to her husband about everything on her plate, she made a list of all the things she was currently doing. When they went through the list together, the only thing Rachel felt her husband was capable of doing was emptying the diaper pail. She realized that she contributed to their unequal responsibilities because she did not want her husband to do things if he was not going to do them to her standards. Claire did more parenting than her husband on weekends. Even though she felt it would be beneficial for her to get a break, she had a hard time doing that because her husband's parenting style never met her standards or expectations. I have consistently found that people who want control over a particular domain or have higher standards about how things should be done do more work.

Women who wanted to have more equality in their relationship often kept track of what they did in relation to their partner. Women usually felt as if they did more work than their spouse, so sometimes noticing when their husband was not contributing was a catalyst for having a conversation about their respective roles, and sometimes it created resentment. Jan and her husband, who both worked full time, acknowledged that they were not going to have a fifty-fifty split. They each expected that they would contribute more to the household labour, which Jan felt made them less likely to monitor and feel resentful of the other partner's contributions.

"You can't do everything fifty-fifty because fifty-fifty is based on your own perception," Jan explained. "But if you always try to give 60 percent and only expect 40 percent, and if you are both doing that, then you're probably going to end up closer to a fifty-figty shared relationship."

THE WORK OF KINSHIP

Even though many couples are committed to egalitarian roles, it is interesting to look at the tasks that women are more likely to do: buying clothes for children; scheduling play dates; keeping the family calendar; choosing activities for child to participate; and buying presents (Brown). This is a demonstration of Michaela Di Leonardo's concept of "the work of kinship." Di Leonardo argues that in addition to housework, childcare and paid work, women also consciously engage in kin work. She defines kin work as the following:

> the conception, maintenance, and ritual celebration of cross-household kin ties, including visits, letters, telephone calls, presents, and cards to kin; the organization of holiday gatherings; the creation and maintenance of quasi-kin relations; decisions to neglect or to intensify particular ties; the mental work of reflection about all these activities and the creation and communication of altering images of family and kin vis-à-vis the images of others, both fold and mass media. (443)

She further argues that kin work is "crucial" for the functioning and maintenance of kinship systems; is a potential source of "women's autonomous power" and "emotional fulfillment;" and can also be a vehicle "for actual survival and/or political resistance" (441). In the five tasks that women are most likely to do, three of them—scheduling play dates, keeping the family calendar, and buying presents—could be classified as kin work. This suggests that for the women in this sample, the "work of kinship" was predominantly a gendered activity, as they did more work to maintain social ties.

SHIFT IN RELATIONSHIP DYNAMICS

There are many factors that can challenge a couple's relationship after having children, such as the following: sleep deprivation, increased workload, incorporating children into the primary relationship, each partner's new roles and responsibilities, work-family conflict, disagreements about parenting, financial constraints, resentment over uneven domestic and childcare responsibilities, and many other things. It is important for couples to be aware of potential postpartum relationship challenges so that they can figure out strategies to navigate these situations should they arise.

Increased Workload for Both Partners

One of the biggest issues for new parents and for parents having subsequent children was the increased workload. When Catherine and Sue adopted a second baby, Catherine felt it was an especially difficult time because their children were relatively close in age and had special needs. "We were so busy, and we didn't have family in town, so it was just Sue and I that had to do it all," explained Catherine. Jessica and her husband split childcare responsibilities. "We both feel the same way," observed Jessica. "We're either working or we're with our son. That's a big difference. It used to be that we were either working or relaxing." Her schedule was exhausting for both of them, but she liked the fact that they were equally responsible for making money and childcare.

Work-Family Conflict

Celeste found it extremely challenging when both she and her husband had high-stress corporate jobs that required long hours, demanding workloads, and frequent travel. They had a full-time nanny and a cleaning person, but it still was difficult for both of them. "My husband is the love of my life," exclaimed Celeste. "But when we were both working hard and running in different directions, our quality of family life just exploded." During this stressful time, Celeste's husband said, "Something has got to give. We just can't keep this up. Either you have to quit or I have to." Celeste quit her job to stay home for a few years, and then got a position in a company that did not require travel. When both partners' work schedules created work-family conflict (WFC), women were more likely than men to scale back their workload to accommodate family work demands. This is in line with other research that shows that when a married father experienced higher levels of WFC, his wife would assume more responsibility at home. However, when a woman experienced higher levels of WFC, her husband did not increase his domestic contributions (Hoobler et. al.).

Bridget and her husband frequently negotiated who got to stay at work late to finish their work commitments. "We often have conversations where one of us will say, 'You worked late last night, so I should be able to work late tonight,'" remarked Bridget. The traditional split the United States has had between the home and market spheres means that women balance family work and paid work amid the broader expectations that "good" mothers are intensive and that "ideal" workers can work "full time and overtime and takes little or no time off for childbearing or childrearing" (Williams 1). Joan Williams notes that although the attributes of the "ideal worker" are not necessary for all jobs, these attributes are essential for "good" jobs, both full-time blue-collar jobs and white-collar executive jobs. The structure of the marketplace prohibits caregivers from being "ideal workers" and, therefore, marginalizes caregivers by prohibiting them from social roles of responsibility and authority (Williams).

Disagreement over Work Status

Most of the women were in alignment with their husband or partner on figuring out their overall household strategy for making money and caring for children. However, when a couple fundamentally disagreed about this issue, it created significant conflict. Vanessa hated her job and desperately wanted to quit after their baby was born, but her husband, who was self-employed, wanted her to continue working because she carried the family's benefits. She did quit her job shortly after their first child was born, which made her husband into "a very nervous person" because he did not have a steady income. She felt passionate about staying home and feared going back to work. "There would be times when the money would be really low, and I'd think, 'Oh my God, he's going to say something again,' but I would turn my face away from it because I wasn't leaving my kids." Ultimately Vanessa and her husband came to the agreement that she would work part time out of the home for his business. In this instance, Vanessa wanted to adhere to traditional gendered expectations of the mother as a primary caretaker and the father as a primary breadwinner, whereas her husband envisioned that they would share these responsibilities more equally.

Change in Work Status

When Maggie transitioned from part-time work to staying home full time, she felt frustrated because her husband "assumed" that the she would be in charge of childcare, even when they were both home. "My husband would never think to ask if it's alright to leave when we're both in the house," she exclaimed. "I always feel that I need to ask if I can leave, or at least let him know, where he just leaves." Tracy, who quit a job she loved to stay home full time, found the transition to parenthood challenging because her life changed significantly, whereas for her husband, things stayed the same, especially since he continued to play softball three nights a week after the baby was born. Many first-time stay-at-home mothers echoed this sentiment that they experienced more significant life changes than their husband did because they had to adjust to losing their work identity and restrictions on their freedom because of caring for an infant.

Competition and the Challenges of Incorporating Multiple Relationships into a Family Unit

Vanessa felt that even though having children initially made her and her husband closer, there was also "a lot of competitiveness on our parts." "We were both so madly in love with the baby, but I always would win out because I was the nursing mother, and she always needed her Mama. Now that we're divorced, I see that as the beginning of some resentment." Amy's "honeymoon baby" had a profound effect on her first marriage. "It was different in that you didn't have the one-on-one relationship time. I think that is probably what dissolved the marriage. The focus was on the baby and there was a lack of money, and so many worries and pressures.

So you just grow apart." Tracy felt that their relationship changed so much because "it wasn't all about us anymore." She laughed as she noted that her husband sometimes referred to her as "Mom." "He'll say, 'Where's Mom?' and I think, 'I used to be your wife, now I'm the Mom,' it's so weird."

Carla, who stays home full time, felt that she and her husband had not quite figured out how to incorporate their relationship with their parental roles. "I usually don't like dinner with my family," commented Carla. "We seem to function really well as a family of three, either me and the children or my husband and the children, but we don't know how to function as a family of four, which is pretty sad." Carla got frustrated because she felt that she and her husband could not have a conversation at dinner because their children kept interrupting them. When Katie experienced a health crisis, her husband Steve took on most of the childcare responsibilities for their middle-school daughter, which made Katie feel lonely and isolated. "I felt like they had their own thing going on," remarked Katie. "They're working out homework and rides and stuff like that, but I felt so much on the outside. It really triggered a lot of jealousy for me and feeling like the third wheel, so we talked about that, and we fought about that, and eventually went to a counsellor to work through it." These stories show how relational dynamics between partners can be intensified when a couple has children.

Changes in the Focus of Attention

Sabrina and her husband experienced relationship challenges after their baby was born. She confided in a quiet voice that some of the conflict may be because she felt more devoted to her child than her husband. Sabrina's comment raises an interesting issue about how sometimes the affection a parent feels for a child takes precedence over the affection they feel for their spouse. In a *New York Times* column, Ayelet Waldman notes that in a variety of mother's groups, in which Ms. Waldman herself was a member, she seemed to be the only mother who had a satisfying sex life with her spouse. Waldman states that women are exhausted from childcare responsibilities; however, she argues that "the real reason for this lack of sex, or at least the most profound, is that the wife's passion has been refocused. Instead of concentrating her ardor on her husband, she concentrates it on her babies.... Libido, as she once knew it, is gone, and in its place is all-consuming maternal desire" (Waldman). Jessica had seen Ms. Waldman on an *Oprah* show before she had a child, and she vowed that she would never lose touch with her husband. When she and her husband experienced a difficult time after their son was born, a part of her felt that she and her baby were "buddies," whereas at the same time, she "couldn't even deal" with her husband. "I could see how you could get so into your kid that you ignore your spouse, especially if your spouse is being a pain," commented Jessica.

Decreased Leisure Time

In women's recollections of what their life was like before children, many recounted all of the activities they did with their spouse or partner. They felt that the biggest change from having children was the difficulty to find the time and energy to schedule a babysitter and have regular dates with their spouse or partner. Maggie said that she and her husband would occasionally get a sitter to go to a movie or to a friend's house to play cards; however most of the time when they did get a babysitter, they would go to political and fundraising events, which was how they met. Maggie was solely responsible for lining up childcare and was more aware of how much time they had been away from their children than her husband. She would rarely attend events on a school night. This was hard on her husband because her husband saw her reduced participation as a sign that she did not value the political activism as much. Maggie, though, felt her husband did not understand that she could only devote so much time to the various causes they supported because the time commitment was difficult to balance with children. Many women were mindful of making it a priority to spend time with their children, and women often felt guilty if they did not spend enough time with a child.

Sabrina and her husband used to have a busy social live, as they saw every new movie release. Now they rarely get a babysitter and do not see movies until they come out on *Netflix*. Tracy felt it was hard to spare two hours to go to a movie or plan a dinner date. "We've been trying to get better about that, even if it is just a couple of times a month, where we have grandma and grandpa come over for an hour and watch the kids." Jody and her husband were married for over ten years before having their first child in their late thirties. During the first ten years of their marriage, they spent nearly every weekend participating in various extreme sports. Even though Jody knew that their ability to travel, sail, and skydive would be curtailed after having a child, she was surprised that their active and busy social life "backed off pretty significantly." She speculated that it was harder to hang out with their childless friends because their friends were used to being able to do things on a whim. She and her husband had neither a consistent babysitter nor a family in town to rely on for help, so doing things without their toddler was not an option for them. During the week, she and her husband were both tired and did not have "quality adult time" because by the time they finished dinner, got their child to bed, finished their own work, it was time for them to go to bed so they could "wake up and do it all over again."

Katie noticed that her husband Steve could easily relax at home, whereas she could not because there was "always a load of laundry to throw in." She vividly recalled how hard her mother worked to cook, clean, do laundry, and deal with seven kids. She, therefore, had a deeply engrained sense that there was always housework to do. One of the main tensions between her and Steve when their daughter was young was negotiating who was going to get time do their own thing on weekends. Every Saturday and Sunday Katie wondered, "Okay, who's going to get the time? Who's going to get the time that they need?" Katie and Steve competed for that time, which was "really hard and challenging" because they both felt that "if one person gets it then the other person for sure is not going to get enough." Eventually, they figured out that Steve was okay if he had two or three hours away, whereas Katie needed five or six hours to come home and feel like "Oh good, I got filled up." Katie explained that it was not that she did not want to be home with their daughter; she just needed to be away for a while. Some couples experienced relief when they found ways to incorporate their children into leisure time activities. Examples of this included running or biking with children in a stroller or bike trailer, taking babies out to dinner with friends, and finding fun "child friendly" things to do as a family.

NURTURING THE PRIMARY RELATIONSHIP AND FRIENDSHIPS

Many women thought that it was essential to put time and energy into maintaining a good relationship with their partner. "There's a school of thought that you can't be a good parent unless you're a good spouse," commented Bridget. "You should focus on the state of your marriage first, and make sure you take time out to nurture it and continue to connect with your spouse, even if it means going out on dates and leaving your children with a babysitter." Bridget believed that it was important to role model having a good relationship to her children, and felt that creating a strong connection with her husband made them both better parents.

Jan and her husband Pat made an effort to maintain a connected relationship with each other. Jan's parents were married for nearly forty years when they got divorced. Even though Jan's parents never fought, she felt they did not nurture their relationship and as a result, once the children left home, they had nothing in common and nothing to talk about. Even though Jan and Pat did not "have things exactly in common," they made an effort to do things together. She was mindful that at some point, their children would leave home, and it would just be her and Pat again. "If we don't have anything in common, and if we don't like hanging out with each other anymore, and if we grow apart, then there's not going to be anything left to keep us together." As with Bridget, Jan felt that role modelling a healthy relationship, in which she and Pat did not focus all of their attention solely on the children, was important for her children to see. All of the women who sought counselling noted that their relationship counsellor recommended scheduling regular date nights.

Sheila felt that she and her husband Tom had been successful at having a good relationship and a good marriage to show their children. Sheila's own parents divorced when she was young, but Tom's parents were "still very joyful and loving ... expect[ing] that you are going to love this person always ... and treat them well." She saw how her in-laws' modelling of a good relationship to Tom had a direct impact on how he viewed marriage, and the love and respect for her that he brought to their marriage. Sheila and Tom also allowed each other the freedom to pursue their own lives, in addition to being married and being parents. "We both do a lot of stuff separately, and pursue our talents and interests," commented Sheila. "I think that's a huge gift to give your kids that people underestimate. People think the best thing to give your kids is to be constantly focused on them, and I think that a greater gift is to show them what it means to focus on yourself and make yourself a whole person whose happiness isn't completely wrapped around somebody else." Current middle-class mothering norms—identified as "intensive mothering" (Hays) or the "new momism" (Douglas and Michaels)—expect that a woman should prioritize mothering over her other identities and devote a significant amount of time, energy, and financial resources to ensure the wellbeing of her children. Most women in my study sacrificed their personal leisure time to accommodate their busy schedules, which often included overseeing children's activities.

Women also felt it was important to continue to do things with their friends, although for many women this was hard to schedule, and many felt guilty for taking time away from their child. I found that women who positively framed the things they did that took them away from their children were less likely to feel guilty. For example, one woman said that exercising was the best thing she can do to stay physically and mentally healthy and that going out with her friends filled her emotionally so that she could be a better mother and partner. Several women noted that they had been able to keep up with friendships but felt their husband did not have enough support outside of their relationship. Leslie's husband did not go out with friends, which Leslie found strange. "I keep telling him, wouldn't it be nice to go out with your guy friends for a beer and bitch about me for a few hours." Leslie loved getting together with her friends to laugh and vent, and felt sad that her husband did not have the same release valve.

TWENTY-FIRST-CENTURY PARTNERSHIPS

We live in an era in which there is little institutionalized support for families. Many people do not live close to extended kinship networks, and there are high expectations for both workers and parents. Many couples aspire to be equal parents, yet they find the reality of implementing egalitarian parenting roles challenging, especially when commercialized representations make it seem "natural" for women to be primarily responsible for childcare, domestic and consumer responsibilities, and the work of kinship. On top of this, there is little accurate information about what becoming a parent will really be like, in part because popular representations of new parenthood often depict a romantically blissful time or an intensely negative experience. New parents face extra strain when they do not have clear expectations of how their primary relationship needs to evolve or strategies in place to nurture their relationship as they accommodate the increased workload, reduced leisure time, and other facets of parenting. The stories in this chapter illustrate some of the ups and downs couples have experienced as they navigate their transition to being first-time parents or having subsequent children. When couples have realistic information about the challenges they may face as parents, they can create a plan that will increase their chances of successfully navigating the transition to parenthood and having a more successful marriage.

ENDNOTES

[1]All names are pseudonyms.

[2]Overall, 140 women from forty zip codes participated in this study. Of the eighty women who participated in an interview or focus group 12.5 percent identified themselves as African American; 3.75 percent identified themselves as Asian American; 3.75 percent identified themselves as biracial; 73.75 percent identified themselves as Caucasian; 5 percent identified themselves as Latino; and 1.25 percent identified themselves as "other" but did not specify their racial category. Women had a variety of work experiences—ranging from being home full time with their children, working part time, working full time—and some were the primary breadwinner for the household. The majority of women were married or living with a partner at the time of the interview, and the majority of these

partnerships were heterosexual. Approximately 15 percent of the interview sample were single or had been single for a significant amount of time while raising children. Women were single because of divorce, being widowed, or because they had never been married. Every participant had a high school degree, and some college or technical training. The majority of women had a college degree, and at least 25 percent of the sample reported having a graduate degree or some graduate training.

WORKS CITED

Arendell, Terry. Conceiving and Investigating Motherhood: The Decade's Scholarship. *Journal of Marriage and Family*, vol. 62, no. 4, 2000, pp. 1192–207.

Brown, Solveig. *All On One Plate: Cultural Expectations on American Mothers*. Paragon House, 2016.

Davis, Shannon, et al. "Effects of Union on Division of Household Labor: Do Cohabitating Men Really Perform More Housework?" *Journal of Family Issues*, vol. 28, no. 9, 2007, pp. 1246–72.

Di Leonardo, Michaela. "The Female World of Cards and Holidays: Women, Families, and the Work of Kinship." *Signs*, vol. 12, no. 3, 1987, pp. 440–53.

Diefenbach, Heike. "Gender Ideologies, Relative Resources, and the Division of Housework in Intimate Relationships: A Test of Hyman Rodman's Theory of Resources in Cultural Context." *International Journal of Comparative Sociology*, vol. 43, 2002, 45–64.

Doucet, Andrea. "'You See the Need Perhaps More Clearly Than I Have': Exploring Gendered Processes of Domestic Responsibility." *Journal of Family Issues*, vol. 22, 2001, pp. 328–57.

Douglas, Susan, and Meredith Michaels. *The Mommy Myth: The Idealization of Motherhood*. Free Press, 2005.

Hays, Sharon. *The Cultural Contradictions of Motherhood*. Yale Press, 1996.

Hochschild, Arlie. *The Second Shift*. Penguin, 1989.

Hoobler, Jenny, et. al. "Do Workers Who Experience Conflict between the Work and Family Domains Hit a 'Glass Ceiling?': A Meta-Analytic Examination." *Journal of Vocational Behavior*, vol. 77, no. 3, 2010, 481–94.

Kluwer, Esther., et al. "Marital Conflict about the Division of Household Labor and Paid Work." *Journal of Marriage and the Family*, vol. 58, no. 11, 1996, pp. 958–69.

Lawrence, Erika, et al. "Prenatal Expectations and Marital Satisfaction over the Transition to Parenthood." *Journal of Family Psychology*, vol. 21, no. 2, 2007, pp. 155.

Johnston, Deirdre, and Debra Swanson. "Invisible Mothers: A Content Analysis of Motherhood Ideologies and Myths in Magazines." *Sex Roles*, vol. 49, no. 1, 2003, pp. 21–33.

Murphy, Bren. "Women's Magazines: Confusing Differences." *Differences That Make a Difference: Examining the Assumptions of Gender Research*, edited by L. Turner and H. Sterk, Bergin and Garvey, 1994, pp. 119–27.

Sanchez, L., and E. Thomson. "Becoming Mothers and Fathers: Parenthood, Gender, and the Division of Labor." *Gender and Society*, vol. 11, no. 6, 1997, pp. 747–72.

Shapiro, Alyson, et., al. "The Baby and the Marriage: Identifying Factors That Buffer against Decline in Marital Satisfaction after the First Baby Arrives." *Journal of Family Psychology*, vol. 14, no. 1, 2000, pp. 59.

Waldman, Ayelet. "Truly, Madly, Guiltily." *New York Times*, 27 Mar., 2005, www.nytimes.com/2005/03/27/fashion/truly-madly-guiltily.html. Accessed 18 July 2017.

Walzer, Susan. *Thinking about the Baby: Gender and Transitions into Parenthood.* Temple University Press, 1998.

Williams, Joan. *Unbending Gender: Why Family and Work Conflict, and What to Do about It.* Oxford University Press, 2001.

6.
Sexuality, Intimate, and Parenting Relationships

Women Maintaining Same-Sex Relationships in Poland

MALGORZATA KOT

IN THIS CHAPTER, I am going to analyze the sexuality, intimate, and parenting relationships of women who maintain an intimate relationship with a woman and raise a child from a previous, heterosexual relationship in Poland. I explore how women shape sexuality beyond socially accepted norms, how it influences the relationship they create and maintain, and whether the intimate relationship with a woman, after leaving a heterosexual relationship, leads to a same-sex parenting relationship or not. I also discuss whether women who are in a relationship define themselves as homosexual, bisexual, or heterosexual, or whether they reject all the labels, and if there is a causal relationship between the sex of the partner and the embraced sexual identity. In order to examine these questions, I conducted semi-structured interviews with same-sex women couples in Poland. Furthermore, I intend to analyze the engagement of "social mothers"—understood here as female partners of biological mothers involved in the process of raising the children—and ways the parental roles are negotiated within the couple.

The sociocultural concepts of motherhood, mothering practices, and characteristics of mother identity have been a point of interest particularly for feminist and queer researchers for decades, deriving from a proliferation of identities, sexualities, intimacies, kinships, and relationships. The variety of relationship constellations, along with widening of the reproduction options, has opened the field for the research of families beyond heteronormative ones.[1] Thus, researchers have reflected on the relationship between woman identity, sexuality, and motherhood, and they have explored social patterns and power relations behind them (Rich; Weston; Dunne). Feminist and queer research conducted on women's identities, sexualities, and relationships has revealed a patriarchal mechanism of domination hidden behind theories of women's identity. The general construct of woman identity is perceived as related to motherhood and marriage and is built upon heteronormative principles. As Anne Woollett explains, "Motherhood is important in all women's lives, whether or not they are or want to be mothers, because women are defined in terms of their relationship to motherhood" (62).

Various societal changes have led to the creation of LGBTQ social movements. According to Maureen Sullivan, the following events were especially significant: separating sexuality from procreation, and the development of sexual identities, and the assimilation policies of homosexual people and separateness from mainstream culture (3). The change of the labour system was one factor separating sexuality from procreation. Labour has moved from the home to the outside world, which has made the home a place of consumption rather than production. Children were not work helpers anymore; they became the responsibility of parents, whereas the multigenerational and large family ceased to be a model. Intimacy and relationships started to be associated with personal pleasure and feelings. Such expanding of relationships allowed some to discover their desires in same-sex relationships and led to changes in the relationship dynamics of heterosexual and homosexual individuals. Regarding heterosexual and same-sex relationships, these dynamics worked in the following way: some people entered heterosexual relationships because of fear of stigmatization, whereas some left heterosexual patterns and created same-sex intimate relationships, including parenting relationships and families (Sullivan 24).

Then, the dilemma of same-sex families' assimilation into heteronormative culture appeared, as homosexual persons were supposed to function as heterosexual families, adjusting into a pattern of a white, patriarchal, heterosexual family (Sullivan 29). Instead, researchers proposed the model of a "family of choice," which rejected the necessity of adjusting to heteronormative models and encouraged individuals to remain open, to focus on experiences and family practices, and to create one's own patterns. Nonheteronormative families, thus, have developed new patterns and new family structures, which have redefined the parenting roles. Families of choice have challenged the heterosexism and division of gender roles in same-sex families, as the division was supposed to be more fluid. These families are more flexible and have a bigger network of social contacts, as more people are involved in child upbringing (Clunis and Green 16). Also, as Gillian Dunne has argued, in lesbian's partnerships, "Their sexuality and the gender dynamics of their relationship, both necessitates the transformation of the boundaries, meaning and content of parenthood and facilitates the construction of more self-reflexive, egalitarian approaches to financing and caring for children" (13). Two abovementioned strands of studying same-sex families—assimilative and transformative— nevertheless have put heterosexual families as a point of reference. Studying same-sex kinships and families in their contexts, exploring privilege and marginalization, may provide a more productive way forward, which does not position them as the "other" (Ryan-Flood 186).

As different people participate in the child's upbringing, two aspects are highlighted in the literature on lesbian families: the role of the female partner as a parent and the involvement of a biological father (in the case of families in which a child comes from a previous, heterosexual relationship). A woman whose partner is a biological mother cannot be assigned to any cultural category of a legitimate parent (Sullivan 158). These women are regarded as friends, sisters, cousins, aunts, or as strangers. To mark their presence, they function as persons important in the family, and they need to create their own identifications, with no clues or possibility to refer to already existing patterns, as there are not any. The term "mother" and her role are, thus, reserved only for the person who gave birth to a child or adopted it. Additionally, the lack of legal security in many countries and lack of recognition of a social mother as a legitimate parent can cause tensions in relationships and can influence social mothers' engagement in taking care of a child.

Another problematic area in the case of previous heterosexual relationships is the presence of a man in a child's upbringing. A father's relationship with his children can vary—from active participation in a child's life through indifference to disappearance from a child's life. The biological mother's decision is crucial here, as she decides whether or not to maintain a child-father relationship (Clunis and Green 48). If such a relationship is possible, then the family model is extended. The "social mother" is then a person taking care of a child on a daily basis and the father is a visitor from time to time. Parenting relationships among same-sex women can be characterized by autonomy of choices, practices, and decisions. It is worth considering, if families of choice develop their own patterns or refer more to heteronormative rules. What is certain, however, is that they face issues resulting from a heteronormative reality: the invisibility of the social mother and lack of recognition, legal or otherwise, for the family structure.

Polish research in the field of nonheteronormative relationships, motherhood, and mothering practices and experiences has reflected on how compulsory heterosexuality underlies patterns of motherhood (Mizielińska). It is, however, mostly focused on the social functioning of queer families and families of choice. It looks at new kinship patterns created by nonheteronormative families and how they operate on a daily basis in a (mostly) homophobic environment in which lesbian women are expected to have children as women but are denied as lesbians to have the right to reproduce (Majka-Rostek).

The reality and societal approaches that nonheteronormative families have to manage while raising a child prove to be marked by heteronormativity and a lack of understanding for different concepts of a family. According to a survey of public opinion in Poland regarding the present meaning and understanding of the family, the heteronormative image remains persistent, as 69 percent of respondents do not agree to treat a same-sex couple raising the child of one of the partners as a family (CBOS, *Rodzina*). The right of same-sex couples to adopt a child is also denied by 87 percent of respondents (CBOS, *Stosunek*). The societal denial to treat a queer family as legitimate is rooted in prejudices and stereotypes regarding nonheterosexual individuals. Homosexuality is argued as abnormal and is not tolerated by over one-fourth of Polish society (CBOS, *Stosunek*). This attitude could entail further discrimination, harassment, and violence, evidenced in the research. A 2013 LGBT survey, conducted by the European Union Agency for Fundamental Rights, shows that Polish lesbians routinely experience discrimination or harassment because of their sexual orientation. Therefore, nonheteronormative couples with a child prefer to hide their relationship from the child's surroundings or sometimes even from the child himself (Mizielińska et al. 135, 139).

The exclusionary societal approach to queer families is also found in Polish family law, as same-sex couples and families remain invisible. They can neither get married nor get registered. Also, nonheterosexual couples do not have the right to adopt a child; this privilege is reserved to married couples and individuals (although in practice, it is extremely difficult for individuals to adopt, as agencies prefer married couples). In cases of nonheterosexual women couples, their reproductive options have been strictly limited since 2015, when the law on in-vitro fertilization was changed. Since then, this law has enabled the refunded procedure only to heterosexual couples. When a same-sex couple raises a child together, only the biological or adoption parent holds parental rights. According to the law, a social parent remains a stranger, which can cause serious problems in case of a biological parent's sickness or death.

DATA AND METHODS: SAME-SEX FEMALE COUPLES' INTIMATE AND PARENTING RELATIONSHIPS

In order to explore the realities of families of choice established and maintained by women in Poland, I conducted a qualitative study among women being in a same-sex relationship and raising a child of one of the partners from a previous heterosexual relationship. I aimed to study women's construction of their sexualities and their effects on a partner choice. I wanted to check factors important for a partner selection, to examine the experience of heteronormativity and strategies to overcome it, and to discover if the relationship with a woman led both women in the relationship to identify as nonheterosexual, lesbian, bisexual, or queer. I also sought to explore how both women partners were involved in taking care of a child, how a father was present or absent in a child's life, whether both women identified equally with the mothering role, and what difficulties they faced in everyday life.

Sample and Setting

I conducted an exploratory study among five nonheterosexual couples living in different cities in Poland. The couples were chosen so that one of the partners was in a heterosexual relationship before and had a child or children. Interviewees were above twenty-five years of age, and the median age was thirty-five at the time of a study. All the couples were white, as ethnic Poles constitute over 90 percent of ethnic composition in Poland (CIA).

In summary, I conducted ten semistructured interviews, separately with each partner so as to allow women to freely express their feelings and opinions. All interviewees had maintained an intimate relationship with a woman for an average of four years at the time of the study.

FINDINGS

For the majority of both biological and social mothers, the personality and emotional aspects were most important in a relationship with a woman; these attributed included closeness, sensitivity, and mutual understanding. As one interviewee explained, "During a talk with a man I don't feel this possibility of getting to know another person, which I feel while talking with a woman; it's an emotional, spiritual getting to know someone."[2]

For interviewees, having a close emotional contact was only possible with women, but they paid attention to the fact that specific features of character were person dependent. The erotic side of a relationship also came into play. However, for women who talked about their same-sex desire as being there from childhood, the sexual sphere of a relationship was important. Some of the interviewees claimed that they could have a sexual relationship with both men and women, but having a relationship of mutual understanding was only possible with women.

Although both grew up in a heteronormative world, the experiences of biological and social mothers were different. Women who were in a relationship with a man previously admitted that the heteronormative model of sexuality and relationships significantly influenced their choice of a male partner. A man was chosen because of family pressure (in one case it was pressure because of pregnancy), awareness of homophobia, and difficulties that a same-sex relationship would entail. For some of the interviewed women, who were the biological mothers, the choice of a man was easier because of social ostracism:

> I decided that I want to be normal and will be with men. And when I was with a man, I said, that it was great, I had peace; I didn't need to wonder about anything that someone would see me, that I didn't have to hide, be cautious about what I said—a relief that parents will get off my back, that it's easier. I sometimes needed such normalcy, easiness in life, and I was fed up with women, this mess. It wasn't that I was fed up with women, but it was easier, as with a woman it was difficult, mentally exhausting.

Another interviewee claimed that she felt that something was wrong with her, regarding her sexuality, but she did not decide to call the wedding off: "I had a fiancé already. I was thinking—it will work out somehow, as it's often said. That I would suppress it, everyone thinks that most often. And I got married."

It can be observed that some of the women chose a man because of the adjustment to social norms and to avoid discomfort, fear, and stigma. One of the respondents treated a relationship with a man as temporary: "I thought he was a guy for a moment only – and suddenly a husband, a child—and I still waited for a woman, for the one."

For another subject, a choice of a man was related to the willingness to experiment, as she had had a bad experience with a first relationship with a woman. It needs to be highlighted that the choice of a male partner was not always because of pressure; some interviewees argued that character traits were also important. During a relationship with a man, some of interviewees tried to have a relationship with a woman. One of the respondents had contact with women through an online forum for nonheterosexual women, but she underscored that it was only a friendship. Two of the interviewees had sexual and intimate relationships with women during their marriage. In one case, the relationship was without the knowledge of her husband, and it was later revealed to him. The interviewee argued that her sexuality was suppressed and silenced. She stopped herself from desiring women for the sake of her marriage, but she could not have a sexual relationship with her husband. As it turned out, the sexual relationship with the woman helped her to fulfil her desires. In the other case, the woman had a sexual relationship with women, but her husband knew about it and approved it. She preferred such a relationship, since she did not have to face the social stigma related to an open relationship with a woman. Relationships with women that were established and maintained during the marriage did not survive, but they were also the main reason as to why marriages fell apart. Two interviewees justified their breakup with their male partner because of a lack of understanding, contact, and support. As one of the women explained, "I had a feeling of such lack, that it wasn't it. There was such a contact with my husband, which I didn't grasp. It all fell apart when the child was born, I felt so alone with all of it and I made the decision to break up."

In the case of an interviewee, whose husband found out about her relationship with another woman, the breakup was traumatizing, as he attempted to terminate her parental rights and stigmatize her as a sick person and as undeserving of being a mother because of her nonheterosexual orientation: "I was accused of being sick, mentally ill, that I fooled everyone. My husband thought that it'll pass; he sent me to psychologists, psychiatrists."

The sexuality of the interviewee was stigmatized and framed in the medical discourse because of her nonheterosexuality. With the support of medical representatives, the husband aimed to prove that her desire needed medical treatment. The nonheteronormative desire of his wife, in his view, was incompatible with a mothering role.

Although biological mother respondents were in relationships with men, none of them labelled themselves as heterosexual. At the time of the study, while being in a relationship with a woman, they also did not want to identify with any specific sexual identity.

They simply said "I just am and I am with a woman." Initially, they tried to identify themselves as bisexual, as it seemed to be safer and not radical as lesbian. Some of them did define themselves as lesbians, but after experiences and contacts with other LGBTQ persons, this definition was too limiting. Some of the interviewees claimed to use the lesbian identity in their activism. When undertaking activities within nongovernmental organizations and acting publicly, they claimed it was useful to speak of oneself as lesbian in order to be a part of representative group.

When talking about intimate and parenting relationships with a woman, the majority of biological mothers tried to divide the intimate relationship from child upbringing. Two interviewees explained it in the following way:

> I don't feel that when I enter the relationship we will bring up my child. It is that I am going to bring up my child, I give him orders and bans, and we are just together.

> I feel that it's my child, not ours. I ask her for help and she always helps me. I don't want to burden her with duties, which are mine. If it were our child, it would be different. It would be our decision.

Biological mothers justified this division so to protect partners and to remove the responsibility for a child from the social mother, which in their understanding had two parents. Parental norms claiming that a child has a mother and a father influenced this division a lot. Blood ties were also regarded as important—the feeling that a child was not a result of a decision made together with a female partner, but it was brought up earlier in a different family system. Biological mothers also paid attention to the age of a child and claimed that the family structure would be different if the child was raised by two women from the earliest years of life:

> M. has a mother and a father, and A. is with me because of me. Surely I wasn't thinking that we will be both mothers, as I have this feeling that if M. was with us from the earliest years, that it would be different.

Biological mothers were convinced that a younger child would get used to a new guardian more quickly and that establishing a child's relationship with a female partner would be easier than in the case of an older child, who was already raised by a heterosexual couple. In one of the cases, the age of the children was important for a better relationship between them and the biological mother's partner. The children were two and three years old respectively, when the women entered into the relationship, so they got used to a new partner more quickly and started treating her partner as another mother. The age of a child was not the only factor for the quality of child-social parent relationship, though. What mattered as well, particularly for biological mothers, was the autonomous decision of a partner as to whether or not she wanted to take care of a child. What's worth noting is that both partners dedicated a huge amount of time to discuss all possible scenarios; all of the partner's needs and limitations in regards to the children were discussed as well as how to best nourish their relationship as a couple.

Although biological mothers divided the intimate relationship from a parenting one, saying that intimate relationship and parenting relationship are two different worlds, female partners participated in the child's raising to some extent. They were involved in home duties and in the child's life. The relationship between a child and female partner was friendly and open but included clear rules.

On the other hand, biological mothers admitted that they sometimes needed more engagement from a partner regarding the upbringing and care of the child. One interviewee explained the need in a following way:

> My partner distances herself, and I think it is a difficult area for us. I wish she would treat my child as hers. I don't put pressure on her now, but I used to do that. I think I expected that she would be a favourite aunt for my child, that she would be engaged more. She hasn't become such a person, such a favourite aunt, but she's a constant element of my daughter's life.

One of the respondents, who had a child with a disability, expected care and greater involvement from her partner, as she was afraid about her child's future: "I wish she would engage more as I would feel safer. A partner doesn't want to take responsibility for a child— and okay, I get it, but it's difficult for me as my son will always need care."

Interviewed couples had their rules regarding upbringing; they were aware of difficulties and limitations, but it was a difficult area for both of them. Female partners participated in a child's upbringing, but at the same time, the biological mothers tried to divide the intimate and parenting relationship so as not to burden their partners and respect their decision of being uninvolved. They justified their decision with the argument that the child had parents already.

Regarding the fathers, their involvement varied and depended mainly on their individual decision. In one case, the biological mother claimed that her relationship with her ex-husband was good, as he had a caring relationship with and financial responsibility for their child. For other interviewees, this relationship was challenging, or there was no relationship. In one family, the father did not participate at all, and his role was taken by the female partner. In another, the father had a new family and ignored his child. And in yet another, the man was addicted to alcohol and drugs, and did not fulfil his parental responsibilities at all. The interviewee claimed that she could not count on him:

> He gets in touch from time to time and that's all. At the same time, in areas where he holds some legal power and can mark it, even symbolically, where he can take advantage of us being together, for example to have lower child support—he does it. He is like "take care of him, and if I can sort something out for me thanks to this, I will."

The lack of fathers' involvement might have caused the need for greater involvement from female partners. The biological mothers evaluated the care work done with a female partner as better than that done with a man, mostly because of bad parenting experience they had with their husband. Even though partners distanced themselves from a parenting role, mothers defined the division of care as equal. Interestingly, this division was often related to gender stereotypes—a mother was more caring, whereas a female partner was described as actively spending time with a child, in a sports manner. Describing the activities undertaken by each of the partners in relation to stereotypical women's traits may be related to a heteronormative environment, which pressures biological mothers to define themselves and their partner. It can be also linked to the effect of previous heterosexual relationships, in which a man's role as a father and a woman's as a mother were clearly defined in line with gender stereotypes. Applying these stereotypes in same-sex relationships may be a normalization strategy, trying to prove that a family led by two women is no different than one led by a man and a woman.

Talking about problems and fears related to shared parenting with a female partner, mothers identified fears related to discrimination by school representatives. Interviewees were aware of a common heteronormativity at schools, the worldviews of headmasters and teachers, so they were afraid of bad treatment toward their children. One of the interviewees had a good experience, in general, but she also experienced a situation, where her partner was ignored by the school headmaster:

> I was scared how we would manage with discrimination and people, how we would behave. This fear was about society, not us. It's better than I thought it would be-cause, I wouldn't say that we are accepted, but we are "of our own." We are always invited together to Christmas eve or other parties. But as for teachers, there is some mocking. Once there was an unpleasant situation when I heard "as you decide" not "as you both decide," although my partner was with me.

Interviewees were also afraid of other children's parents, as a group that transfers heteronormative values, resulting in discrimination and mocking by other children. However, the remarks of two interviewees below show that there is no need to be afraid of children. The mothers pointed out that they were not afraid of children, as children themselves do not have prejudices. Two interviewees elaborated in the following manner:

Children react positively; there's no aggression or surrounding comments. Friends come to visit my children and ask who my partner is. My children respond "distant mum," and there's no problem, but I worry about parents, as they shape an attitude.

> I'm afraid how much difficult it can be for my child when she sees that her family is untypical. She's at such a point, experiences it. A peer group is the least predictable; they are a random group, but peers will become more and more important and I don't know what I'll do. I worry about discrimination, pointing fingers.

Regarding the definition of a relationship as a family, it was observed that the term was conflictual. The perception of biological mothers was that they were family, whereas female partners, as social mothers, distanced themselves from such a term. Two interviewees explained this phenomenon in the following way:

> I think we are family, and but my partner doesn't. This is our conflict. I think of us, regardless how we call ourselves, as a family. For me, a family is people who create bonds. I develop a bond with my partner and with my daughter; my partner also develops a bond with my daughter because they live together, and my daughter creates bonds with both of us.

> Family consists of people who are close with one another. A stranger made me aware that I didn't think of us as a family, that if we don't exist legally then we don't exist—but we are family.

The most important factors that defined a family were bonds, feelings of closeness, and trust, and these were not necessarily blood ties, as a child's father was not usually regarded as a family member because of his lack of involvement in childcare and daily life. Only in one case was the father seen to be a family member, as he was regularly engaged in parenting duties. In other cases, the interviewees claimed that a father was family for a child, but in these relationships, the bonds were not nurtured because he was mostly absent. It can be said that he was a family to a child only because of blood ties. Interviewees were also speaking about an "accompanying" family, which was defined as family members who supported a biological and a social mother in the child's upbringing. The accompanying family was made of grandparents, parents of the biological mother, and a social mother. Rarely, the ex-husband's parents were mentioned, as these contacts were dependent on the relationship with the father.

For biological mothers, the intimate and parenting relationships were theoretically divided, but it cannot be said that no parenting relationship existed, as one of the interviewees argued: "We both try to participate in upbringing, when you live with each other on a daily basis, it's impossible not to participate."

The strength of heteronormativity could be also observed here, as a child has a mother and a father. Undoubtedly, the distance of female partners had its influence on the parenting relationship. The greatest difficulty encountered was homophobia toward the family from the environment. It needs to be highlighted that although the parenting relationship was not clearly defined, biological mothers argued that their triad was a family.

Female partners defined themselves as a partner of a person who has a child, rather than wanting to be identified as a mother. Three of the interviewees described their experiences in the following way:

> I'm not a parent. A child has a mother and a father, and every third person is not a parent, and it shouldn't be artificially changed. A daughter of my partner is important to me, but she is not my child.

> Surely, I don't call myself a mum. For me, a person who gave a birth is a mum. I, not giving birth, cannot define myself as a mother. Besides, I feel the inequality of parental power. I have a feeling that her son will never listen to me as he does to his own mother. I can order him to do something, but I also feel that he can say: "don't give me orders. You're not my mother."

> There are areas that I don't enter. It's the decision related to what I want and what I don't want. I don't wonder about if I should or shouldn't be a mum; there are simply things I don't decide for. The basis for me not defining as a parent of a child is that if something happened to my partner, I wouldn't raise her child afterward.

In the majority of cases, partners were hesitant to define themselves as a child's parent. Heteronormative values had a strong influence, as these partners believed that a mother can only be a person who gives birth and that the parental dyad is a closed system. Nevertheless, biology was not the only reason. Women also felt that because they were not parents, they did not have the parental power entitled to a mother or a father. Legal regulations, which made taking care of a child impossible for a female partner, were also a cause; female partners knew that if a biological mother died, they would not have any rights to the child, as he or she would be given to a father or to the grandparents. Partners accepted being unrecognized as guardians by the rest of a child's family, as one interviewee expressed: "I would like to have a bigger influence, but there is a resistance from child's parents and grandparents. Here at home I have influence, but there I don't have any."

All these factors resulted in the female partner deciding not to be involved in taking care of the child to a great extent, but she still took care of the child on a daily basis. For one of the women, the parental role was something natural, resulting from an intimate relationship:

> I think that I have children, but I don't know if I am a mum, a guardian (I don't want to call it that way), or I am with a person who has children. It's too much to say that I'm a mum, but I entered relationship with my partner, knowing that she has children, and I said okay, we will bring them up together.

Because a parenting relationship was ambiguous, defining the triad of mother, partner, and child was also problematic for some interviewees: "Family—this term is too difficult for me. I don't know if we are family. Family is a constellation of persons who are most important for one another, and there are various decisions, and I couldn't make any decisions as related to child upbringing."

As the statements above show, the parenting relationships created were ambiguous. On the one hand, both women argued that they were not two mothers, and the responsibility was on the mother and the father. The female partner participated in the child's upbringing, but at the same time, she distanced herself from the mothering role. On the other hand, these women were involved in daily duties, and they sometimes took on the father's duties, who existed only symbolically, as he did not fulfil his role.

CONCLUSIONS

The partners' personal decisions and heteronormative patterns shaped their relationship with the child in an area related to childrearing. Interviewees internalized the nativist belief, claiming that only a woman who gives birth is a legitimate parent. They, therefore, positioned themselves as illegitimate guardians, as almost strangers. Heteronormative patterns also had their impact through societal reactions and legal limitations, which do not recognize a partner as a guardian. Interviewees experienced difficulties with school educators, who did not recognize them as guardians and as a member of the child's family. They often treated them as invisible or as only a friend but not as an another parent and life partner. Also, the father figures were very strong and shaped the parenting relationship, although they were rarely present in the child's daily life. Their presence powerfully underscored that the child had biological father, a "real" parent. However, social mothers were still involved in the day-to-day care of the child, so the parenting relationship was present regardless of how the relationship was defined. What seemed important was the personal agreement in an intimate relationship, as to how to manage the parenting relationship and what duties were required of both partners. Both partners regarded communication on this topic as very important and devoted a lot of time to it, which also strengthened their intimate relationship.

Parenting practices, the dynamics of sharing childcare, and the differences in involvement of biological and social mothers are also factors that influence not only parenting but also intimate relationships. Biological mothers spoke about partners distancing themselves from childcare and had difficulty naming their relationship a "family" Some of them pointed, also, to the need for more involvement from their partner's side. This imbalance in childcare and emotional distance can cause tensions within the intimate relationship; in one case, the different understanding of the term "family" was called a "conflict" by one biological mother. The confluence of factors causing the distance, such as the presence of a child's father or legal obstacles, may additionally increase the tension and discomfort in both parenting and intimate relationships and potentially lead to a split. Exploring the intimate relationship dynamics within same-sex families, the emotions of partners toward one another, and everyday negotiations should not be neglected within studies on families of choice, as they provide an important insight into the experiences and challenges of nonheterosexual partnerships.

Nonheteronormative relationships have been a point of interest for researchers and should be studied further. These relationships show that parenting relies on individual agreements and negotiations, and is not limited to biological parents but involves other parties willing to be involved in childrearing to a degree negotiated and agreed upon with other family members.

As I have tried to prove through this study, sexuality, intimate, and parenting relationships are constructs shaped by patterns and individual decisions; these are not monolithic structures but processes that change during life. Interviewed women had a chance to talk about their experiences, which had been invisible and stigmatized. Giving voice to lesbian mothers in relationships, to speak loudly about their experiences, desires, sexualities and relationships, will allow for fuller and more diverse analyses of sexualities, identities, and relationships. An acknowledgment of the variety of experiences, a critique of existing definitions, and an extension of terms are all necessary if we want, as researchers, to show the diverse mosaic of modern realities of human identities and relationships.

ENDNOTES

[1]Heteronormativity is understood in this article as "the view that institutionalized heterosexuality constitutes the standard for legitimate and prescriptive sociosexual arrangement" (Ingraham 204), which limits the recognition and understanding of nonheteronormative relationships and families.

[2]All Polish-to-English translations are my own.

WORKS CITED

CBOS (Public Opinion Research Centre), (2013), *Stosunek do praw gejów i lesbijek oraz związków partnerskich*. Komunikat z Badań Centrum Badania Opinii Publicznej, BS/24/2013.

CBOS (Public Opinion Research Center), (2013). *Rodzina—jej współczesne znaczenie i rozumienie*. Komunikat z Badań Centrum Badania Opinii Publicznej, BS/33/2013.

Central Intelligence Agency. *The World Factbook*, 2017, www.cia.gov/library/publications/the-world-factbook/geos/pl.html. Accessed 19 July 2017.

Clunis Merilee, D., and G. Dorsey Green. *The Lesbian Parenting Book. A Guide to Creating Families and Raising Children*, Seal Press, 1995.

Dunne, Gillian. *Opting into Motherhood: Lesbians Blurring the Boundaries and Redefining the Meaning of Parenthood and Kinship*. LSE Gender Institute, 2000.

Hallett Nicky. *Lesbian Lives: Identity and Auto/Biography in the Twentieth Century*. Pluto Press, 1999.

Ingraham, Chrys. "The Heterosexual Imaginary: Feminist Sociology and Theories of Gender, in Sociological Theory." *Sociological Theory*, vol. 12, no. 2, 1994, pp. 203-19.

Majka-Rostek, Dorota. "Macierzyństwo lesbijek—wybrane konteksty społeczne." *Studia Socjologiczne*, vol. 4, no. 215, 2014, pp. 59-76.

Mizielińska, Joanna. (2012), "Czy macierzyństwo jest już od zawsze heteroseksualne? Próba refleksji." *Pożegnanie z Matką Polką? Dyskursy, praktyki i reprezentacje macierzyństwa we współczesnej Polsce*, edited by R. Hryciuk and E. Korolczuk,

Wydawnictwa Uniwersytetu Warszawskiego, 2012, pp. 235-66.
Mizielińska, Joanna, et al. *Families of Choice in Poland. Family Life of Non-Heterosexual People*. Warsaw: Instytut Psychologii Polskiej Akademii Nauk, 2015.
Rich, Adrienne. "Compulsory Heterosexuality and Lesbian Existence." *Signs*, vol. 5, no. 4, pp. 631-60.
Rich, Adrienne. *Of Woman Born: Motherhood as Experience and Institution*. Norton, 1976.
Ryan-Flood, Róisín. *Lesbian Motherhood: Gender, Families, and Sexual Citizenship*. Palgrave Macmillan, 2009.
Sullivan Maureen. *The Family of Woman. Lesbian Mothers, Their Children, and the Undoing of Gender*. University of California Press, 2004.
The European Union Agency for Fundamental Rights. *EU LGBT Survey: European Union Lesbian, Gay, Bisexual, and Transgender Survey*. Publications Office of the European Union. 2013.
Weston, Kath. *Families We Choose Lesbians, Gays, Kinship*. Columbia University Press, 1991.
Woollett, Anne. *Having Children: Accounts of Childless Women and Women with Reproductive Problems. Motherhood: Meanings, Practices and Ideologies*. Sage, 1991.

7.
"Hopefully He Puts the Ring On It"

Teenage Mothers' Voiced Desire for Marriage

SARAH BEKAERT

WHILE I WAS INTERVIEWING teenage mothers in East London to explore the social and cultural context of their pregnancy decision making, the young women voiced a keen desire for marriage. However, this goal stood in tension to the reality of their lives, evident in their narratives, which attested to the effectiveness of creative family formations—but not marriage. In these narratives, the young mothers presented a positive account of their "baby father's" involvement in their family life despite his financial, emotional, and childcare support being sporadic. All stressed the committed nature of their relationships, which countered the stereotype of the absent young father. In an astute move by the young women, it seemed that by valuing what the young men do rather than lamenting what they do not do, they keep the young father close and promote the growth of their new family. However, despite this early, and in my opinion, exciting, creative challenge to the stereotypical nuclear family model, all the young mothers expressed a desire for the traditional: marriage and living as a nuclear family unit. A simple desire to marry and/or practical considerations to ensure the young father's continued support may be a contributing factor to this voiced goal; however, I will consider how pressure to prove themselves as a "good citizen" (Kidger 490) in response to social stigma regarding teenage parenthood, may also push them toward expressing a desire for marriage.

Through eight in-depth interviews with young mothers, or mothers to be, who had previously had an abortion, this exploratory study examined the influencing factors on pregnancy decision making in relation to becoming a mother soon after an abortion while in the teenage years. The study considered these factors in a UK context; however, the findings may be relevant to other international contexts with similar societal expectations for motherhood and childhood. These contexts might be those that favour the scholarization of the child (Mayall, "The Sociology" 250); where young people spend increasing time in education in preparation for the workplace. This supposedly precludes motherhood in the teen years, which is assumed to hinder this expected trajectory. Family-formation expectations to be within a financially supportive nuclear family unit also exist; this model is assumed to make no financial demands on the state and is therefore favoured by government and popular opinion (Craig and O'Dell). This narrow view of what family should look like ignores positive aspects of varied family formation—such as extended family supporting the new mother or apprenticeship in which the early parenthood years are spent with the grandparents, and the new parents learn to parent with support close at hand.

My research questions evolved from my growing unease with the assumptions and goals of the UK's Teenaged Pregnancy Strategy, which focused on reducing teenage pregnancy. The government viewed young parenthood as leading to social exclusion and poverty. The policy constructed teenage pregnancy and parenthood as a risk to be fixed through appropriate intervention. I had become increasingly unsettled by the risk discourse surrounding young parenthood through meeting many young mothers who were successfully parenting, and through noting how parenthood could mark a positive change in their lifestyle. Similarly, research attests to teenage parenthood as frequently positive and restorative. Teenage parenthood can lead to reengagement with education (Theriot et al. 355; SmithBattle, "Teenage" 35); a restoration of relationships with family (Furstenberg 79; Bassey-Etowa 32); and withdrawing from negative lifestyles (Kaye et al. 182). Furthermore, motherhood can be experienced as a valued social role (Phoenix 119). In poorer socioeconomic environments in which career opportunities are few, the responsibility of raising children gives young women a recognized role. The "transgression" of becoming pregnant in the teen years is forgotten as the importance of a mother's responsibility in providing a positive environment for their child takes precedence.

There are, without doubt, challenges inherent to young or early motherhood, highlighted most recently in the report by the Young Women's Trust, which notes such issues as poverty, isolation, poor experience with employers, and the prohibitive cost of childcare. However, the same report highlights that young mothers' main challenge is negative judgment because of their age. The terms "young" mother or "early" motherhood are troublesome in themselves. They suggest a right timing for motherhood against which the young mother falls short. Pam Alldred has noted that although media is rife with judgement regarding the wrong time to have a child, it is less clear when the supposed right time may be. The difficulties encountered by young mothers tend to be rooted in dominant popularized psychological and social discourses that find the young mothers wanting.

Deficit psychological models are mobilized to suggest that young mothers are not yet adult—such as teenage egocentrism purported by Elkind (1025)—and are, therefore, unprepared for parenthood (Garcia Coll and Vàzquez García 283). Erica Burman has critiqued deficit psychological models of child development that suggest that children are adults in waiting, and Gerison Lansdown has suggested considering the "capacities of the child" based on social context and life experience (3). Lee SmithBattle has proposed that young mothers may have developmental needs, but this growth can occur through having a child ("Teenage" 22). More specifically in relation to being able to care for their children, Arlene Geronimus has noted that previous childcare work has shown to have better prepared young mothers for motherhood ("What" 323).

Berry Mayall has discussed how young people are viewed as "socialization projects" in preparation for full participation in society ("Understanding" 313). Consequently, further assumptions are levied against young mothers: they have not completed education and, therefore, are not ready for the workplace and assumed financial independence; they are often neither cohabiting nor married to their partner and, thus, are drawing on scant governmental resources. However, these assumptions are often unfounded. Ann Phoenix has noted the financial astuteness of the young mothers she interviewed; the young women decided to parent at a time when it would have the least financial impact on their lives. Maximizing on extended family support, when available, is also a consideration in the face of high childcare costs (SmithBattle, "Intergenerational" 56). Assumptions about single-parent status are also often erroneous; Simon Duncan et al. has noted that many young parents are "living apart together": the fathers support the family even though they do not live in the same residence. In summary, there is significant evidence that the actuality of young mothers' lives often stands in contrast to the negative picture drawn by policy and popular opinion.

I had been working as lead nurse in a young people's clinic in Hackney, East London. This service was instrumental in trying to achieve government targets to reduce teenage pregnancy rates locally over the ten-year duration of the Teenage Pregnancy Strategy. As part of the local plan, an assertive outreach pathway to reduce repeat pregnancy among young women who had a pregnancy in their teenage years was piloted by the community teenage health service. An audit of this pathway, while indicating the effectiveness of the pathway overall, also highlighted a small group of young women who became pregnant, had an abortion, then became a parent within two years of the first pregnancy. Commissioners saw these young women as "hard to reach" and a "failure" of our outreach attempts. The phenomenon was also a conundrum for practitioners. I wished to follow this thread, not so much to contribute to a reduction in the teenage pregnancy rates, but to explore what appears to be a mismatch in the young women's decisions—deciding to abort the first pregnancy yet to carry on with a subsequent pregnancy despite still being in their teenage years.

Teenage parenthood in the UK sits within a general trend toward delayed fertility, a consequence of which is that younger pregnancy becomes more noticeable. Also, as mentioned above, teenage mothers are often assumed to be single, yet many are in an ongoing relationship with the baby's father but not necessarily married or cohabiting. In this way, they reflect relationship trends across the age range. According to the latest figures from the UK Office of National Statistics, marriage is becoming less popular in the UK—just over half of parents registering a child's birth are married. Far fewer couples marry in the younger age groups; nearly all twenty-year-old, or younger, respondents registering a birth were unmarried. In contrast to this, however, there have been increasing numbers of joint birth registrations by both mother and father, which suggests a committed parenting relationship but not necessarily marriage. Andrew Cherlin has observed the deinstitutionalization of marriage over recent decades, which has contributed to its declining popularity (849). With women's increasing participation in the workforce, the clear division between breadwinner and homemaker has changed and the practical importance of marriage has declined—the decision to marry becoming more an act of personal choice and self-development. Furthermore, childbearing outside of marriage has become increasingly acceptable.

Contemporary policy constructs teenage mothers within a discourse of social exclusion and marginalization, requiring action and intervention to solve the problem of teenage pregnancy, yet young women's accounts demonstrate a different story. Young women might have a wealth of childcare experience rather than being unprepared for parenthood (Geronimus, "Clashes" 322; Bennett-Murphy 300). Early parenthood does not necessarily lead to disengagement with school, as this lack of engagement often exists before the pregnancy (SmithBattle, "Teenage" 23). In fact, becoming a parent often encourages a reengagement with education to raise the chances of finding a better-paid job (SmithBattle, "Teenage" 30; Tabberer et al. 23), or to be a role model for their children. One of the young mothers in this study wanted to train as a midwife, saying; "I don't want her [daughter] to be like, oh my mum she doesn't do anything with her life." Similarly, young parenthood does not lead to poverty; a life lived in poverty tends to preexist the pregnancy (Geronimus, "Teenage" 466; SmithBattle, "Teenage" 29). Overall, the literature attests to teenage parenthood as a frequently positive and restorative event that represents inclusion rather than exclusion.

My methodological approach to exploring young women's pregnancy decisions was based around exploring the social structures and cultural contexts that shape young people's and young parents' lives and to focus on where resistance may be present in response to these expectations. I took a social constructionist stance to this research: we, and our narratives, are shaped by the social structures and cultural contexts in which we live. I have drawn on Foucauldian thought regarding power in society, personal interaction, and management of self. In *The History of Sexuality*, Foucault observes how sovereign power, that of a monarch for example, has been devolved and is executed and negotiated by agents of the state (136). Expanding on this concept in *Security, Territory, and Population*, he identifies government agents as a devolved form of state power, which he calls "biopower" (108). These could include social care and health practitioners. In *Discipline and Punish*, Foucault draws on Bentham's panopticon prison as an illustration, where inmates self-regulate, since their behaviour is being monitored at all times; in a similar way, he suggests that we modify personal behavior in respect of state norms (202-3). I suggest that this theory has had resonance for this study in how the young women narrated their accounts to me—a nurse researcher and state employee—and in relation to expected norms for the teenage years and from the recent Teenage Pregnancy Strategy. Foucault suggests that people negotiate power at these "capillaries" in a relationship of equality; however, women, mothers and children, despite recent rights movements, are not in a position of equal power in society. Therefore, I have also drawn on the work of feminist thinkers who have critiqued Foucault's assumption of equal power negotiation with regard to women (Hartsock 24; Deveaux 223) and children's disempowerment (Burman 67; Mayall, "Understanding" 313). The young women taking part in this study are women, mothers, and teenagers—a considerable intersection of marginalization.

This social constructionist stance is reflected in a narrative inquiry approach that recognizes that people's narratives are "historically, culturally and linguistically mediated" (Willig 7). I used the listening guide as data analysis method (Gilligan 71; Mauthner and Doucet 419). The listening guide reflects a relational ontology and a feminist reflexive methodology. It sits within a narrative framework and entails layered readings of transcripts focusing on the personal, interpersonal, and social structures and cultural contexts within the young women's stories.

In this dialectic, I first discuss how the young women presented the fathers in a positive light by emphasizing their commitment to the young women and the child. I suggest that offering positive feedback to the young fathers encouraged their continued support in the future. This was a proactive approach to strengthening their family for now and in the future. I then explore the young couples' creative family formation and the strengths and limitations of these ways of operating as a family. I then discuss how, despite successful creative family formation and their exploring of new ways of commitment within a relationship, the young women's narratives attested to a desire for a nuclear family and, ultimately, marriage. I theorize on the motivation for these desires, which I suggest may be a consequence of trying to avoid the current stigma associated with teenage pregnancy.

PRESENTING THE GOOD FATHER

The mothers were keen to present a positive account of the fathers' involvement in the child's life. All stressed the committed nature of the relationship, countering the stereotype of the absent young father. I suggest that this was an astute move by the young women, taking what David Dollahite et al. would call an assets rather than a deficit approach to the young fathers' involvement. By valuing and encouraging what the fathers do provide rather than lamenting what they did not, the young women kept the fathers close and promoted the growth of their new family. For example, Danielle[1] was full of praise for her partner who provided for her material needs while she was pregnant:

> Danielle: Yeah he's a brilliant dad like I must say cause I thought he would be like a typical dad. He's not... He looks after her, provides for her, and provides.... He's a good guy. He's a really good dad ... If I say to him, I haven't got no money, he'll say how much do you need? Or whatever, and he'll give me money or he'll buy me. When I was pregnant, I said I ain't got no clothes cause obviously my belly was big he gave me money for clothes and stuff so he was, at the end of the day, he's been really good.

Susannah stressed how her partner was willing to take full responsibility for childcare while she finished school: "So eventually when we decided on it, we decided that if anything once I've had the baby he'll stay at home with the baby full-time while I'm at school, and then I would have the baby in the evening and he can do what he can do."

Mai's partner also seemed keen to get work and sort out their finances in preparation for their child's arrival: "He's sorted his money out; he wants to pay for my ... he wants to pay for me to get a car, pay for my theory [driving lessons] and that, because he says he doesn't want his child on a bus so he wants to pay for everything."

These women highlighted the various ways that fathers were involved in family life, including financial, emotional, childcare, and other practical support. The ways the young women voiced their satisfaction with their partners' involvement showed how they valued a range of participation beyond the purely financial. The financial provision by fathers for their children has recently been a topic of intense debate in the UK, which has been linked to political concerns over single motherhood and the consequent supposed financial impact on government funds. The Child Support Act and Agency was introduced in 1991 to ensure that absent parents contributed financially to the upbringing of their children. Alldred has discussed how this was a problematic move—for example, it can force contact with violent ex-partners. It also defines fatherhood in biological terms and casts its primary responsibility as financial (Alldred 100). As the dominant discourse for fathers was understood as an economic one, other ways of being in relationship with their children remained unarticulated.

According to the young women's accounts in this study, fatherhood seemed to be a catalyst for change in the young men's lives in the same way as it had been for them. The young men expressed a desire to be a role model for their child, to change negative behaviours, and to reengage with education and work. Three of the young women described how the news that their partners were to become fathers prompted the young men's withdrawal from gang involvement, although, as Sandra's words indicate, this was not without risk: "Before he used to do gang things, but now he's come out of it, but you see when you come out of it, not everybody knows."

Mai described how her partner had left gang life and was now focused on finding work to provide for his new family: "Now he's on a course and apparently not many people got onto the course but he managed to get onto it because he passed the [entrance] test. He got a job interview this morning." Angelique's partner, as another example, was ready to leave his criminal background behind and start afresh: "He's like I'm going to change and he needs someone to support him and stuff."

Dollahite et al. critique the literature on deficit perspectives to fatherhood for overemphasizing fathers' inadequacies and ignoring their strengths. Similar to the findings in this study, other research highlights the positive involvement of young fathers. Linda Davies et al. challenge the stereotype of the absent or irresponsible teenage father; they observe that some contribute money or resources, provide regular or intermittent childcare, and have consistent or periodic contact with their children. The young mothers in a study by LaRon Nelson et al. thought a father's presence is in the best interests of the child, with less emphasis on provision of material resources. Dollahite et al's strengths-based view of fathering counters a deficit approach to fathers' involvement in their children's lives, which they have suggested is too focused on social roles such as provider and breadwinner rather than on facilitating personal transformation into fatherhood. A deficit approach ignores that most fathers have strong desires and motivations to be a good father—illustrated in the examples above—and creates barriers to change by maintaining low expectations for fathers.

An "assets" view of fatherhood, however, does not excuse a father's poor involvement in his child's life. It does, however, facilitate a critical examination of what this involvement should and could be. In previous generations, the fatherhood ideal was to be supportive in family life but not necessarily be directly involved, act as gender role model, and be a distant breadwinner. Currently, there are high expectations of men's involvement in the everyday lives of their children. The constantly evolving approach to parenting and what might be the ideal is a ripe area for discussion;

however, in relation to this study, it is society's focus on fathers' apparent failings rather than their positive contributions to family life that I wish to debate and challenge.

Most of the women in this study presented their child's father in a positive light, considering a range of benefits over and above the breadwinner or co-parent role. Perhaps, by encouraging the father's involvement, the young mother avoids the stigma of being seen as a single teenage mother, consequently increasing her self-esteem. Having an affiliation with a man may also be protective and offer a sense of security, which could relate to the uncertain social contexts in which the young women live—where violence is a real possibility. This is evident in the words of Ally, whose partner often accompanies her to the metro station for work:

> but you don't want to go walking around at 4:30 in the morning and see them [men] there because it is scary. Because sometimes the man won't think "oh she's pregnant" ... being round this area now, cause I'm going to get raped or stabbed or someone taking my phone ... I don't actually walk with my bag sometimes when I'm going work and I know that my boyfriend is not here to walk me down...cause if I'm staying out earlier I always ask him to come and stay over and walk me down the next day.

This sense of security provided by their partner is also illustrated in Angelique's choice of a partner with a violent criminal background. He provided protection from her unpredictable, violent ex-partner and her brother, who was physically threatening to her in the past. Having a strong partner ensures that violence from these perpetrators was kept at bay. When she described her new partner it is more as a foil to stop her violent ex-partner getting to her than his positive attributes:

> But now even though I have love for him [ex-partner] a little bit, I don't love him or feel that thing I had before, because I've got something else to love ... that love has gone to [new partner] and my unborn baby. Yeah like he's

> different; he's so different. So I just want to get away from [ex-partner] really. And like now he can't text me and stuff.

Overall, the young women focused on the father's material, practical, and emotional support, playing down any negative aspects, such as a criminal history. This might be an attempt to normalize their family arrangements by stressing that they are a two-parent family. Here, I foreground how the young women take an assets approach to the fathers' involvement. The young women were accepting of, and even celebrated, the level of provision the young men can offer. As a consequence, the young women facilitated a similar transformation and growth through parenthood for the young fathers that they described having experienced for themselves. This facilitative approach was conducive to the growth of positive family relations and demonstrated new ways of showing commitment and being a family.

CREATIVE FAMILY FORMATION

Several of the young women desired living as a nuclear family unit with their child's father and their child. Sandra was adamant that she would not be able to move her life onto the "next chapter" if she could not secure a council property for her, her partner, and their child to live in:

> Like right now, with me right now, I ain't got a house and it's like this is the biggest thing. I need my house, to give, to have a little time and be sorted out and everything. And then move onto the next chapter. If I don't have my house, I'll feel like I'm still on the same chapter.

Despite being a little nervous about how things might work out, Angelique and her partner had their names jointly on the housing list to move in together:

> Cos I told him that if we live together one of us has to come off the housing list, and we can't ever go separate again. Do you understand what I mean? So we're together now

> as partners in the housing. So we might as well do what we have to do. And if we feel comfortable living together then we'll do it. Cos we're first timers.

In Mai's relationship, it was her partner who is keen for her to apply for housing: "The day of the [pregnancy] scan he come here and was filling out job applications on my laptop and was telling me yeah I need to go get a job ... that he's on to me about getting a job, and going housing [going to the Housing Department of Social Services]."

The young women's narratives reflected desires for nuclear family living, likely perceived as the norm for family living, although many families live in a non-nuclear arrangement. Despite the demise of the nuclear family, politicians have tended to focus on its reestablishment because it is assumed to make no financial demands on the state, as one or both parents usually work (Craig and O'Dell). However, Kelly Musick and Ann Meier argue that a two-parent family is no guarantee of a healthy, financially independent unit. It may also be that these young parents prefer this arrangement, as it marks a final move away from parents and toward independence, autonomy, and perceived maturity.

Although moving toward a nuclear family arrangement is a legitimate desire for the young parents, it does little to acknowledge their successful and creative alternative family arrangements. None of the young women I interviewed were living as a nuclear family. Several were living with their parents. Some were in their own accommodation through being in the Leaving Care System, in which young people who have been in care are entitled to their own accommodation from the age of eighteen. Although the majority of the young fathers were supportive and involved, none were permanently living with their partner.

Interestingly, the three young women who had already had their babies were all either living with family members, or they were very close by. They drew on the support of parents both for advice and practical support. Sandra was acutely aware that she could not live the life she had, where she could meet with friends and have a social life, "without the help of my parents." Danielle also recognized how her mother's support enabled her to have free time in the evening: "she helps out like every time she comes home she takes her [daughter]." Cadeen had her own place and had requested a flat very close to her mother. She was reconciled with her mother since having a child, and they spent a lot of time together: "Yeah, because I've matured and she's like I'm a big girl now and she has to respect that."

This more fluid approach to family formation reflects varied models evident in the literature pertaining to teenage parenting. For example, an apprenticeship approach is when the young woman remains with her family in a safe and nurturing environment and learns the motherhood role with the close support of her family (Furstenberg 78; Burton 124; SmithBattle, "Intergeneration" 60); or the extended family model is when childrearing is shared by family members, usually the maternal grandmother (Furstenberg 78; Geronimus, "What" 337; Owen et al. 302). There is also the visiting relationship in which the children's father does not live with the mother and child but supports the family in terms of childcare and finances, and is in a relationship with the mother (Clarke 61).

The apprenticeship approach can be positive in that it gives protection to the young mother so that she does not face all the realities of adulthood in one sudden transition (Apfel and Seitz 424). However, this approach can exclude the young fathers from the emerging family. In this arrangement, young fathers have to negotiate the approval of the mother's parents and the changing relationship with the mother, as well as their own feelings about fatherhood. This may explain why a couple of the young women's partners were keen to apply for social housing for their new family unit, so they no longer had to negotiate their baby's maternal grandmother on a day to day basis. For some young fathers, the challenge of negotiating access and involvement with his new family may be too difficult and they may withdraw from day-to-day contact.

Another tension exists within the apprenticeship approach. Sharon Tabberer et al. have noted that although grandparent support is welcome, it could also engender continued dependence on the family of origin. Ironically, the help offered may keep young mothers dependent on their families and prevent them making the transition to adulthood in the same way as other teenagers. A lack of social housing stock in recent years, a particular issue in the UK, may perpetuate this problem, as it is difficult for young parents to continue their parenting as a nuclear family unit if that is desired.

The visiting relationship model describes unmarried couples living in separate households (Clarke 61). The rights and responsibilities of these unions are ill-defined but are usually shouldered by the mother. Jean Clarke has also stated that typically in visiting unions, the man is already married. A variation of the visiting relationship can be seen in several of the young women's relationships. None of the partners were married, but several of the young women were accepting of their partners having relationships with other women. In a field note regarding a discussion with one of the young women, when the interview had finished and the recording stopped, Danielle spoke about her partner's probable recent unfaithfulness. She explained how she had been contacted on Facebook by a female friend who said Danielle's partner had slept with someone else. When she confronted him with this, he admitted it, but said that he had been drunk and had not really done anything. Although she was not convinced, she said she was prepared to put this aside considering how long they had been together.

Susannah described how her relationship with her partner cooled after her first miscarriage, although she said their relationship was never officially over. During this time, he had a relationship with another girl and fathered a child with her.

> Interviewer: So how long were you not together?
> Susannah: We weren't together for about six months. Cause after I had the miscarriage things were a bit rocky, and I think that's where it all kicked off from. So we weren't talking as much.
> Interviewer: "So does that mean that you weren't together. Did you actually say "right, we're not together?"
> Susannah: No, we just weren't seeing as much of each other. And then I think I heard that he was going out and being with other girls so I was like fine if you want to do that go ahead but I don't want to be part of it....He's got

> a daughter already from a previous relationship. She's two.
> Interviewer: Okay, so that happened while you were on a break?
> Susannah: Yeah.

Shonda's partner also had a relationship with another girl, which prompted a violent reaction from Shonda. However, despite this, she seemed resigned to being together forever as a couple: "We're on good terms now but because so much has happened in the space of time, so many things. It's like, it's hard to get rid of him."

The young women seemed to value their partner's commitment to them through emotional support, material provision or time, which overrode sexual fidelity or exclusivity as the mother of his child. It may be that the young women ascribed less importance to faithfulness in relationships, and demonstrated a constructive approach to building family. Instead of driving fathers away through accusation and rule setting, and by responding positively to what they did provide, they drew in their support, which was more effective for family building.

This more fluid approach to family formation challenges policymakers and many professionals who favour the nuclear family arrangement. Carol Smart has explored a more fluid approach to emotional commitment beyond the waning institution of marriage. She suggests an understanding of family as a "range of flexible practices" rather than as an institution (Smart 25). She does, however, focus on the concept that within this range of flexible practices, there is a sense in which commitment has to start somewhere, but this is not always with marriage. She reflects that some couples choose a precise moment for a ceremony that could be recognized by the family or community, and this may be marriage; however, there are other moments at which commitment can be said to have started—for example moving in together (Smart 71). Susannah recalled the time her mother talked with both Susannah and her partner about their plans for a family holiday and its significance as a marker for him joining the family:

> Her [mother] main concern was meeting my boyfriend properly because I was always "oh mum this is my friend," sort

> of. So when she met him, they've had their talk. I just made sure I was just like out of the room, and then the same day he met my aunty and my cousin, so when the little ones like someone they like someone. I knew that was a good sign. My mum seems to like him ... so at least she likes him. My aunty likes him. So we were planning a trip to go away for the weekend and they all invited him as well, so....

In relation to these young women's narratives, I suggest that having a child together, or having had a pregnancy together, even when that pregnancy was miscarried or aborted, could mark a commitment between the young women and their partner. This commitment is strengthened with a subsequent pregnancy and by the young women's positive and encouraging approach to the father's involvement to the growing family.

A DESIRE FOR MARRIAGE

Despite a contributing and supportive partner, and effective and creative family formation, some of the young women, notably the ones with children, voiced a desire for marriage. Both Sandra and Danielle—who had children over a year old and were in a long-term supportive relationship—expressed a desire to marry and live with their partner:

> Interviewer: So where do you see your future with [partner], or your future generally?
> Sandra: Where do I see ... hopefully, hopefully right about now our relationship's perfectly fine; we're working on it and everything, no rush, no nothing. Hopefully my future will still be the same ... keep having kids.
> Interviewer: So you'd like more children?
> Sandra: Yeah.
> Interviewer: Okay.
> Sandra: Hopefully he puts the ring on it ... hopefully ... but for now it's great.
> ...
> Interviewer: So do you guys have plans for the future?

> Danielle: We don't know, we've not really thought ahead like that. About anything. I keep on saying I want to get engaged, get a ring. But he keeps on saying yeah, maybe.

Cadeen also discussed marriage with her baby's father despite acknowledging that their relationship seemed to be breaking down: "He's planning to marry me apparently. His mum wasn't supposed to tell me but she told me. He was supposed to engage me before he went to university, but because his mum told me, he wanted it to be a surprise."

Carol Smart observed that some couples in her research were not happy with the idea of allowing commitment to emerge over years as it was seen as risky. They felt that their relationship might not survive long enough without some kind of external support. For them, the ceremony and the vows of the marriage ceremony were like an "external adhesive to help them bond the long-term relationship they wanted" (Smart 74). Perhaps the young women I interviewed, a year or so into motherhood, also felt this uncertainty and desired marriage as a binding contract for their relationships. The public commitment of marriage can bring less fear of abandonment.

I further suggest that by expressing a desire for marriage and consequently adhering to normalized expectations for committed relationships and family living, the young mothers assured wider society of their good citizenship, despite their "transgression" in becoming a teenage parent (Kidger 490). Judi Kidger has explored peer education in which teenage mothers went into classrooms to discuss the realities of being a teenage mother (488). The intention was to speak of both positive and less positive aspects of teenage parenthood. Despite the opportunity to tell of the good parts of being a mother, the young mothers stressed how it would have been better to wait until they were older and established in the workplace before starting a family. As such, they perpetuated social norms for delayed motherhood and ensured their role of good citizen by promoting these norms, despite the opportunity to give a more honest account. Consequently, this hid certain positive truths of their lives.

This situation reflects Deborah Lupton and John Tulloch's exploration of narratives of self-improvement and self-control that are "mediated through discourses, or social and cultural frameworks of understanding" (115). Teenage pregnancy and parenthood are viewed negatively in society, with parallel assumptions of single parenthood and financial dependence on the state. I suggest that the young mothers in my study were keen to offer socially acceptable narratives of marriage and nuclear family living to counter these judgments. These narratives may have been shaped by prevailing societal moral and ethical values and have been offered as a way of reassuring the research audience that they were "good citizens" and not feckless single teenage parents.

CONCLUDING THOUGHTS

In this chapter, I have explored how the young women's narratives demonstrated how parenthood can be a catalyst for positive change in their partner's life, prompting engagement with work and leaving gangs. I have highlighted how the young women presented the "good father," describing his day-to-day involvement in their lives. I have suggested this "assets" (Dollahite et al.) approach was an astute approach by the young mothers that encouraged the continued involvement of their partner in their lives for the future. I have also explored the young women's effective family formations, through apprenticeship, extended family support, and visiting relationship. Despite a creative challenge to the stereotypical nuclear family model, all the young mothers expressed a desire for marriage and living as a nuclear family unit. Practical considerations to ensure their partner's continued support may be a contributing factor to this goal. However, I have also suggested that these narratives appear to be actively mobilized in order to resist the stereotype of the feckless single teenage mother. Unfortunately, as a consequence, celebrating how their lives are demonstrating new ways of showing commitment and being a family is stymied.

ENDNOTE

[1]The young women's names have been changed to protect their confidentiality.

WORKS CITED

Alldred, Pam. *"Fit to Parent": Psychology, Knowledge, and Popular Debate*. University of East London, 1999.

Apfel, Nancy H., and Victoria Seitz. "Four Models of Adolescent Mother-Grandmother Relationships in Black Inner-City Families." *Family Relations* vol. 40, no. 4, 1991, pp. 421-29.

Bassey-Etowa, Josephine. "Becoming a Mother: The Meaning of Childbirth for African-Canadian Women." *Contemporary Nurse* vol. 41, no. 1, 2012, pp. 28-40.

Bennett-Murphy, Laura M., et al. "Unintentional Injury among Very Young Children: Differential Risk for Children of Adolescent Mothers?" *Children's Health Care*, vol. 30, no. 4, 2001, pp. 293-308.

Burman, Erica. *Deconstructing Developmental Psychology*. Routledge, 2007.

Burton, Linda. "Teenage Childbearing as an Alternative Life-Course Strategy in Multigeneration Black Families." *Human Nature*, vol. 1, no. 2, 1990, pp. 123-43.

Cherlin, Andrew J. "The Deinstitutionalization of American Marriage." *Journal of Marriage and Family*, vol. 66, no. 4, 2004, pp. 848-61.

Clarke, Jean. "Repeated Teenage Pregnancies—The Meanings Ascribed by Teenagers—A Comparison between London and Two Caribbean Islands. Brunel University." British Library, ETHoS, 2002.

Craig, Gill, and Lindsay O'Dell. "Mothering on the Margins: Special Issue Editorial." *Radical Psychology*, vol. 9, no. 2, 2011, openaccess.city.ac.uk/1296/. Accessed 20 July 2017.

Davies, Linda, et al. "On My Own: A New Discourse of Dependence and Independence from Teen Mothers." *Teen Pregnancy and Parenting: Social and Ethical Issues*, edited by D, Checkland and J. Wong, University of Toronto Press, 1999, pp. 38-49.

Deveaux, Monique. Feminism and Empowerment: A Critical Reading of Foucault. *Feminist Studies*, vol. 20, no. 2, 1994, pp. 223-47.

Dollahite, David C., et al. "Fatherwork: A Conceptual Ethic of Fathering as Generative Work." *Fatherwork*, 1997, fatherwork.

byu.edu/old/sage.htm. Accessed 20 July 2017.

Elkind, David. "Egocentrism in Adolescence." *Child Development*, vol. 38, no. 4, 1967, pp. 1025-34.

Foucault, Michel. *Discipline and Punish: The Birth of the Prison*. Random House LLC, 1977.

Foucault, Michel. *Security, Territory, Population*. Palgrave, 2007.

Foucault, Michel. *The History of Sexuality*. Volume One. Vintage, 1990.

Furstenberg, Frank. "Burdens and Benefits: The Impact of Early Childbearing on the Family." *Journal of Social Issues,* vol. 36, no. 1, 1980, pp. 64-87.

García Coll, Cynthia, and Heidi Vàzquez García. "Definitions of Competence during Adolescence: Lessons from Puerto Rican Adolescent Mothers." *Rochester Symposium on Developmental Psychopathology: Opportunities and Challenges*, edited by D. Cicchetti and S. Toth, University of Rochester Press, 1996, pp. 283-308.

Duncan, Simon, et al. (2013). "Living Apart Together: Uncoupling Intimacy and Co-residence." *Research Gate*, 2013, www.researchgate.net/publication/294444860_Living_apart_together_uncoupling_intimacy_and_co-residence. 20 July 2017.

Geronimus, Arlene. "What Teen Mothers Know." *Human Nature*, vol. 7, no. 4, 1996, pp. 323-52.

Geronimus, Arlene. "Clashes of Common Sense: On the Previous Child Care Experience of Teenage Mothers-to-Be." *Human Organization*, vol. 51, no. 4, 1992, pp. 318-29.

Geronimus, Arlene. "Teenage Childbearing and Social and Reproductive Disadvantage: The Evolution of Complex Questions and the Demise of Simple Answers." *Family Relations*, vol. 40, no. 4, 1991, pp. 463-71.

Gilligan, Carol. "The Listening Guide Method of Psychological Inquiry." *Qualitative Psychology*, vol. 2, no. 2, 2015, pp. 69-77.

Hartsock, Nancy. "Postmodernism and Political Change: Issues for Feminist Theory." *Cultural Critique*, no. 14, 1990, pp. 15-33.

Kaye, Dan K., et al. "Escaping the Triple Trap: Coping Strategies of Pregnant Adolescent Survivors of Domestic Violence in Mulago Hospital, Uganda." *Scandinavian Journal of Public Health*, vol.35, no. 2, 2007, pp. 180-86.

Kidger, Judi. "Stories of Redemption? Teenage Mothers as the New Sex Educators." *Sexualities*, vol. 8, no. 4, 2005, pp. 481-96.

Lansdown, Gerison. *The Evolving Capacities of the Child. UNICEF*, 2005, www.unicef-irc.org/publications/pdf/evolving-eng.pdf. 20 July 2017.

Lupton, Deborah, and John Tulloch. "Life Would Be Pretty Dull without Risk: Voluntary Risk-Taking and Its Pleasures." *Health, Risk and Society*, vol. 4, no. 2, 2002, pp. 113-24.

Mauthner, Natasha, and Andrea Doucet. "Reflexive Accounts and Accounts of Reflexivity in Qualitative Data Analysis. *Sociology*, vol. 37, no. 3, 2003, pp. 413-31.

Mayall, Berry. Understanding Inter-generational Relations: The Case of Health Maintenance by Children." *Sociology of Health & Illness*, vol. 37, no. 2, 2015, pp. 312-24.

Mayall, Berry. "The Sociology of Childhood in Relation to Children's Rights. *The International Journal of Children's Rights*, vol. 8, no. 3, 2000, pp. 243-59.

Musick, Kelly, and Ann Meier. "Are Both Parents Always Better Than One? Parental Conflict and Young Adult Well-Being." *Social Science Research*, vol. 39, no. 5, 2010, pp. 814-30.

Nelson, LaRon E., et al. "Black Adolescent Mothers' Perspectives on Sex and Parenting in Nonmarital Relationships with the Biological Fathers of Their Children." *Journal of Obstetric, Gynecologic, and Neonatal Nursing*, vol. 41, no. 1, 2012, pp. 82-91.

Office National Statistics. "Marriage, Cohabitation, and Civil Partnerships." *Office for National Statistics*, 2015, www.ons.gov.uk/peoplepopulationandcommunity/birthsdeathsandmarriages/marriagecohabitationandcivilpartnerships. 20 July 2017.

Owen, Jenny, et al. "Ethnicity, Policy and Teenage Parenthood in England: Findings from a Qualitative Study." *Social Policy and Society*, vol. 7, no. 3, 2008, pp. 293-305.

Phoenix, Ann. *Young Mothers?* Polity Press, 1991.

Social Exclusion Unit. *Teenage Pregnancy Strategy*. Stationery Office, 1999.

Smart, Carol. *Personal Life*. Polity Press, 2007.

SmithBattle, Lee. "Intergenerational Ethics of Caring for Adolescent Mothers and Their Children." *Family Relations*, vol. 45, no, 1, 1996, pp. 56-64.

SmithBattle, Lee. "Teenage Mother's Narratives of Self: An Examination of Risking the Future." *Advances in Nursing Science*, vol. 17, no. 4, 1995, pp. 22-36.

SmithBattle, Lee. "The Vulnerabilities of Teenage Mothers: Challenging Prevailing Assumptions." *Advances in Nursing Science*, vol. 23, no. 1, 2000, pp. 29-40.

Tabberer, Sharon, et al. *Teenage Pregnancy and Choice*. Joseph Rowntree Foundation, 2000.

Theriot, Judy G., et al. "Revelations of Adolescent Mothers: An Intensive Case-Study Approach. *Adolescence*, vol. 26, no. 102, 1991, pp. 349-60.

Willig, Carla. *Introducing Qualitative Research in Psychology.* McGraw-Hill International, 2013.

Young Women's Trust. *What Matters to Young Mums?* Young Women's Trust, 2017.

8.
Making Marital Face(book)

Husband Posts and Face Management on Facebook

LORIN BASDEN ARNOLD

ANYONE WHO REGULARLY spends time on Facebook has surely seen the number of posts that occur each day praising spouses, particularly husbands. Searches of posts in September 2016 showed 86,544 people talking about "best husband ever"; 100,000 talking about #besthusbandever; 96,028 talking about #besthubbyever; and 93,648 talking about #besthusbandaward. The posts range from individualized, seemingly heartfelt, tributes to a spouse to chain posts shared repeatedly across users with an exhortation to others to "share if your husband is wonderful."

Given the social expectation that women should operate as the primary caretakers of relationships, it is not surprising to note that the rate of relationship-focused posts seems to be higher among female Facebook users than male ones (Park et al.). Most of us, however, do not frequently enumerate the wonderful qualities of our spouse in casual face-to-face conversation with large groups of friends. As a Facebook user, spouse, and family communication scholar, I began to question what the purpose or function is of such posts and what the effects of these messages may be for others who post and read on Facebook.

Consideration of how adult partner relationships are portrayed in mediated communication, including social media settings, is important to our understanding of the social construction of relational beliefs and expectations (Holmes). Such beliefs about relationships significantly affect our evaluations of self and other, and can have long-term impacts on relational partners and our larger social structures (Casad et al.; Kelly and Burgoon).

In this chapter, I consider some of the research regarding presentation of self on Facebook, examine a sampling of these posts, use face management theory in an attempt to address how the posts may function for the user, and address the potential effects of such posts for both the spousal pair and those who read the posts.

PRESENTING THE SELF ON FACEBOOK

One of the often made claims regarding online communication is that people use and enjoy it because of the anonymity it offers. However, with some social media platforms, including Facebook, the primary function is not to connect with strangers but to connect with individuals who are already friends, family, acquaintances, or work associates. Although one may make new friends on Facebook, this is not generally the goal. Even new friends tend to be known by name, often with pictures associated, and are typically only limited degrees of separation away by virtue of connection through other known individuals.

Although Facebook does not offer anonymity, it does give an opportunity to show elements of your day-to-day life to friends, who may not otherwise be privy to those parts of life. As such, Soraya Mehdizadeh argues that friend-networking sites, such as Facebook, are prime settings for engaging in impression management efforts because they are not anonymous; however, they remove the "now self" and place focus on the "hoped-for possible self" (358). Other scholars have conducted research that supports this argument (Park and Lee; Steers et al.). The selves constructed in Facebook posts can be the selves that we wish to be, not the selves we are in any moment. In the process of creating this "hoped-for" self on Facebook, participants are likely to write more posts reflecting positive emotional states than negative (Bazarova et al. 13; Qiu et al. 571). We can remove the fit of temper we had when a loved one was being obstinate. We can erase the troubled relationships with family or friends by blocking those we do not wish to interact with and simply not discussing them. We can have pets that are not uncontrollable beasts but adorable rascals (and children that are the same).

Based on this research regarding self-presentation on online friend network sites, we would expect that for people who discuss current spousal or romantic relationships on Facebook, the posts are likely to strongly emphasize the positive, showing the best possible side of the partner. This is seen in many of the posts regarding husbands that show up regularly on Facebook feeds. In looking at such posts occurring on my personal Facebook page over a period of several months, and conducting searches for publicly available posts on Facebook,[1] I noted that husband posts are fairly equally divided between "spousal chain posts" and "best husband posts."

SPOUSAL CHAIN POSTS

Recently, a common Facebook spousal chain post has been the "love your spouse challenge." For the purpose of this examination of posts, I defined spousal chain posts as posts that appear on the pages of many authors; are nearly identical in nature; and either involve tagging—or selecting for continuation—specific others to participate in the chain or exhorting the reader to continue the chain by reposting the message. Two examples of the "love your spouse challenge" post can be seen below. With only small stylistic differences and the addition of details regarding the spouse, the messages are very similar:

> Day# three of Love your spouse challenge. I was challenged by XX to post photos of my amazing spouse, XX for seven days and tag two people each day to keep the celebration of love and the positive aspects of marriage going.

> Day six—Love your spouse challenge! I was challenged by my friend to post pictures of my handsome husband XX for seven days and challenge two people each day to keep the Celebration of Love and promotion of marriage going. I challenge XX and XX to do the same. My husband is a disabled army vet and I am so proud of my soldier!

The "love your spouse challenge" contains the elements of a spousal chain post. The post has appeared on many user's streams.

In early October 2016, a search for the challenge showed almost 100,000 recent posts on Facebook, including dozens of posts that appeared on pages of my individual Facebook connections during the summer and early fall. Each iteration is very similar, often varying by little more than names and sometimes the addition of a sentence or two. The challenge specifically charges others (typically two per day) to continue the process. If followed to its full extent, each participant would repost the challenge seven times, tagging fourteen friends to continue. Although the challenge is not specifically limited to wives posting about husbands, I encountered few examples of men being tagged or posting the challenge.

The "love your spouse challenge" is a named chain post. However, there are many others that circulate with regularity on Facebook without an official name being designated. A post of this type that circulated in February 2016 was shared over 15,000 times. The post read "Share this if you have an awesome husband. It just might brighten his day." This directive was followed with the image of the lower torso of a man holding a construction hat and wearing a reflective vest. Text on the image states "I'm blessed with a husband that works hard for his family. Thank you, for all that you do!"

In the summer of 2016, posts of this type appeared on Facebook with frequency. Although details of the chain messages varied and some posters individualized the text to some degree, consistent features were present. The messages are reproduced from account to account with a high degree of redundancy; they state the exemplary characteristics of the husband; and they encourage other wives to repost the status (copy the message and reproduce it as their own statement on their Facebook timeline) in recognition of their own spouses:

> My husband has made me laugh. Wiped my tears. Hugged me tight. Watched me succeed. Seen me fail. Kept me strong. My husband is a promise from God that I will have a friend forever. Put this as your status if you love your husband.

> If you have an Awesome husband who works hard to take care of you and would do anything for you, then re-post

> this as your status to give the honest good men out there the recognition that they deserve. Cause great men are very few; I'm proud to say my husband is one among them.

Although chain posts like this are reproduced across many women's Facebook accounts and represent a shared story of good husbands, wives also post individual tributes to their spouses. While the posts are individual, it is possible to see recurrent patterns within them. By far, the most common of these is a type that I have termed the "best husband post."

BEST HUSBAND POSTS

> Who has the best husband? I do!!!

> I just wanted to thank you @XXX for being the best husband in the world, being with me through the good times and the bad times...even when times have been really bad and may have tested your patience to the limit, you've always stayed strong and put up with me through thick and thin!..you're the best thing that has ever happened in my life and I'll love you always.

Best husband posts typically invoke the specific language of "best husband." Whereas some are simply a statement of having the best husband, many include a discussion of the reasons why the husband is being characterized as best.

The most common type of best husband post indicates that the husband is the "best husband" and then reveals the action that earned him that title:

> Best husband in the world! He planted my favorite flower!

> Best husband in the world Award!! He got up and cooked for us all.

Reasons for the designation of "best husband" vary, yet many are related to a purchase or the completion of some household task. Some wives provide text to describe the particular behaviour that has earned the title, as with the two posts above. Others post an image to show the item purchased or the work completed. In the examples collected for this analysis, wives state that they have the "best husband ever" for reasons including purchases—such as a new ring, a new dress, candy, food, a gun safe, flowers, a puppy—and tasks completed—such as changing a tire, installing an air conditioner, organizing a surprise party, cleaning the house, and ironing. As can be seen in these examples, wives call husbands "the best" for significant purchases or work done, as well as more day-to-day examples.

In addition to best husband posts related to specific purchases or tasks completed, many examples relate to special occasions, such as birthdays and anniversaries:

> Happy birthday to the best husband in the world. I feel so blessed to have found true love in your arms. I feel so proud to call you my husband!!!

> Happy Birthday to the Best Husband, Best father. If my life was a ship, you would be the anchor that holds me in place and the sails which take me on a beautiful journey.... You are a loving husband, wonderful father or a great husband. But you are much more than that—an example of a perfect man.... Every single day that I spend being your wife, I realize how lucky I am to live such an amazing life, Thank u for everything....I love you so much Hon

> Happy Birthday to the best husband in the whole world!! Eric isn't on FB, but I had to post anyway! #lovemyhusbandwithallmyheart

"Happy birthday" or "happy anniversary" best husband posts are often not posted on the page of the husband. In fact, as the last example indicates, it is not particularly unusual for the husband to not be tagged in the post or to not see the post at all. Instead, the writers tend to post the message on their own pages, suggesting that the intended audience is less the spouse than others. This calls into question the intent and outcomes of these messages. Considering the posts within the frame of face management theory can provide some useful understandings regarding how such messages function.

FACE MANAGEMENT AND FACEBOOK HUSBAND POSTS

Erving Goffman has defined "face" as "the positive social value a person effectively claims for himself by the line others assume he has taken during a particular contact" (*Interaction Ritual* 5). We may understand this as a positive image that an individual desires to represent in his or her interactions with others. Goffman has further defined facework as "the actions taken by a person to make whatever he is doing consistent with face" (12). Face-saving actions, or those behaviours we engage as we attempt to present the face we wish to have seen, are present as we reinforce face and also as we attempt to counter potential threats to face (13). We can also act to preserve and support the face of others on an ongoing basis or in response to threats. Face can be threatened when something occurs that disrupts the self being presented. Face threats may be the result of the actions of the threatened individual (i.e., social gaffes or behaviour inconsistent with face). Face threats may also occur because of the actions of another, who challenges the face presented in some way. Goffman notes that face threats can happen as a result of purposeful action but can also result through unintended or incidental offense to face (14).

Face Saving and Facebook Husband Posts—Facebook spousal posts can be seen as facework in support of both the face of the poster and the face of the spouse. The potential value of such posts to spouse's face is perhaps the most obvious. In presenting the husband as the "best husband" in the world and as a "good man," these posts validate the man's performance of the social role of good husband, much valued in cultures where Facebook is used. Because men are frequently presented in mass mediated messages as poor husbands—who are inept, insensitive, and philandering—to reaffirm a man's status as a "good" man and husband is a positive act to protect and enhance his face. Given the shared social networks often experienced by spouses on Facebook, these positive facework messages enhance and support the husband's performance of face for his social network as well as the network of the wife. Because men are less likely to post messages related to their relationships (Park et al.; Wang et al.), it may seem even more important for wives to validate and support the husband's face in terms of this particular role.

Although spousal chain posts and best husband posts may be most easily seen as a face-saving act for the face of the husband, such messages also act to support the face of the poster. To choose a "good man" and have a "good relationship" reflect positively on the face of the woman in the same way that staying in a relationship with a "bad man" can create a courtesy stigma that devalues a woman in social settings (Goffman, *Stigma* 30-31). Additionally, as the societally defined relationship experts (Cancian 699-702), women may feel a particularly strong need to show that they are part of a good and healthy relationship, and these posts may operate in just that way. In their study of relationship visibility and disclosure on Facebook, Linda Emery and colleagues have found that more relational visibility and high levels of relational disclosure are predictive of others having stronger beliefs that the relationship is high in quality (5-6). As such, when a woman posts her positive feelings about her husband, it not only suggests that he is good but also supports her image as a wife and as a woman.

Face Threats and Facebook Husband Posts—It is perhaps most obvious that Facebook posts praising a husband act as positive facework for the spousal pair, but these posts can also act as incidental threats to the faces of the spousal pair and to the faces of others. Goffman notes that incidental offenses to face "arise as an unplanned but sometimes anticipated by-product of action—action the offender performs in spite of its offensive consequences, although not out of spite" (*Interaction Ritual* 14).

Spousal chain posts and best husband posts may threaten the face of the husband if the face presented is not the image he is attempting to project within his social sphere, regardless of the laudatory nature of the posts. In my own Facebook network, I have seen not a small number of posts that acknowledge a spouse's dislike of relational information, even positive in nature, being shared on social media. Some spouses may feel that the marital relationship is private and should not be part of the public face presented. Others husbands may believe that posts acknowledging them for doing particular kinds of work or engaging in certain behaviors, more associated with the female role, represent a threat to the presentation of face as strong males.

Even though these Facebook messages may generally function to support the face of the poster as a loving wife and a good person, they may incidentally act to threaten the face that the poster is attempting to present. A recent study suggests that individuals who disclose more about their relationships on Facebook are perceived as less likeable (Emery et al. 6). Although the study does not indicate the reasons for this response, it is possible that frequent disclosure is perceived as inappropriate attention seeking or bragging. Thus, while a woman supports the view of her husband as extremely wonderful, she may be inadvertently rendering herself less likeable to her Facebook connections.

Perhaps most significantly, when a woman presents a spousal chain post of positive affirmation for her husband, it creates an incidental threat to friends who have unhappy (or less overwhelmingly happy) marriages or to those who are not married. Women who are not married can experience a threat to face via an implication that a single, unmarried life cannot be as wonderful as this happy marriage. Other women not posting such glowing messages about their spouses may appear to be less loving or grateful by comparison. In fact, the failure to repost such messages has the potential to threaten the face of both partners in a couple if it is seen as indicating a bad marriage, whether that is actually the case or not. As such, when messages are passed within a friend group and reposted by members, it can begin to appear as if everyone's marriage is very strong, except for the relationships of wives who are not participating in the posts.

These incidental face threats are probably, in most cases, unintended. However, the medium of these messages may increase the likelihood of them occurring. A recent study of social networking site behaviour has found that participation in such sites as Facebook may promote an egocentric focus that reduces concern about others and associated prosocial behaviour (Chiou et al. 71-72). In face-to-face interaction with friends, the physical presence of the other may encourage a speaker to take into account the relational status and recent life experiences of the listener, and to adapt the message within that framing. Most of us would be hesitant to rave about an amazing spouse or romantic partner to a friend who had recently been through a nasty divorce or who we knew was in an unhappy marriage. However, in removing the friend from the room, Facebook has the potential to remove some of that attention to the face—and the feelings—of others.

This may seem to be of little consequence; however, studies have suggested that such messages can have a strong impact on readers. In a survey of 425 undergraduate Facebook users, Hui-Tzu Chou and Nicholas Edge find that the longer and more frequently individuals spend time on Facebook, the more they believe that their friends are happier and have better lives than they do. Similarly, another group of scholars has found that spending significant time on Facebook is "positively related to comparing one's self to others, which in turn is associated with increased depressive symptoms" (Steers et al. 723). Thus, the common appearance of these posts on social networking sites may contribute to reduced satisfaction in life for all participants.

Facebook and the Marital Stage—In his seminal work of sociology, *The Presentation of Self in Everyday Life,* Goffman argues that individuals enact identities for others on an everyday basis, as if social interactions were a stage upon which we perform the roles expected of us. Goffman states that for each role, there is a frontstage and a backstage. The frontstage consists of social interactions in which our audience expects that role performance of us (107). Thus, these are the times where we attempt to present a particular face for others. For example, at work, I must be the teacher, scholar, and administrator. The backstage consists of periods in which the importance of that role has retreated (112). In those times, we may present an alternative face (based on a different social expectation). For example, at home, the importance of my teacher/scholar role is diminished, but I am expected to enact the role of spouse and the role of mother. When one is completely alone, this may be thought of as the ultimate backstage, where the roles we are called upon to enact for others fade in importance.

However, the internet has to a significant degree changed our understandings of where and when we are being called upon to play our roles, which has created a much larger frontstage for many of the roles we enact, as well as new roles that require attention. With social media, we perform for a larger number of people; we have the opportunity do so for more hours a day, and we perform for a more diverse audience, thus having to enact a variety of roles simultaneously. My Facebook connections include people who know me primarily through my spousal relationship (making wife the most heightened role in that relationship); nonspousal familial relationships (making daughter, sister, mother the most salient roles); work relationships (making scholar/teacher the most crucial role); yoga practitioner/teacher (making yogi the most important role); and so on. Thus, we find ourselves attempting to perform a multitude of roles simultaneously in one social space. Because Facebook allows us to enact more roles with greater frequency and for more people, it creates more frontstage for each individual role, and it exacerbates the potential conflict in performing multiple roles. Wives on Facebook find themselves performing the spousal role for audiences that they would not have been expected to "be a wife" in the presence of before social media. Since the Internet is never closed, the performance is also all day, every day. As the frontstage grows, the backstage shrinks, reducing the time in which we are not attending to social expectations. With near constant connection to social media, the pressure of performance is increased, and even time spent physically alone can become a frontstage experience.

The change in stage presented by Facebook creates a relational complexity for wives that cannot be overlooked. Because our roles and the concomitant frontstages are not based only upon our desires but also upon the expectations of the audience, a married woman will be, by default, performing the role of wife on Facebook if her connections are people who know her in that role and expect that performance of her. Thus, electing not to post about a spouse, not to repost chain spousal posts, or not to make claims about the happiness of the relationship is a performance that becomes laden with meaning about the spousal relationship for the viewer.

That this pressure is felt by participants can be seen in the number of posts and articles—on and off of Facebook—that explicitly discuss a refusal to participate in the Love Your Spouse Challenge and the reasons for that refusal. Writers describe not wishing to participate because of a spouse who does not wish to have pictures posted online, a desire not to hurt others who are not in good relationships, or a worry that participating in such chain posts creates unrealistic expectations about marriage. As stated by Sarah Williams, "My marriage actually is fine. But I know many (most?) marriages aren't. I want to be a person who knows people, who sees people. And if someone's marriage isn't fine, I want to be a safe place for that to be said."

A Google search shows that Sarah's perspective on this is not unique, as a variety of bloggers discuss the reasons they chose not to participate, or the fact that they did participate and had friends or family question that participation. That women feel such a strong pressure for participation in such posts on Facebook that it requires a discussion of reasons not to is an indicator of how strong the expectations are of spousal role performance in that venue.

In the end, spousal Facebook posts appear to be part of the process of creation of an ideal self in this social media form. As couples, particularly women, achieve social value for the quality of their romantic relationships, as well as reflected approval from the close association with an admirable person, it is reasonable that these posts appear as a common method of securing and maintaining face on Facebook. However, these messages may have both positive and negative effects on the lives of the poster, the spouse, and others. The posts can promote the idea of happiness that can be found in a committed romantic relationship, and this may be a positive outcome. Alternatively, they may simultaneously cause feelings of shame or dissatisfaction because of an overidealized presentation of marital bliss. As we communicate about the "happily ever after" of marriage in public forums such as Facebook, we create myths of relationships and spousal partners that are difficult or impossible to realize. These mythic representations can have strong effects on how we evaluate our own relationships, the relationships of others, our relational partners, and ourselves. Additionally, in their celebration of monogamous heterosexual marital relationships, the heteronormative character of most husband posts may act to contribute to the cultural disenfranchisement of same-sex partners by appearing to diminish the value of their relationships.

Finally, it is important that we understand that the motivations for spousal chain posts and husband posts are complex and variant. Although these posts appear to be a voluntary act of disclosure, the social milieu of Facebook, with the role of spouse in the frontstage for many participants, exerts a pressure to produce such messages. This, in turn, becomes a self-replicating process that reproduces artificial understandings of the true complexity of marital relationships.

ENDNOTE

[1]All discourse reprinted here is from publically available pages or posts. However, author names, spousal names, and other identifying information have been removed to maintain confidentiality of the writer and spouse.

WORKS CITED

Bazarova, Natalya N., et al. "Managing Impressions and Relationships on Facebook: Self-Presentational and Relational Concerns Revealed Through the Analysis of Language Style." *Journal of Language and Social Psychology*, vol. 20, no. 10, 2012, pp. 1-21.

Cancian, Francesca M. "The Feminization of Love." *Signs*, vol. 11, no. 4, 1986, pp. 692-709.

Casad, Bettina J., et al. "The Real Versus the Ideal: Predicting Relationship Satisfaction and Well-Being from Endorsement of Marriage Myths and Benevolent Sexism." *Psychology of Women Quarterly*, vol. 39, no. 1, 2015, pp. 119-29.

Chiou, Wen-Ben, et al. "Does Facebook Promote Self-Interest? Enactment of Indiscriminate One-to-Many Communication on Online Social Networking Sites Decreases Prosocial Behavior." *Cyberpsychology, Behavior, and Social Networking*, vol. 17, no. 2, 2014, pp. 68-73.

Chou, Hui-Tzu, and Nicholas Edge. "'They are Happier and Having Better Lives than I am:' The Impact of Using Facebook on Perceptions of Others' Lives." *Cyberpsychology, Behavior, and Social Networking*, vol. 15, no. 2, 2014, pp. 117-21.

Emery, Lydia F., et al. "Do We Look Happy? Perceptions of Romantic Relationship Quality on Facebook." *Personal Relationships*, vol. 22, no. 1, 2015, pp. 1-7.

Goffman, Erving. *Interaction Ritual: Essays in Face to Face Behavior.* Aldine Publishing, 1967.

Goffman, Erving. *Stigma: Notes on the Management of Spoiled Identity.* Simon & Schuster, Inc., 1963.

Goffman, Erving. *The Presentation of Self in Everyday Life*. Doubleday Anchor, 1969.

Holmes, Bjarne M. "In Search of My 'One-And-Only': Romance-Related Media and Beliefs in Romantic Relationship Destiny." *The Electronic Journal of Communication*, vol. 17, no. 3-4, 2007, pp. 1-29.

Kelly, D. L., and Judee K. Burgoon. "Understanding Marital Satisfaction and Couple Type as Functions of Relational Expectations." *Human Communication Research*, vol. 18, no. 1, 1991, pp. 40-70.

Mehdizadeh, Soraya. "Self-Presentation 2.0: Narcissim and Self-Esteem on Facebook." *Cyberpsychology, Behavior, and Social Networking,* vol. 12, no. 4, 2010, pp. 357-64.

Park, Namkee, and Seungyoon Lee. "College Students' Motivations for Facebook Use and Psychological Outcomes." *Journal of Broadcasting and Electronic Media*, vol. 66, no. 4, 2014, pp. 601-20.

Park, Gregory, et al. "Women are Warmer but No Less Assertive than Men: Gender and Language on Facebook." *PLoS One*, vol. 11, no. 5, 2016, /journals.plos.org/plosone/article?id=10.1371/journal.pone.0155885. 20 July 2017.

Qiu, Lin, et al. "Putting Their Best Foot Forward: Emotional Disclosure on Facebook." *Cyberpsychology, Behavior, and Social Networking,* vol. 15, no. 10, 2012, pp. 569-72.

Steers, Mai-Ly, et al. "Seeing Everyone Else's Highlight Reels: How Facebook Usage is Linked to Depressive Symptoms." *Journal of Social and Clinical Psychology*, vol. 33, no. 8, 2014, 701-31.

Wang, Yi-Chia, et al. "Gender, Topic, and Audience Response: An Analysis of User-Generated Content on Facebook." *CHI '13 Proceedings of the SIGCHI Conference on Human Factors in Computing Systems, Paris, 2013.* Edited by Susanne Bødker, et al., ACM, 2013, pp. 31-34.

Williams, Sarah. "You Are Fine. I am Fine. We Are All Fine. Except We Aren't Fine." *The Huffington Post*, 22 Aug. 2016, www.huffingtonpost.com/entry/you-are-fine-i-am-fine-we-all-fine-except-we-arent_us_57bb61bce4b029a9a4671261. Accessed 1 Oct. 2016.

9.
Tending the Privacy Boundary between the Married Couple and the Husband's Mother

Its Impact on Marital Satisfaction and Relationship Solidarity

KRISTEN M. NORWOOD AND LYNNE M. WEBB

MARRIAGES CAN EXPERIENCE a variety of problems. One of the most widely acknowledged problems is troubled relationships with in-laws. Mothers-in-law, specifically, are often ignored, disliked, joked about, and frequently perceived as problematic members of the family (Fischer). Social scientists noted the concern as early as 1954 (Duvall); in the interim, researchers have documented and investigated the phenomenon (Fischer; Serewicz, "Getting"; Silverstein). Mother-in-law issues extend to multiple countries—including Belgium (Datta et al.), China (An), India (Gangoli and Rew), Japan (Harris and Long), and Taiwan (Sandel, "Narrated," "Enacted")—into cyberspace (An and Chou; Ford), and beyond the marriage into postdivorce relationships (Frisby and Sidelinger). The privacy issues that surround mother-in-law disclosure (Rittenour; Serewicz et al.) and intrusiveness are common mother-in-law concerns (Lopata; Nastasee-Carder; Rittenour and Kellas). Can a husband and wife find their "happily ever after" in the face of mother-in-law problems? Can these issues be resolved in ways that support the marriage?

The purpose of this study was to examine communication phenomena surrounding the potentially intrusive and problematic relationships among sets of mothers-in-law, daughters-in-law, and the husbands in heterosexual marriages in the United States. Specifically, we empirically assessed potential relationships among a set of key variables: the permeability of the communication boundary between married sons and their mothers, the interpersonal solidarity between mothers-in-law and their daughters-in-law, and the marital satisfaction of the married son and his wife.

REVIEW OF LITERATURE

For purposes of this study, we adopted Sandra Petronio's definition of privacy: perceiving ownership rights over private self-information (*Boundaries*). Recently, one theory has emerged as the most widely accepted explanation for maintaining privacy within families (e.g., Mikucki-Enyart; Young et al.): Petronio's privacy management theory. The theory provides a description of and potential solution to the problem of in-law intrusiveness.

Privacy and Boundary Management

Petronio posited a theory initially called "communication boundary management theory," now "communication privacy management" or CPM ("Communication"). It focuses on privacy rules within relationships. Petronio originally employed the theory to explain how marital couples transform personal information into dyadic information based on their expectations surrounding disclosure and privacy rule coordination. CPM theory focuses primarily on how individuals use communication to regulate and maintain private information—how they create and regulate information boundaries via communication. There may be risks associated with revealing information of a private nature to others. These risks motivate individuals to be aware of and manage what information others know about them. Thus, spouses, for example, may work to keep some information private and within the privacy boundaries of the dyad (Petronio, *Boundaries*).

CPM theory uses a boundary metaphor to describe the regulation of private information. The theory assumes that communication boundaries are established, made more rigid, or permeated by the exchange and flow of personal information. The flow of information, in turn, is regulated by rule management systems. CPM proposes that there are three management processes within the rule-based management system. The first management process, privacy rule foundation, focuses on the development process for rules governing boundaries and the attributes of those rules. The second, boundary coordination, refers to the way individuals regulate privacy boundaries by sharing ownership in collectively owned boundaries. The third process, boundary turbulence, occurs when individuals do not effectively coordinate boundaries; they may experience asynchronized understandings or executions of privacy rules (Petronio, *Boundaries*). Mother-in-law intrusiveness likely involves the second and third processes in that mothers and sons may disagree on which information is mutually owned (e.g., Does the mother have the right to know her son's household finances?). And they may have oral arguments concerning those contested privacy boundaries (e.g., The son may tell his mother to stop asking him, his spouse, and his children about their household finances; the mother may reply that as a loving and concerned mother, she has a right to know).

According to CPM theory, boundary ownership refers to the rights and privileges a person has over what he or she considers private information. Personal or collective boundaries may be relatively permeable (easy to breach) or they may be relatively rigid (stringent). Lines of ownership may be unclear for two reasons: because permeability of boundaries exists and because linkages exist among multiple boundaries. Thus, when multiple individuals co-own information, such as the marital dyad's financial information, both co-owners must coordinate terms of the boundary to achieve clarity and make decisions as co-owners (Petronio, *Boundaries*). For example, during a joint discussion of finances, a spouse may explicitly state that the information should not be disclosed to other family members, such as a mother-in-law. The ability to coordinate a collective boundary depends on the ability to reach a level of synchronicity in the degree of permeability (Petronio, *Boundaries*). However, when two or more individuals (such as spouses) co-own boundaries, privacy rules must be unambiguous to avoid abuse or misuse of boundary ownership. Furthermore, co-ownership of private information "is accompanied by an obligation ... to contribute to boundary maintenance by adherence to privacy rules" (Petronio et al, "Family Privacy" 28). Thus, we can imagine a wife saying to her husband, "I'll tell my parents to stop asking personal questions of you, if you tell your parents to do the same."

Boundary turbulence may occur if the coordination process does not progress smoothly, prompting interpersonal conflict (Petronio, *Boundaries*). When individuals experience such turbulence, they may attempt to reduce conflict through increased boundary coordination (Afifi). "Some [family] members may expect to be recipients of private information from other members, whereas others do not" (Petronio et al., "Family Privacy" 29). For example, a mother-in-law may expect to be included in intimate knowledge of any illness her son, daughter-in-law, or grandchildren experience. In contrast, her daughter-in-law may desire to not be included in the intimate details of her mother-in-law's medical situations. Furthermore, "managing [privacy] dilemmas may become complicated because there are times when ownership markers are unclear and family members do not endorse collectively held rules, are uncertain about the rules, or make mistakes and do not follow the rules" (Petronio, et al., "Family Privacy" 29). Thus, a mother-in-law who is diagnosed with breast cancer may consider the diagnosis "family business" rather than "personal business," especially if her son is her only child or if she has granddaughters who may share her genetic makeup. In the face of established and articulated family rules to keep health information private, cancer patients may question whether the regular rules apply to potentially lethal diagnoses or they may simply elect to violate the rules because they desire social support or need financial assistance.

Many scholars have studied the negotiation and communication surrounding boundary issues among family members (Afifi; Caughlin and Afifi; Caughlin, et al.; Golish and Caughlin; Madden-Derdich et al.; Mazur and Hubbard; Petronio, "Privacy Binds"; Petronio et al., "Family Privacy"; Petronio et al. "Family and Friends"), including in-law relationships (Mikucki-Enyart; Young et al.) and marital dyads (Chan; Craddock; Petronio, "Communication"; Serewicz and Canary; Silverstein). However, only two previously published studies examined disclosure among the triangulated relationship between the two spouses and an in-law (Serewicz, "Toward"; Serewicz et al.). Thus, the present study has followed in the tradition of previous communication researchers to advance the line of research examining boundary issues among marital dyads and in-laws. Our study adds to the research by focusing on the question of what the mother-in-law could do communicatively to enhance and support the marriage of her son and his spouse. We examined this question from the perspectives of the potentially most immediately affected parties—the son and his spouse. Rather than assume that a bride will "live happily ever after" with her husband and his family, and rather than assume that the mother-in-law relationship will always be problematic, we endeavoured to discover how communication with the mother-in-law could enhance the marital experience.

Interpersonal Solidarity

We hypothesized that a close and positive relationship between a mother-in-law and her daughter-in-law may mitigate mother-in-law intrusiveness. We assessed this possibility using Lawrence Wheeless's measure of interpersonal solidarity. Wheeless has defined solidarity as a

> generally symmetrical relationship derived from five sub-relations: relations involving (a) similarities in personal characteristics such as age, attitudes, and occupation; (b) closeness in physical space and social space (status); (c) pleasant sentiments such as liking, loving, attraction, sympathy, and trust; (d) behaviors such as cooperation, frequent interaction, confiding in one-another, and beneficent actions; and (e) symbolic expressions of similarity, proximity, or intimacy such as wedding rings, secret symbols, and secret handclasps. ("Self-Disclosure" 48)

Communication scholars have previously examined the interpersonal communication surrounding relationship solidarity among family members—including blended families (Braithwaite et al.), siblings (Rocca and Martin), and grandparent-grandchild dyads (Downs; Harwood). The present study extends this line of research to examine solidarity between daughters-in-law and their mothers-in-law. Other researchers have examined alternative aspects of overall relational quality in the pairing (Datta et al.; Rittenour; Rittenour and Soliz; Santos and Levitt; Wang; Young et al.) but not in interpersonal solidarity. Measuring solidarity allows for an overall assessment of liking, trust, closeness, and satisfaction (Wheeless, "Self-Disclosure").

Previous findings about the influence of social networks—including Susan Sprecher's ("Investment Model") finding that perceived network support for the relationship predicted commitment level in dating, cohabitating, engaged, and married couples—have led us to believe there may be a relationship between the interpersonal solidarity levels of a wife and her mother-in-law and the marital satisfaction of the wife and her husband. Such a relationship would be consistent with previous research (Rittenour and Kellas; Serewicz, "Getting"; Timmer and Veroff) documenting potentially "positive effects of in-law relationships on marriage" (Serewicz, "Getting" 111).

Marital Satisfaction

Marital satisfaction can influence and be influenced by family and marital communication (Lavner, Karney, and Bradbury). Indeed, the numerous studies examining communication and marital satisfaction continue to appear (Bravo and Martinez). Three previous studies closely examine the influence of relations with in-laws on marital satisfaction. First, Mary Claire Morr Serewicz asserts that marital quality can "influence the type and amount of aid exchanged" between in-laws and their children ("Getting" 110). Second, Christine Rittenour and Jody Koenig Kellas have discovered a positive association between marital satisfaction and the husbands'/wives' similar attributions for mothers-in-law's behaviour; in short, the more the husband and wife are "on the same page" about why the mother-in-law behaves as she does, the higher their marital satisfaction. Finally, Chalandra Bryant and colleagues have reported that the quality of the mother-in-law relationship is associated with marital satisfaction—but only for the husband. Our study builds on these findings that issues surrounding mothers-in-law can influence marital satisfaction and advances this line of research by examining the influence of maintaining communication boundaries with mothers-in-law on marital satisfaction. Furthermore, we have included an additional, potentially positive factor: the level of interpersonal solidarity between the mother-in-law and daughter-in-law.

Purpose, Hypotheses, and Research Question

The purpose of this study was to examine communication phenomena surrounding the potentially intrusive and problematic relationships among mothers-in-law, daughters-in-law, and the husbands in heterosexual marriages. To this end, we posed one research question and hypothesized a three-way relationship among three variables that may influence the quality of the relationship between mothers-in-law and their daughters-in-law as displayed in Figure One below.

Hypothesis one (H1): As the permeability of the communication boundary between the married son and his mother increases, the interpersonal solidarity between the mother-in-law and the daughter-in-law (the son's wife) decreases.

Hypothesis two (H2): As the permeability of the communication boundary between the married son and his mother increases, the marital satisfaction of the son and his wife decreases.

Hypothesis three (H3): As the interpersonal solidarity between the mother-in-law and daughter-in-law increases, the marital satisfaction between the daughter-in-law and her husband (the married son) increases.

Research question (RQ): As the son's perception of the mother's intrusiveness increases, does the son report more frequently verbalizing to his mother the communication boundary between them?

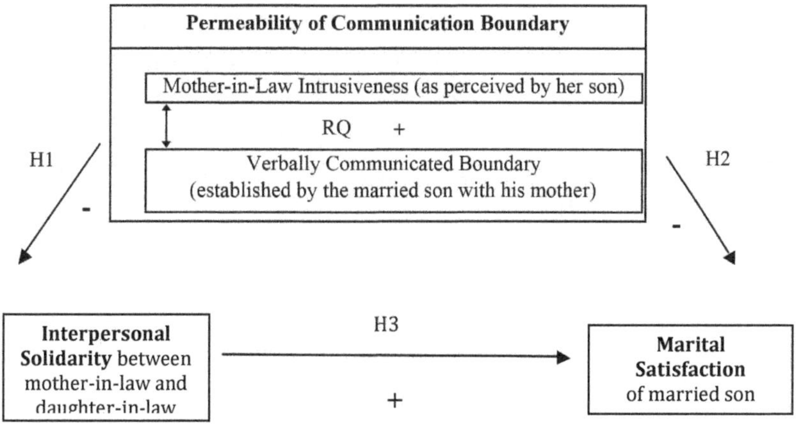

Figure 1: Tested Relationships.

METHODS

Participants

We recruited our convenience sample of 102 marital dyads from two sources. We obtained thirty-five dyads by distributing surveys to married friends of the first author, who completed surveys and also distributed surveys to their married friends. Additionally, we provided extra credit to students enrolled in two upper-division undergraduate classes in communication at a large, flagship university in the southeastern U.S. who distributed questionnaires to sixty-seven married couples who ultimately completed the survey. The student-collected data included a telephone number for confirmation of the couples' marital status.

Our sample contained 102 self-reported heterosexual, marital dyads (102 males and 102 females) between the ages of twenty and sixty-one, living in seven of the United States of America: Arkansas, Illinois, Missouri, New York, Oklahoma, Tennessee, and Texas. The majority of the participants (Ps) were Caucasian ($N = 181$), but the sample also included African Americans ($N = 11$), Latinos ($N = 5$), and individuals who indicted an ethnicity of "Other" ($N = 7$). Women in this sample ranged in age from twenty to fifty-six years ($M = 35.19$; $SD = 10.96$).[1] Men in this sample ranged in age from twenty to sixty-one years ($M = 37.20$; $SD = 11.14$). The couples reported being married for less than one year to thirty-six years ($M = 11.09$; $SD = 10.64$); over half of the sample had been married for eight years or less. Couples typically reported raising two children ($M = 1.88$; $SD = 3.09$). In our incident-rich sample, the couples reported talking to the husband's mother on average 3.90 times a week ($SD = 3.68$), or about once every other day. The couples visited the husband's mother an average of 66.19 times a year ($SD = 102.39$), or about once every 2.5 weeks. The couples reported living zero (typically living together or next door to one another) to 1450 miles from the husband's mother ($M = 142.98$, $SD = 267.95$), or on average about a 2.5-hour drive away.

PROCEDURES

Each spouse signed an informed-consent form and completed

three questionnaires. Wives completed a short demographics survey, the modified version of the ENRICH Marital Satisfaction Survey (Fournier et al.), and the Interpersonal Solidarity Scale about their relationship with their mother-in-law (Wheeless, "A Follow-Up"). Husbands completed a short demographics survey, the modified version of the ENRICH Marital Satisfaction Survey (Fournier et al.), and two modified versions of the Permeability of Boundaries Scale (Olver et al.) with reference to his mother's potential intrusiveness into his marriage and his establishment of a verbally communicated boundary with his mother on the topic of his marriage. To ameliorate order effects, spouses received the questionnaires in random and counterbalanced orders. We collected the data from our participants during two two-week periods occurring in sequential semesters.

After receiving approval from our university's Institutional Review Board on the Use of Human Subjects, we placed the questionnaires inside envelopes marked "husband" and "wife" so that each spouse received the appropriate questionnaires. The envelopes and surveys were coded to avoid the use of names while allowing us to match spouses' surveys. We asked spouses to complete the questionnaires alone and not to share their answers with their spouses. Finally, we asked them to seal the envelopes and return them to the person who solicited their participation, who then returned the instruments to the first author. We removed and separated the surveys from the envelopes so that we could not associate names with the data.

MEASURES

The Modified ENRICH Marital Satisfaction Scale assessed marital satisfaction. Using a scale of one (strongly disagree) to five (strongly agree), spouses rated fifteen statements, such as "I am very happy about how we make decisions and resolve conflicts." Based on Bryant and colleagues' findings that the quality of the in-law relationship is associated with marital satisfaction only for the husbands, we measured the husbands' and the wives' marital satisfaction separately; we did not calculate a joint or collective measure of marital satisfaction. Using a cross-validation assessment, Blaine Fowers and David Olson report evidence of the scale's discriminant validity and a Chronbach's alpha of .86. Our Chronbach alpha scores for male and female spouses were slightly less at .74 and .83, respectively. Males' ENRICH scores ranged from 15.34 to 83.50 (M = 54.85; SD = 10.35); females' scores ranged from 14.00 to 76.68 (M = 55.26; SD = 11.53).

The Interpersonal Solidarity Scale, a twenty-item questionnaire, assessed the wife's perceived interpersonal solidarity with her mother-in-law. The female spouses rated twenty items (e.g., "I feel very close to this person"; "I distrust this person") from one (strongly disagree) to seven (strongly agree). Our Chronbach's score of .93 was similar to Wheeless's ("A Follow-Up") report of a .96 alpha score. Our female-only solidarity scores ranged from 1.15 to 7.00 (M = 4.45; SD = 1.16).

The Permeability of Boundaries Scale (Olver et al.) originally consisted of seventeen-items rated from one (never) to five (often) and assessed the permeability of boundaries between a mother and her college-age child. We reworded items to address boundary permeability between mothers and their married sons concerning information about the son's marriage. Our male spouses rated these items according to frequency of occurrence during the last few years on a scale from one (never) to five (often). Parts A and B produced Chronbach alpha scores of .89 and .96, respectively—larger than Rose Olver and colleagues' Cronbach's alpha of .77 originally reported for the scale.

Part A assessed mother-in-law intrusiveness, and Part B assessed the verbally communicated boundary. Part A assessed the son's perception of his mother's tendency to penetrate the boundary between her and her son by inappropriately discussing his marriage (e.g., "My mother comments critically about my marriage"). Our male-only spouses' "intrusiveness" scores ranged from 1.00 to 3.88 (M = 1.56; SD = 0.54). Part B of the scale contained parallel items reworded to assess the sons' boundary management, such as "I have told my mother not to comment critically about my marriage." Our male-only spouses' "verbally-communicated-boundary" scores ranged from 1.00 to 3.88 (M = 1.36; SD = 0.65).

All spouses completed a brief demographics questionnaire to assess age, sex, ethnicity, and state of residence. We posed these questions to gather data to describe the sample.

RESULTS

Researchers employ two types of valid, statistical analyses for hypothesis testing: parametric and nonparametric statistics. Scientists prefer parametric analyses because they possess more statistical power and allow for more confidence in the outcomes. However, parametric statistics require assumptions about measurement and data sets, which nonparametric statistic do not; chief among these assumptions is that the variables of interest are normally distributed (i.e., assume the shape of a bell curve). We examined our data arrays to determine the normalcy of each variable and, thus, to identify which relationships in Figure One should be assessed via parametric statistics. Because the data arrays for our variables displayed non-normal distributions, we conducted nonparametric analyses. A series of Spearman's rho analyses assessed associations among the variables of interest. Given that non-parametric analyses may lead to less powerful outcomes than parametric analyses, it is appropriate to assess the power of a given nonparametric statistic compared to its parametric counterpart. "The efficiency of the Spearman rank correlation when compared to the most powerful parametric correlation, the Pearson *r*, is about 91 per cent" (Siegel, 213)—which we deemed acceptable. Our analyses yielded six significant relationships displayed in both Table One and Figure Two. The next logical step in analyses (i.e., path analysis to test the revised model displayed in Figure Two) was not appropriate, given the non-normal distributions.

DISCUSSION

Summary of Findings

Our analysis revealed the six significant associations depicted in Figure 2. However, the results provided no support for H1; we documented no direct association between permeability of the communication boundary (between the married son and his mother) with interpersonal solidarity in the mother-in-law to daughter-in-law (the son's wife) relationship. Conversely, and consistent with Bryant et al., our findings provided direct but limited confirmation for H2. Increases in both indicators of boundary permeability (i.e.,

Table One

Spearman Rho Associations

Variable	1	2	3	4	5
1. intrusiveness	1.00				
2. verbally-communicated boundary	.724**	1.00			
3. interpersonal solidarity	.007	-.124	1.00		
4. wife's marital satisfaction	-.181	-.198*	.299**	1.00	
5. husband's marital satisfaction	-.100	-.077	.264**	.512**	1.00

Note: The *N* for all analyses = 102 couples.
***p* < .01; **p* < .05

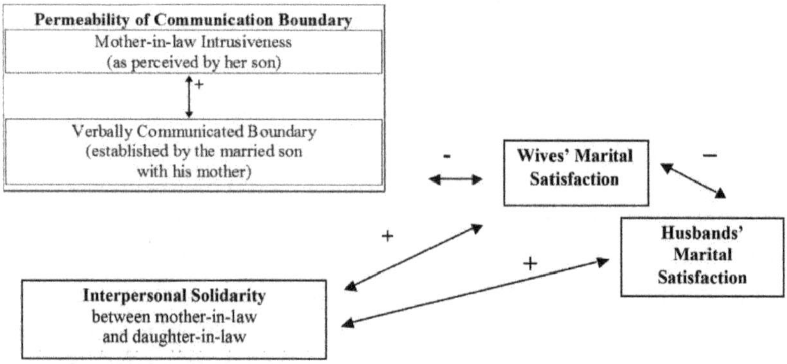

Figure Two: Confirmed Relationships

Figure 2: Confirmed Relationships.

mother-in-law intrusiveness and husband's verbal communication of the boundary) were associated with decreases in wives' marital satisfaction; however, the marital satisfaction of the son/husband was not directly associated with either measure of the permeability of the communication boundary with his mother.

In contrast, our results provided unconditional support for H3, indicating that as the interpersonal solidarity between the mother-in-law and daughter-in-law increased, the marital satisfaction of both the daughter-in-law and her husband (the married son) increased. Finally, our findings answer RQ in the affirmative: As perceived mothers' intrusiveness increased, the sons reported talking more frequently with their mothers about the communication boundary between them.

Interpretation of Findings

Overall Findings. Our results provide evidence that married sons maintain and manage communication boundaries with their mothers; their success in this endeavour is associated with their wives' marital satisfaction. Our results augment the findings of previous studies examining issues of privacy and boundary management among marital dyads (Chan; Craddock; Petronio, "Communcation"; Serewicz and Canary; Silverstein). Whereas Alan Craddock found that privacy within the dyad had minimal impact on marital satisfaction, our study provides initial documentation that privacy with other family members (i.e., the husband's mother), as assessed by two indicators of permeability of communication boundaries, is associated with wives' marital satisfaction.

Furthermore, our finding that husbands reported managing communication boundaries with their mothers provides further confirmation of Ying-Keung Chan's (2000) report that individuals desire to maintain privacy with their in-laws. Finally, our finding that interpersonal solidarity in the mother-in-law/daughter-in-law relationship was associated with marital satisfaction for both husband and wife confirms previous findings (Rittenour and Kellas; Serewicz, "Getting"; Timmer and Veroff) that in-law relationships can affect marital quality.

Individual Findings. Our results (see Figure Two) indicated that the more the son perceived his mother as intrusive, the more frequently he reported verbalizing the communication boundary. The son may be attempting to change his mother's behaviour to reduce turbulence and achieve coordination (Afifi).

Perhaps our most counterintuitive finding was the discovery of a negative association between the husband's report of verbally communicating a boundary with his mother and the wife's report of her marital satisfaction. The positive association between the mother-in-law's intrusiveness and the husband/son's verbally communicated boundary, as well as the negative association between intrusiveness and wife/daughter-in-law's marital satisfaction, may help explain this counterintuitive finding (i.e., the more frequently the husband verbally established the communication boundary with his mother, the more his wife's marital satisfaction declined). When the son verbalizes the communication boundary more frequently, he may be responding to the rising level of mother-in-law intrusiveness, given the positive association between the two variables, and he may, therefore, be engaging in boundary management or renegotiation prompted by boundary turbulence (Afifi; Petronio, *Boundaries*). It is this catalyst to establish the boundary—the mother-in-law's intrusiveness—that may prompt the wife to experience reduced marital satisfaction. Alternatively, the wife may perceive her husband as ineffective in communicating the boundary or "controlling his mother," thus prompting the wife's reduced marital satisfaction.

Interestingly, the wives' marital satisfaction scores were associated with every variable under study in this research project (see Figure Two). The analyses do not indicate directionality (which variable is influencing the other variable or whether mutual influence flows between them). However, the significant relationships may indicate that the mother-in-law can influence her daughter-in-law's marital satisfaction in two ways: in a negative way through her intrusiveness and in a positive way through her solidarity with her daughter-in-law. Similarly, the husband may influence his wife's marital satisfaction two ways: in a positive way through his own marital satisfaction as well as in a negative way through his verbally communicated boundary with his mother. Perhaps the wife's vulnerability to influence can be explained by considering Susan Sprecher and Diane Felmlee's notions about the influence of social networks. These researchers reported that individuals who perceive disapproval from their partner's social network are less likely to experience positive thoughts about the relationship than those who perceive approval. When a wife becomes aware of the phenomena here discussed (i.e., her interpersonal solidarity with her mother-in-law, her mother-in-law intrusiveness, her husband's verbal communication of boundary permeability, and her perception of her husband's marital satisfaction), she may perceive these factors as indicators of her mother-in-law's approve or disapproval of her actions as a wife. This perceived approval or disapproval may influence her marital satisfaction. Specifically, she may be happier in her marriage when she experiences interpersonal solidarity with her mother-in-law and when she perceives her husband as happy with the marriage. She may be less satisfied with her marriage when she perceives her mother-in-law as intrusive and when she perceives her husband as engaging in frequent attempts to manage that intrusiveness.

Finally, our findings also provide evidence that the greater the interpersonal solidarity between the mother-in-law and daughter-in-law, the higher the marital satisfaction of both the son and his wife. Conversely, the less interpersonal solidarity between the mother-in-law and daughter-in-law, the lower the marital satisfaction for the son and his wife. The results do not reveal the direction of influence; that is, we cannot know whether the interpersonal solidarity prompts the marital satisfaction or vice versa. However, it appears that when a man's wife and mother do not get along, then he and his wife may find their marriage less satisfactory. Thus, our findings provide evidence that a mother may influence her son's marriage through at least the two channels examined in this study: through her intrusiveness with her son and through her relationship solidarity with her daughter-in-law.

Our findings continue fifty years of research documenting that mothers-in-law can serve as problematic forces in families. Conversely, our results also indicate that mothers-in-law may serve as positive forces in their sons' marriages by respecting boundaries and by maintaining positive relationships with their daughters-in-law. Thus, the mother-in-law may influence her son's marriage in both negative and positive ways. Our findings also are consistent with Petronio's (*Boundaries*) theory of boundary management, coordination, and turbulence.

LIMITATIONS AND FUTURE RESEARCH

Perhaps the greatest limitation of our study was our sample's national and ethnic consistency. Our sample contained only participants living in the United Sates and only 11.3 percent non-Caucasians. Furthermore, we surveyed marital dyads from seven states who self-reported as ages twenty through sixty-one and as married from less than one year to over thirty-six years, but over half the sample reported being married eight years or less. Additionally, we examined only heterosexual marriages; given recent, legal changes, gay and lesbian marriages are likely to become increasingly common and also warrant examination. Finally, we employed self-administered questionnaires—a methodology associated with multiple known limitations, including issues of recall, honesty, and possible collaboration.

Given the scope of our study, we surveyed only daughters-in-law and sons. A future study could examine mothers-in-law's perceptions of solidarity with their daughters-in-law to discover if the relational partners concur. Another future study could identify variables that facilitate interpersonal solidarity between mother-in-law and daughter-in-law. Perhaps women with positive relationships with their own mothers are more likely to establish interpersonal solidarity in their female in-law relationships. Alternatively, perhaps women with absent mothers or challenging relationships with their mothers embrace the mother-in-law relationship as a venue for meaningful mother-daughter interaction. Additionally, perhaps positive relationships with "outsiders" can influence multiple kinds of personal and familial relationships. Finally, we recommend expanding research examining communication in in-law relationships beyond the current focus in parents-in-law to include the many in-law relationships within the marital dyad's social network, including but not limited to siblings-in-law, grandparents-in-law, and aunt/uncles-in-law (Floyd and Moor).

CONCLUSIONS

Despite the previously mentioned limitations and the many issues surrounding in-law communication that remain unexplored, our study contributes to an understanding of family communication in numerous ways: This study offers preliminary insights into the potential for problematic as well as positive relationships between mother-in-law and daughter-in-law. Specifically, the significant association between the daughters-in-law's perceptions of interpersonal solidarity with their mothers-in-law and marital satisfaction with their husbands adds to our knowledge about the mother-in-law and daughter-in-law relationship. Our findings offer both brides and mothers-in-law a pathway to supporting the sons' heterosexual marriages—to develop solid, personal relationships between the two women.

Our study furthers a small but growing line of research examining issues of privacy and the management of communication boundaries among marital dyads and with in-laws. Specifically, our findings provide support for Petronio's (*Boundaries*) incongruent privacy rule orientation, which explains the influence of social networks on marital functioning. For example, the significant findings associated with boundary management provide a communicative explanation for decline in marital satisfaction.

Our study provides preliminary insights into one largely unstudied area in family communication: interactions between mothers and their married sons. Specifically, the significant association between intrusiveness and communicated boundaries adds to our knowledge of privacy and disclosure in the mother-son relationship. Furthermore, the significant association between husbands' communication boundaries with their mothers' and their wives' marital satisfaction add to our knowledge of possible associations between mother-son relationships as well as husband-wife relationships.

ENDNOTE

[1]*M* refers to mean or arithmetic average. Grade-point-average is an example of a mean. *SD* refers to standard deviation, a measure of disbursement of the data set. It specifically assesses the extent to

which, on average, individual data points deviate from the mean. A small SD indicates that most data points clustered around the mean. A large SD indicates that the data points vary widely and the sample is diverse.

WORKS CITED

Afifi, T. D. "'Feeling Caught' in Stepfamilies: Managing Boundary Turbulence through Appropriate Communication Privacy Rules." *Journal of Social and Personal Relationships,* vol. 20, no. 6, 2003, pp. 729-55.

An, Z. "The Dilemma of Receiving Support from In-Laws: A Study of the Discourse of Online Pregnancy and Childbirth Support Groups." *China Media Research*, vol. 10, no. 3, 2014, pp. 32-42.

An, Z., and C.P. Chou. "Social Support for First-Time Chinese Mothers in Contexts of Provider-Recipient Relationships." *Health Communication*, vol. 31, no. 4, 2016, pp. 504-12.

Braithwaite, D.O., et al. "'Becoming a Family:' Developmental Processes Represented in Blended Family Discourse." *Journal of Applied Communication Research*, vol. 29, no. 3, 2001, pp. 221-47.

Bravo, C.S., and A.W. Martinez. "Profiles Using Indicators of Marital Communication, Communication Styles and Marital Satisfaction in Mexican Couples." *Journal of Sex & Marital Therapy*, vol. 43, no. 4, 2017, pp. 361-76.

Bryant, C.M., et al. "The Influence of In-Laws on Change in Marital Success." *Journal of Marriage and Family*, vol. 63, 2001, pp. 614-26.

Caughlin, J.P., and T.D. Afifi. "When Is Topic Avoidance Unsatisfying?: Examining Moderators of the Association between Avoidance and Dissatisfaction." *Human Communication Research*, vol. 30, 2004, pp. 479-513.

Caughlin, J.P., et al. "Intrafamily Secrets in Various Family Configurations: A Communication Boundary Management Perspective. *Communication Studies*, vol. 51, no.2, 2000, pp. 116-34.

Chan, Y.K. "Privacy in the Family: Its Hierarchical and Asymmetric Nature." *Journal of Comparative Family Studies*, vol. 31, no, 1, 2000, pp. 1-17.

Craddock, A.E. "Relationships between Marital Satisfaction and Privacy Preferences."*Journal of Comparative Family Studies*, vol. 25 no. 3, 1994, pp. 371-83.

Datta, P., et al. "Parent Care by Indian and Belgian Caregivers in Their Role of Daughter/Daughter-in-Law." *Journal of Cross-Cultural Psychology*, vol. 34, 2003, pp. 736-49.

Downs, V.C. "Grandparents and Grandchildren: The Relationship between Self-Disclosure and Solidarity in an Intergenerational Relationship." *Communication Research Reports*, vol. 5, 1988, pp. 173-79.

Duvall, E. *In-Laws: Pro and Con; and Original Study of Interpersonal Relations*. Association Press, 1954.

Fischer, L.R. "Mothers and Mothers-in-Law." *Journal of Marriage and the Family*, vol. 45, 1983, pp. 187-92.

Ford, S.M. "The Mother-in-Law Effect: Managing the Publicity of Personal Content Online." *Journal of Broadcasting & Electronic Media*, vol. 56, no. 4, 2012, pp. 550-61.

Fournier, D.G., et al. "Assessing Marital and Premarital Relationships: The PREPARE/ENRICH Inventories." *Marriage and Family Assessment*, edited by E.E. Filsinger, Sage, 1983, pp. 229-50.

Fowers, B.J., and D.H. Olson. "ENRICH Marital Inventory: A Discriminant Validity and Cross-Validation Assessment." *Journal of Marital and Family Therapy*, vol. 15, no. 1, 1989, pp. 65-79.

Floyd, K., and M.C. Moor. "Human Affection Exchange: VII. Affectionate Communication in the Sibling/Spouse/Sibling-in-Law Triad." *Communication Quarterly*, vol. 51, 2003, pp. 247-61.

Frisby, B.N., and R.J. Sidelinger. "Parents' Post-Divorce Relationships: Maintenance and Former In-Laws." *Ohio Communication Journal*, vol. 47, 2009, pp. 77-95.

Gangoli, G., and M. Rew. "Mothers-in-Law against Daughters-in-Law: Domestic Violence and Legal Discourses around Mother-in-Law Violence against Daughters-in-Law in India." *Women's Studies International Forum*, vol. 34, 2011, pp. 420-29.

Golish, T.D., and J.P. Caughlin. "'I'd Rather Not Talk about It': Adolescents' and Adults' Use of Topic Avoidance in Stepfamilies." *Journal of Applied Communication Research*, vol. 30, 2002, pp. 78-106.

Harris, P.B., and S.O. Long. "Daughter-in-Law's Burden: An Exploratory Study of Caregiving in Japan." *Journal of Cross-Cultural Gerontology*, vol. 8, no. 2, 1993, pp. 97-118.

Harwood, J. "Communicative Predictors of Solidarity in Grandparent-Grandchild Relationships." *Journal of Social and Personal Relationships*, vol. 17, no. 6, 2000, pp. 743-66.

Lavner, J.A., et al. "Does Couple Communication Predict Marital Satisfaction, or Does Marital Satisfaction Predict Communication?" *Journal of Marriage and Family*, vol. 78, no. 3, 2016, pp. 680-94.

Lopata, H. Z. "In-Laws and the Concept of Family." *Marriage & Family Review*, vol. 28, no. 3-4, 1999, pp. 161-172.

Madden-Derdich, D.A., et al. "Boundary Ambiguity and Co-parental Conflict after Divorce: An Empirical Test of a Family Systems Model of the Divorce Process." *Journal of Marriage and the Family*, vol. 61, 1999, pp. 588-98.

Mazur, M.A., and A.S.E. Hubbard. "'Is There Something I Should Know?': Topic Avoidant Responses in Parent-Adolescent Communication." *Communication Reports*, vol. 17, no. 1, 2004, pp. 27-37.

Mikucki-Enyart, S.L. "Parent-in-Law Privacy Management: An Examination of the Links among Relational Uncertainty, Topic Avoidance, In-Group Status, and In-Law Satisfaction." *Journal of Family Communication*, vol. 11, no. 4, 2011, pp. 237-63.

Nastasee-Carder, A. "Between Image and Reality: An Analysis of the Mother-in-Law and Daughter-in-Law Relationship." National Communication Association, Nov. 2003, Miami, Florida.

Olver, R.R., et al. "Self-Other Differentiation and the Mother-Child Relationship: The Effects of Sex and Birth Order." *Journal of Genetic Psychology*, vol. 150, no. 3, 1989, pp. 311-21.

Petronio, S. *Boundaries of Privacy: Dialectics of Disclosure*. State University of New York Press, 2002.

Petronio, S. "Communication Boundary Management: A Theoretical Model of Managing Disclosure of Private Information between Marital Couples." *Communication Theory*, vol. 1, no. 4, 1991, pp. 311-35.

Petronio, Sandra. "Privacy Binds in Family Interactions: The Case of Parental Privacy Invasion." *The Dark Side of Interpersonal Communication*, edited by W.R. Cupach and B.H. Spitzberg,

Lawrence Erlbaum Associates, Inc. 1994, pp. 241-57.

Petronio, S., et al. "Family Privacy Dilemmas: Managing Communication Boundaries within Family Groups." *Group Communication in Context: Studies of Bona Fide Groups*, L.R. Frey, Erlbaum, 2003, pp. 23-56.

Petronio, S., et al. "Family and Friends as Healthcare Advocates: Dilemmas of Confidentiality and Privacy." *Journal of Social and Personal Relationships*, vol. 21, 2004, pp. 33-52.

Rittenour, C. "Daughter-in-Law Standards for Mother-in-Law Communication: Associations with Daughter-in-Law Perceptions of Relational Satisfaction and Shared Family Identity." *Journal of Family Communication*, vol. 12, no. 2, 2012, pp. 93-110.

Rittenour, C., and J.K. Kellas. "Making Sense of Hurtful Mother-in-Law Messages: Applying Attribution Theory to the In-Law Triad." *Communication Quarterly*, vol. 63, no. 1, 2015, pp. 62-80.

Rittenour, C., and J. Soliz. "Communicative and Relational Dimensions of Shared Family Identity and Relational Intentions in Mother-in-Law/Daughter-in-Law Relationships: Developing a Conceptual Model for Mother-in-Law/Daughter-in-Law research." *Western Journal of Communication*, vol. 73, no. 1, 2009, pp. 67-90.

Rocca, K.A., and M.M. Martin. "The Relationship between Willingness to Communicate and Solidarity with Frequency, Breadth, and Depth of Communication in Sibling Relationships." *Communication Research Report*, vol. 15, 1998, pp. 82-90.

Sandel, T.L. "Enacted Social Support and Cultural Practices among Women and Families Observing a Postpartum Rest in Taiwan." *China Media Research*, vol. 10, no. 2, 2014, pp. 48-59.

Sandel, T.L. "Narrated Relationships: Mothers-in-Law and Daughters-in-Law Justifying Conflicts in Taiwan's Chhan-chug." *Research on Language and Social Interaction*, vol. 37, 2004, pp. 365-98.

Santos, J.D., and M.J. Levitt. "Intergenerational Relations with In-Laws in the Context of the Social Convoy: Theoretical and Practical Implications." *Journal of Social Issues*, vol. 63, 2007, pp. 827-83.

Serewicz, M.C.M. "Getting Along with the In-Laws: Relationships with Parents-in-Law." *Widening the Family Circle*, edited by K. Floyd and M.T. Morman, Sage, pp. 101-16.

Serewicz, M.C.M. "Toward a Triangular Theory of the Communication and Relationships of In-Laws: Theoretical Proposal and Social Relations Analysis of Relational Satisfaction and Private Discourse in In-law Triads." *Journal of Family Communication*, vol. 8, no. 4, 2008, pp. 264-92.

Serewicz, M.C.M., and D.J. Canary. "Assessments of Disclosures from the In-Laws: Links among Disclosure Topics, Family Privacy Orientations, and Relational Quality." *Journal of Social and Personal Relationships*, vol. 25, 2008, pp. 333-57.

Serewicz, M.C.M., et al. "Disclosure from In-Laws and the Quality of In-Laws and Marital Relationships." *Communication Quarterly*, vol. 56, no. 4, 2008, pp. 427-44.

Siegel, S. *Nonparametric Statistics for the Behavioral Sciences*. McGraw-Hill, 1956.

Silverstein, J.L. The Problem with In-Laws. *Journal of Family Therapy*, vol. 14, no. 4., 1990, pp. 399-412.

Sprecher, S. "Investment Model, Equity, and Social Support Determinants of Relationship Commitment." *Social Psychology Quarterly*, vol. 51, 1988, pp. 318-28.

Sprecher, S., and D. Felmlee. "The Influence of Parents and Friends on the Quality and Stability of Romantic Relationships: A Three-Wave Longitudinal Investigation." *Journal of Marriage and the Family*, vol. 54, 1992, pp. 888-900.

Timmer, S. G., and J. Veroff. "Family Ties and the Discontinuity of Divorce in Black and White Newlywed Couples." *Journal of Marriage and Family*, 62, no. 2, 2000, pp. 349-61.

Wang, F. "Role Prospects, Life Mission, Life Cycle: The Frame of Understanding in Relations between Mother-in-Law and Daughter-in-Law." *Journal of China Women's University*, 2011, http://en.cnki.com.cn/Article_en/CJFDTotal-ZNXY201101014.htm. 21 July 2017.

Wheeless, L.R. "Self-Disclosure and Interpersonal Solidarity: Measurement, Validation, and Relationships." *Human Communication Research*, vol. 3, no. 3, 1976, pp. 47-61.

Wheeless, L.R. "A Follow-Up Study of the Relationships among Trust, Disclosure, and Interpersonal Solidarity." *Human Com-*

munication Research, vol. 4, no. 2, 1978, pp. 143-57.

Young, V., et al. "Relationship characteristics mediate topic avoidance and relationship quality with mothers-in-law." Annual Meeting of the National Communication Association, Nov. 2015, Las Vegas, NV.

III. Marriage: Looking Out and Forward

10.
Contracting Out of Legal Protections

How Popular Culture Messaging Clashes with the Lived Realities of Women Entering into Prenuptial Agreements

MARIE L. GORDON AND TIFFANY S. STOKES

AS FAMILY LAWYERS, we have the opportunity to see what happens when the "happily ever after" falls apart. Most of our efforts are devoted to assisting our clients in negotiating acceptable resolutions to matters of parenting, child and spousal support, and a reasonable property division. All of our negotiations take place in the "shadow of the law," and we try to guide our clients to acceptable settlements armed with a set of rules, presumptions, and guidelines, which are the product of the last four decades of progressive development in the family law arena in Canada.

We are also asked, from time to time, to represent parties wishing to enter into prenuptial agreements, which are negotiated before the "happily ever after" even starts. In seeing the ways in which these negotiations come about, and the often problematic exercise of trading away rights in a factual vacuum, we thought it worthwhile to examine the dynamics at play in the prenuptial landscape. Why do people think that prenuptial agreements are a good idea for young women entering into their first marriage? What cultural messages and expectations are in play? Whose interests are served by the process of bargaining legal rights prior to marriage? Are there gendered patterns in women's negotiating behaviours in the premarital phase? Why would women contract out of hard-fought legal entitlements in favour of a private set of rules that would offer fewer rights to them? To what extent are the courts in Canada upholding premarital agreements, even when they clearly place a spouse at a legal disadvantage on marriage breakdown?

Although we certainly do not have all the answers, we thought that these were good questions to ask. We hope to "marry" the power of popular culture messaging (as curious as it is) about prenuptial agreements with a sober understanding of what it means to be a young woman entering marriage today.

CINDERELLA V. GLORIA STEINEM

Young women are no longer confined to their stereotypical gender roles of housewives and caretakers.[1] Traditional gender roles are being redefined as more women are delaying marriage and childbirth (Lundberg and Pollak; Goodwin et al.; Miller). This may lead women to attaining a higher level of education and it likely has a positive impact on their career achievement and earnings (Lehrer 533; Miller 1073). Despite the potential benefit of delaying marriage and motherhood, marriage is still often regarded as the culminating event or a rite of passage in a woman's life that takes her from childhood to female adulthood. Furthermore, in exchange for this "happily ever after," some women are asked to enter into prenuptial agreements that give up or sacrifice legal entitlements.

Young women are currently poised to reap the benefit of years of feminist struggle for equality rights and equal treatment under the law. The gains made in the feminist movement have opened numerous doors for women; women no longer need to be married or remain married in order to have financial stability. In particular, family law has developed over the years to protect a woman's legal entitlement to division of matrimonial property and spousal support, so that she is not confined to a life of poverty in the event her marriage breaks down. Given these monumental achievements for women, it begs the following questions: what is still so attractive about marriage, and why would a woman enter into that union and a marriage agreement in which she waives entitlement to these protections?

THE PULL OF MARRIAGE

Popular culture still views marriage as an "organizing principle of female adult life" (Tolentino). Even if a woman has a postsecondary degree, has lived on her own for many years, or has even purchased her own home, marriage is still the life event that transforms her from juvenile to adult. According to this view, without marriage, a young woman's life is unstable and still in flux. In an interview on her book, *All the Single Ladies: Unmarried Women and the Rise of an Independent Nation*, Rebecca Traistor states, "Marriage is popularly a sign that your life is in order, which contributes to this renewed positioning of marriage as aspirational" (Tolentino).

In addition to the "stabilizing factor" of marriage, the pressure women face is reinforced and strengthened by the corporate bridal industrial complex or what Traistor calls the "fetishization of marriage." "[O]ne of the interesting things that's happened coterminously with the decline in marriage rate is the rise of the wedding industrial complex and the fetishization of marriage as the signal achievement of female life" (Tolentino). The corporate bridal industrial complex is hardest at work in social media platforms, such as Facebook, Instagram, and Pinterest, as well as in television shows and websites geared specifically toward wedding planning. These channels bombard women with images that the perfect, lavish wedding is the crowning achievement in one's life. It hyperfocuses on the details of a wedding (and all the events that go along with it), from the engagement party, bridal showers, photoshoots, wedding attire, place cards—the "must haves" for today's modern wedding are too many to list. It is perhaps the only time family, friends, and the larger society will truly celebrate a woman, notwithstanding she may have several degrees and professional achievements under her belt. The corporate bridal industrial complex acts as a "pressure to correct women's move away from marriage by fetishizing it" (Talentino). The act of getting married, particularly in a self-aggrandizing way, signals to others that a woman has succeeded in life.

PRENUPTIAL AGREEMENT AS A WEDDING ACCESSORY

Among the many details of planning a wedding, women now add one more item to that checklist: the prenuptial agreement. Gone are the days where prenuptial agreements were simply for the uber-wealthy and celebrities. *The Knot*, a popular wedding planning website, includes information about prenuptial agreements amid their articles on seating arrangements and centerpieces. In these articles, women are encouraged to enter into a prenuptial agreement by financial planners, women's interest magazines, and even feminist websites, even if they are entering marriage with no assets.

Prenuptial agreements are sold to women as an example of what a "reasonable" woman would do. Jeff Landers, who specializes in providing financial advice to women going through a divorce, encourages young women to consider prenuptial agreements. "Long considered stuffy, stodgy and even insulting, the prenup is beginning to win favor as a reasonable, practical and smart sign of trust between a woman and her fiancé." Not only are prenuptial agreements hailed for their reasonableness, but they are also seen as a way to exert independence from the state: "If done correctly, a prenup can be an excellent way to supersede your state's marital laws" (Landers).

Furthermore, a prenuptial agreement is presented in popular culture as a way to actually improve a marriage before it even begins, as it encourages open, honest communication. According to Terry Savage, author of *The New Love Deal: Everything You Must Know Before Marrying, Moving In, Or Moving On!*, the greatest benefit of a prenuptial agreement is the heartfelt communication that comes along with it, not necessarily the financial protection: "Just the very act of discussing and trying to come to an agreement—before you even see the attorneys—will help reveal what you have in common, and what might become a 'dealbreaker'.... And you want to know these things before you get married!" (Kane).

A FEMINIST ACT?

Another surprising perspective is that a prenuptial agreement may be viewed by some as an act of feminism. In her article for *Bustle* (a women's lifestyle website), "7 Reasons Getting a Prenup Can Be a Feminist Act," Gabrielle Moss admits that most marriage traditions are not for her— except the prenuptial agreement. Despite the fact that she and her future husband only have "just enough money right now to make a down payment on a plate of taquitos," she states that "Our prenup symbolizes the fact that our independence is ensured, no matter what happens in the future." She declares it a "feminist act," particularly as women are working more outside of the home and are getting married later (and presumably have acquired assets as a single person). It also gives her freedom, Moss states, because having a prenuptial agreement means she is "less likely to get stuck in a marriage that no longer works due to financial concerns." In her view, a prenup creates equality between the spouses, as neither party will fear being "bankrupted by spousal support" or "being stuck with zero financial resources if things end." Because Moss and her future husband do not plan on having children, she insists that "laws designed to protect women who gave up their careers to raise families simply shouldn't apply to [her]," and that she will not "deserve a penny" of her husband's money (Moss). She does not contemplate what would happen if she stopped working because of other circumstances (such as a disability), rather than childrearing. To her, prenuptial agreements are seen as a noble way to avoid financially "destroying" each other.

Karen McCullah, a successful Hollywood screenwriter, also offers a cautionary tale for young women in her article for *Elle*, a magazine marketed to women:

> When I got married at twenty-four, a prenup never even remotely occurred to me. What was there for him to take? My Visa bill? But eighteen years later, when I divorced my husband, I had a successful writing career and some money in the bank. He got to take half of it. But it isn't even the fact that I had to give him half that I find so egregious. It's the alimony he demanded I pay him on top of it that makes me very, very angry.

When repeating one of the first conversations with her lawyer, she insisted her husband would never ask for alimony, as it would be a "pussy move." She implores women to ensure that they sign a prenuptial agreement that eliminates spousal support in order to avoid being "penalized for [their] success" (McCulllah).

The clear message sent to women is that the strides women have made in education and the workforce are enough to protect them in the event their marriage breaks down. Because of these advances, women shouldn't need to depend on anyone but themselves. As Traistor has stated, "It is an enormously rewarding possibility for women, to earn their own money, to support themselves, to not having to be dependent on fathers, on husbands. It is rewarding to meet people, to have colleagues, to be in the public world." Although it makes sense that a career or working outside of the household affords women unique opportunities and can improve their self-esteem and overall wellbeing, this "rewarding possibility" cannot replace legal protections for women. To be fair, Traistor is not suggesting that women should opt out of their legal entitlements. However, the pressure on women to have it all and join the workforce is a one-size-fits-all mentality that does not necessarily work for all women. This burden can also create a stigma against women who do not work outside of the home, or it can lead to feelings of shame and embarrassment for women who rely on their spouses for financial support. This criticism can instill a sense of misdirected pride that women should waive their legal entitlements, not because they are financially capable of providing for themselves but because it is what a modern woman who "has it all" should do. This view suggests that legal entitlements secured by decades of feminist legal activism are no longer necessary for women in today's society.

Interestingly, women who recognize their financially precarious role in their marriage and take steps to protect themselves are heavily criticized, either for being greedy or antifeminist. Wednesday Martin, in her book *The Primates of Park Avenue*, uncovers a "tribe" of women from the upper echelons of Manhattan. These women lead busy, privileged lives as stay-at-home mothers, and in exchange for their hard work, they are remunerated with a "wife bonus." A wife bonus is usually derived from a percentage of the husband's bonus received in his employment, and it is intended to compensate the wife for her efforts in the household as if she were an employee receiving a bonus for good performance. These women are often well educated and may have had at one point successful careers.

Polly Phillips is part of this tribe, not because she lives on Park Avenue but because she is a wealthy, stay-at-home mother who also receives a "wife bonus" from her husband. When Phillips's husband received a job transfer to Australia, she gave up her career as a broker to move with him. She did not resume working and instead they focused on having children. She negotiated with him to receive a "wife bonus," as recognition of the work she does in the home, and to be used at her discretion. They do not have a prenuptial agreement. As Phillips explains, "By not working, I'm financially dependent on my husband, regardless of whether I accept a 'wife bonus.' If anything, by receiving a bonus, I am finally being recognized as my husband's true equal." Phillips has received condemnation from other women, "who feel [she] is betraying the feminist cause" (Phillips).

A "wife bonus" may not be what family law feminists had in mind when they championed for women's rights in matrimonial property and spousal support, but it does recognize that an imbalance of financial resources that can exist between spouses and that a need exists to support the spouse who does not work outside of the home, or earns less, than the other. The push against a fair division of property or spousal support implies that claiming these rights is seen as being greedy and selfish person or a "gold digger."

UNEQUAL FINANCIAL POSITIONS

It is true that there may be good reasons for a couple to enter into a prenuptial agreement. For example, there may be assets that each person brings into a marriage that they want to keep separate. A blanket waiver of entitlement, however, can be particularly disadvantageous to women. Women still earn less than men, acquire less wealth than men, and are more likely to take a leave of absence when having children or caring for aging relatives. Young women entering marriage may believe they will remain gainfully employed through the marriage, but the lived realities of women are that they are still not on equal financial footing with their male counterparts.[2]

Celeste Watkins-Hayes, a professor of sociology and African American studies and chairwoman of the African American Studies Department at Northwestern University, takes the perspective that prenuptial agreements may be useful for a particular socioeconomic group of women, but they are not an adequate financial safety net for all women. She relies on a study by sociologist Mariko Chang, which has found that women in the United States generate only thirty-six cents for every dollar of wealth generated by men. Watkins-Hayes explains the gap as follows: "This is largely because women are more likely to have primary custody of children, making it more difficult to stay out of debt, sustain assets and hold onto cash for making investments. They are also less likely to have jobs that grow and protect their assets through fringe benefits like generous health care coverage and stock options." The financial inequality that still exists between men and women is being left out of, or ignored, in the conversations surrounding prenuptial agreements.

What is missing from all the advice in favour of prenuptial agreements is a clear warning about the consequences of waiving entitlement to hard-fought rights—that women are potentially giving up entitlement to property or spousal support—and the devastation that can cause women who may have to "start over" later in life after a separation. They may be left with very few financial resources because of a prenuptial agreement that was sold to them as a symbol of feminism and independence, or as a way to demonstrate their love over material aspirations. Financial equality is a laudable goal, but it may not be a reality for many women who are taking the leap into marriage.

UNPACKING THE REALITY OF PRENUPTIAL AGREEMENTS

In all of the noise generated about "signing a prenup" in popular culture, there is very little critical analysis about what prenuptial agreements do, and what benefits or detriments they confer upon the contracting parties, especially from a gendered point of view.

This analysis demonstrates that there are many interests, myths, priorities and aspirations at play in the discussion about prenuptial agreements, few of which ever seem to be articulated clearly. In addition, we argue that many of the presumed benefits or imperatives about prenuptial agreements seem to serve outsider or sociocultural narrative needs, rather than the needs of the women who sign them. This gendered analysis is a critical step when looking at a family law topic that involves prospective spouses privately assigning to themselves rights, obligations, and entitlements outside the public family law arena.

A further task, which flows from this, is the need to understand the extent to which courts strictly uphold or refuse to enforce the terms of agreements bargained by individuals prior to marriage. This topic is a massive one, likely beyond the scope of this chapter, but one which we will introduce at the very least.

What Prenuptial Agreements Do

It sounds rather elementary to talk about what prenuptial agreements do, but it's worthwhile to see this private contracting exercise in its historical and legal context.

Prenuptial agreements usually involve a couple rejecting, in whole or in part, a statutory regime that governs their rights to a sharing of property acquired during the course of the marriage and potentially the sharing of income at the end of the relationship. The parties are essentially substituting their own private contract for the public rules that would govern entitlements. Although prenuptial agreements vary in use, they tend to follow predictable and consistent patterns, no matter what state or province the parties live in.

Prenuptial agreements may involve both parties opting out of all statutory rights or obligations, and agreeing to a regime of entire separateness as to their finances. Such an agreement would prevent any claims against the other party for any share of assets acquired during the marriage[3] or for any increase in the value of any premarital assets. Some agreements go even further and include waivers of future claims for spousal support or alimony in the event of the breakdown of the relationship.[4] Very few agreements include any waivers or prearranged outcomes for child support on marriage breakdown, given that courts uniformly reject attempts to opt out of such basic statutory provisions, and will almost always refuse to enforce such terms. Exceptions to this rule may involve couples with stepchildren from another marriage, with parties wishing to make clear their desire not to seek or pay child support for children who are not a product of their marriage. Even then, however, courts will apply the law that may exist in their jurisdiction, relating to the rights of children to support from individuals "standing in the place of a parent."[5]

Some agreements involve partial contracting out of statutory regimes,[6] and may preserve certain statutory rights and obligations in place.

What Benefits or Detriments Are Conferred

These waivers, in whole or in part, usually involve one of the spouses giving up a right to claim a possible financial entitlement upon marriage breakdown. In most prenuptial agreements, the wealthier spouse (often the husband) achieves protection of assets, and the economically vulnerable spouse (often the wife) waives what would otherwise be a statutory entitlement.

The bargain may involve the economically vulnerable spouse receiving some "settlement" amount at the time of signing, or some formulaic entitlement based on years of marriage or some other arbitrary marker. The settlement amount almost never replicates what a spouse could claim in the event of separation after a medium or long-term marriage. It may be payable more as an attempt to bolster the enforceability of the agreement in the eyes of a court than an attempt to quantify and match what the law may offer in a contested scenario at the end of the marriage (Frommer Brod).

What is the problem with this practice? Why would we have any issue with two adults freely contracting their future rights and obligations in the event of a possible future marriage breakdown?

THE HISTORICAL DEVELOPMENT OF FAMILY LAW IN CANADA (THE SHORT VERSION!)

To understand this better, we place this discussion in a historical context and take a look at the development of family law over the last four decades. We write from the Canadian perspective of family law practitioners in Alberta, knowing that legislative developments in other jurisdictions happened at very different times and might have yielded quite different statutory regimes.

Nonetheless, in Canada between 1978 and 1980, most provinces[7] in Canada introduced matrimonial property legislation to provide for a presumptive equal distribution of property upon marriage breakdown. At the time, this was perceived as a radical and, for many, an unwelcome legislative development that would endanger, for example, the viability of the family farm and small businesses upon marriage breakdown.

However, for women, the introduction of matrimonial property legislation was an overdue and a highly positive development. The catalyst for property laws was the widely publicized and controversial decision of the Supreme Court of Canada in *Murdoch v. Murdoch*,[8] in which the court denied a farm wife her claim under constructive trust for an equal share of her husband's ranching operation, saying that she had contributed no more than any other ranch wife would have done. Justice Laskin's dissent, and the outcry from feminists about the unfairness of the case, propelled provincial legislative action across the country. From a gendered perspective, giving domestic labour the same value as paid labour in the general workforce was a revolutionary improvement in women's rights across the country.

Not only did this new legislation change the landscape of outcomes following contested family law trials, but also it profoundly altered the parties' "bargaining entitlements" and the shape of family law negotiations for women in powerful ways. No longer did women start from a position of "zero" and have to beg or argue for equal property entitlement. They started from a presumption of equality, and the onus of seeking anything but an equal division shifted to the other spouse. In addition to property rights, the development of the law in the area of spousal support has had an impact on the financial wellbeing of women following marriage breakdown.

Canada's 1985 Divorce Act[9] introduced a purposive and progressive palette of factors and objectives to be considered in awarding spousal support. The exclusion of "misconduct" as a factor to be considered meant that Canadian spousal support law[10] developed with an understanding of the importance of economic consequences of both marriage and separation for spouses, rather than the old-fashioned "fault" perspective.

In addition, the Divorce Act's objectives[11] go beyond a simple "means and needs" analysis, and include a more sophisticated and progressive "compensatory" approach to understanding the impact of marriage and its breakdown on the players.[12]

Women, who statistically continue to experience negative economic outcomes by virtue of their continuing role as primary caregivers of children during periods of the marriage, continue to be the beneficiaries of developments in the area of spousal support (Gadalla; Moyser). The accommodation of family needs to the detriment of one's own economic and occupational potential is something that continues to have a gendered aspect. Simply put, women tend to earn less and acquire fewer assets if they carry out more of the traditional (but highly valuable) childbearing and childrearing roles in their marriage. Not all women carry out this role, but on average, society continues to expect women to second their own needs for those of their family.

CONTRACTING OUT OF WHAT?

As this brief historical overview indicates, women have achieved substantial gains in Canadian provincial matrimonial property laws since the passage of legislation thirty-five years ago, which recognized the value of unpaid work and the view of marriage as an economic partnership. Women have also benefitted from the development of a huge body of legislation and jurisprudence related to spousal support under not only the federal Divorce Act but also under provincial family law legislation.

These gains are of greatest importance to younger women who may be entering their first marriage and who have yet to experience the impact of marriage on their economic wellbeing. Older women who are entering into a second or subsequent marriage are also affected by these developments in family law, but the impact of childbearing and childrearing is felt most keenly by younger women who are entering domestic relationships or marriage. Accordingly, the prospect of young women being encouraged, either by messages in popular social media or by prospective spouses or family members, to contract out of hard-fought legislative gains is unsettling, to say the least.

This is especially the case when parties fail to engage in a critical cost-benefit analysis of contracting out of (all or a part of) matrimonial property legislation in a prenuptial agreement and are unclear about the long-term impact of a contractual "opting-out" exercise. Early feminists fought for legislative improvements in family law so as to ensure that individualized bargaining for rights might be avoided and so that a public system would, by default, offer enhanced entitlements to spouses who might contribute unpaid labour to the marital venture. The development of these normative legislative rights (most of which include degrees of discretion to achieve individualized fairness in unusual situations) was a long and difficult battle fought by advocates for women's rights over decades in Canada and elsewhere.

CONTRACTUAL SANCTITY VERSUS LIVED REALITY OF WOMEN'S LIVES

A lively debate continues to exist on the issue of whether or not women should be "saved" from bad bargains and contracts that either minimize or do away with their potential entitlements under a legislated set of rules (Leckey).

As the argument goes, women have fought long and hard to achieve recognition of their full independence, autonomy, and ability to assess and determine their own preferences, desires, and wishes. In so doing, they have the ability to enter into contracts of their choosing and the obligation to comply with their contractual undertakings. Having the law and courts intervene to "save" them from bad bargains represents a paternalistic view of women's agency and accountability.

Leah Guggenheimer (156-59) points out a number of reasons why premarital agreements may need to be enforced, regardless of how they affect women following marriage breakdown:

- Certain agreements might advantage a woman's position vis-à-vis the distributive legislation in force in her jurisdiction.
- Women might use premarital agreements to determine rights and duties during the marriage (childcare, housework, management of family finances, etc.) so as to increase their personal wealth maximizing opportunities.
- Denying the enforceability of premarital agreements will

operate to decrease women's abilities to negotiate contracts to their advantage.

•Enforceability promotes a clearer understanding of outcomes, rather than a muddy range of possibilities; it promotes careful consideration based on certainty of enforcement.

•Entering a marriage may, in some situations, actually improve a woman's economic status; maybe the deal is worth it.

•Enforcement remedies substitute a woman's own assessment of her best interests for that of the state and its paternalistic implications.

•Women are seen as needing to be "rescued" from the bad deals they have agreed to.

•Women are seen as less than rational, capable agents; they are seen as having a diminished capacity to contract.

•A conservative or sexist judiciary might fail to detect unfair agreements in any event, and might engage in a highly fact-driven analysis of the facts presented, with no better outcome.

•In this era of overburdened and underfunded Court systems, the idea of inviting challenges to domestic contractual arrangements is counter to the modern development of family law (i.e. the historical development of predictable and consistent rules, presumptions, guidelines, and avoidance of litigation/the trend towards arbitrary measures of fairness rather than highly individualized contests over what constitutes fairness for any individual couple.

There are, of course, many compelling reasons to support the existence of legal remedies to avoid the enforcement of certain prenuptial agreements:

•Prenuptial agreements can operate to "sharpen the existing inequality in the distribution of wealth and resources" between women and men generally (Frommer Broder 235).

•Courts have a strong interest in remedying cases of unconscionability, exploitation and palpable unfairness.

- Courts also have an interest in ensuring that procedural fairness in negotiating of private contracts is promoted and that unfair or exploitative processes are discouraged.
- Prenuptial agreements are owed less deference than agreements negotiated following the breakdown of a marriage; in the former, it is often impossible to prospectively have full knowledge of the value of rights that are being waived or exchanged, whereas in the latter, there is a much better opportunity to calculate and assess the value of a compromise or waiver of an entitlement.
- Domestic contracts between prospective spouses, especially younger ones, have little similarity to commercial or business contracts, given the emotional, cultural, and psychological landscape in which they are negotiated. As well, the power and resource imbalance between many prospective spouses considering prenuptial agreements yields the greater likelihood of unfair bargaining and unfair outcomes.

One prominent 2004 Supreme Court of Canada case in which this topic is discussed is *Hartshorne v. Hartshorne*.[13] In this case, a prenuptial agreement was negotiated in which the wife waived claims to assets acquired during the marriage and obtained a 3 percent per year entitlement to the equity in the matrimonial home. The husband was a successful lawyer, and the wife was also a lawyer but had no income as she was a stay-at-home mother caring for the two children of the marriage (one of whom had special needs). The contract was characterized as "grossly unfair" by the wife's lawyer who strongly recommended against her signing it. A few minor changes were agreed to, and eventually the agreement was signed on the day of the wedding—after the ceremony and before the wedding dinner. At trial, both parties gave evidence that the wife was "very upset and crying when she signed the agreement."[14]

At trial and on appeal, the courts held that that the contract was unfair and intervened to give the wife a greater share of matrimonial property, following the parties' twelve-and-a-half-year cohabitation and marriage.

However, at the Supreme Court of Canada, those decisions were reversed, and the wife was held to the original bargain. The decision evinces the desire of Canada's highest court to uphold and enforce agreements between spouses, unless clear traditional contractual grounds exist to set them aside (e.g., duress, misrepresentation, undue influence, unconscionability etc.). It reinforces individual responsibility for the marking of bargains, and the need to hold individuals to their bargains.[15]

Sarah Whitmore contrasts the rational view of "economic man" (according to which each person acts for themselves in a manner that will maximize their own utility, regardless of what consequences may arise to others) with the often explicitly gendered realities of bargaining in marriage agreements. Her article, "Deconstructing 'Economic Man's' Application to Marriage Agreements: An Analysis of the Method of Contractual Enforcement in *Hartshorne v. Hartshorne*," explores "the many and complex reasons why the content of marriage agreements may not actually reflect the parties' attempts to achieve fairness, but instead may reveal a power struggle waged by one to achieve a windfall and a capitulation by the other to achieve a fragile peace" (328).

Hartshorne v. Hartshorne, though not the only prominent decision in which the policy reasons behind upholding and enforcing prenuptial agreements are discussed, is still a leading authority from the Supreme Court, and signals a clear unwillingness to save people from bad deals, unless traditional grounds exist to set aside their agreements.

THE ROLE OF GENDER IN NEGOTIATIONS

Surprisingly little empirical data exist to give us reliable understandings of the ways in which gender affects negotiations between spouses-to-be (and separating spouses) in the family law context. Most of our knowledge about the role of gender in contractual negotiations comes from the workplace focused field of study. The exercise of grafting that knowledge onto the field of family law is an imperfect one, but it gives us a good place to start.

From an earlier essentialist perspective which sees women and men as different creatures by nature, research and writing has moved us to a much more sophisticated understanding of how gender plays out in various contexts (Gordon). Gender socialization, rather than essentialist features, is now understood to be a powerful force influencing negotiating behaviours. Although it is beyond the scope of this paper to exhaustively survey the various studies on negotiating behaviours seen through the lens of gender, the following issues are relevant to premarital negotiations:

- Women (who historically were denied career opportunities, and were only able to access wealth through marriage) traditionally place greater importance on maintaining good relationships in bargaining, even if it means sacrificing short-term gains (Bedont).
- Women are less likely than men to ask for things in contract negotiations (Babcock and Laschever).
- Culturally mandated/expected behaviours for women still include accommodating the needs of others, deferring to power, willingness to concede points to achieve consensus, using tentative rather than absolute demands, unwillingness to use threats and bluster to achieve aims, etc.
- Women tend to focus on what their negotiation partner needs to close the deal, in addition to what their needs might be.

These points read like something out of a 1950s etiquette book for young women, but they continue to characterize some of the gender behaviours still in play today. None of this is to belittle individual behaviours but to comment on the extraordinarily powerful and long-lasting social and cultural messages that women internalize and act upon. The idea of rejecting a marriage that is conditional upon the signing of a prenuptial agreement—out of a desire to maximize one's own entitlement and to protect one's own financial self-interest—is antithetical to a traditional female socialized bargaining stance.

One of the most interesting and powerful influences on younger women today is the extent to which their identity, status, security and value are perceived to be enhanced through the act of marriage. This cultural ritual continues to be a powerful motivator for women. If a precondition for marriage is an agreement to enter into a private ordering of rights (by way of a prenuptial agreement), some women will trade certain legal entitlements in exchange for marital status. This is all the more likely when we live in an era in which prenuptial agreements are no longer the preserve of millionaires. Instead, they start to look like a normal facet of wedding planning for the modern bride.

In a survey of sixteen hundred members of the American Academy of Matrimonial Lawyers conducted in October 2013, 63 percent of the respondents reported an increase in prenuptial agreements over the previous three years. The top three items most often covered in those agreements were noted as "protection of separate property" (80 percent), "alimony/spousal maintenance" (77 percent) and "division of property" (72 percent).

THE BEST AND THE WORST OF PRENUPTIAL AGREEMENTS

At their best, prenuptial agreements can do the following:

- For older couples with adult children who marry later in life, prenuptial agreements can protect premarital property and can operate to avoid miserable divorce and property litigation late in life.
- Prenuptial agreements can exempt certain assets from distribution.
- Prenuptial agreements can allow couples to engage in a difficult but important premarital conversation about what their expectations are in the event of marriage breakdown; they can learn about their potential rights and obtain full disclosure about their prospective spouse's assets and income. They can test each other's assumptions and actually address common approaches to resolving future disputes.[16] There is an honest and authentic sharing of information and views, without any pressure or coercion. The discussions may result in a prenuptial agreement; they equally may result in no agreement at all.

At their worst, prenuptial agreements may involve:

- An unquestioning agreement to contract out of certain presumptive legal rights, at the request of the other spouse or their family.
- The assumption that there is one kind of prenuptial agreement—a complete waiver of rights to a share of property or future support
- Strong-arm pressure tactics at the beginning of a marital relationship; the use of ultimatums and threats; short-time frames for disclosure and execution of the agreement; toxic and corrosive dynamics that poison the goodwill ordinarily associated with a marriage.
- Lawyers who see their role as aggressively representing the interests of a groom and the groom's family business without any insight into the impact of their negotiating tactics and posture on the couple's relationship.
- An imbalance in resources and power going into a marriage, then cemented into a contractual imbalance for the remainder of the relationship.
- An inequality in bargaining power; a lack of leverage or confidence to call off a wedding.
- A reverse gender impact: what about the rights of those (a minority, but nonetheless a minority society needs to encourage) men who sacrifice paid work in order to stay at home to look after children? Is feminism all about maximizing women's financial positions, or is it about ensuring that marriage does not economically disadvantage either spouse?
- An economically vulnerable spouse (usually the woman) not understanding the long-term impact of waiving certain rights into the future, or (optimistically but unrealistically) underestimating the likelihood of relationship breakdown
- An illusion of equality; women being told that their independence means that they need not rely on legislation in the event of a divorce accepting the view that entering into a prenuptial agreement is a feminist act.

By exploring the meaning and possible impact of prenuptial agreements, we start to see that they never mean just one thing;

the term carries a5 load of cultural expectations, messages about gender and entitlement, and unarticulated assumptions. By trying to unpack some of these, we can gain a much clearer understanding about whether or not they contribute to a "happily ever after."

CONCLUSION

Popular culture continues to promote the importance of marriage in the lives of young women, and the corporate bridal industrial complex remains a multi-billion-dollar enterprise successfully messaging women about what they need for a "happily ever after." In a curious development, prenuptial agreements are increasingly being presented as a form of wedding accessory.

The messages about why such an agreement is a "good idea" are varied and confusing, and they often go unexamined. Advertised as a fail-safe guarantee of "protection," "fairness," and modern independence for women, they frequently involve brides giving up claims or entitlements at law that they may need and likely deserve. Waiving a claim to an equal division of property, or the right to seek spousal support upon marriage breakdown, can be one of the most financially disastrous things a young woman can agree to, especially when there is a possibility of having and raising children in her future. A brief review of Canadian law indicates that prenuptial agreements are very likely to be upheld and enforced in the event of marriage breakdown, even if the terms agreed are highly unfavourable to one of the parties.

Contemporary rules and presumptions governing property division and spousal support claims are the product of four decades of concerted effort on the part of legislators, family law experts, and feminists to fairly acknowledge the value of unpaid domestic labour and to recognize the role of a secondary wage-earner in marriage. Contracting out of and waiving the benefit of these legislative provisions is both a counterintuitive and problematic exercise.

Although prenuptial agreements may represent a worthwhile undertaking for second or later-in-life marriages (to protect existing assets and their growth for first families, for example), the bargaining away of rights for young women is a practice that begs scrutiny and critical analysis. What are women getting in exchange for what they are giving? Surely, they should not be expected to pay a price for the privilege of gaining marital status.

As young women navigate their way through the process of entering marriages, they need to consider their own needs in priority to everyone else's. Prenuptial agreements usually represent a giving up of some or all claims, rights, and entitlements that would otherwise belong to them. The willingness of women to accommodate the needs and priorities of other actors, or to accept the messages in popular culture and social media about what they need to be a happy bride, is concerning on a number of levels. Hopefully, women will engage in a sober analysis of what their own "happily ever after" looks like by not giving up anything.

ENDNOTES

[1]The authors recognize that while young women may not be confined to only the roles of housewives and caretakers, they may still be encouraged to fulfill these roles *in* addition to their career achievement.

[2]For Canada-specific information, see: Tammy Schirle; for United States-specific information, see: "Women in the Labor Force: A Databook."

[3]Where couples acquire assets such as real property in joint names, the law tends to presume joint ownership regardless of disparate contributions, except in jurisdictions that empower a judge to adjust entitlement to equity in property based on a variety of factors.

[4]In Canada, the s. 15.2(4) of federal Divorce Act outlines a number of factors to be considered by the court in determining entitlement to spousal support. The existence of a prenuptial agreement in which one of the spouses purports to waive spousal support is one of a number of factors that the court is directed to consider, but such an agreement is not necessarily determinative and may be overridden depending on the circumstances of the case. See *Miglin v Miglin* [2003] S.C.R. 303 (SCC). Prenuptial agreements, entered into prior to a marriage, are qualitatively different than postseparation settlement agreements, given that spouses in the former scenario have not yet had an opportunity to consider or know the ways in which their lives may be affected by the mar-

riage, and exactly what they are contracting out of or giving up.
[5]For example, s. 2(2) of the Divorce Act 1985 and s. 48 of the Alberta Family Law Act S.A. 2003 c. F 4.5.
[6]For example, an agreement not to seek any increase in the value of premarital assets which might accrue during the course of the marriage, or an agreement not to seek any remedies as against or related to specified assets.
[7]In Canada, provinces have legislative jurisdiction in areas related to property and civil rights (s. 92(13) of the Constitution Act 1867) and the federal government has jurisdiction in the area of divorce. Most matrimonial property legislation excludes assets acquired prior to marriage by either of the spouses from such division.
[8][1975] 1 S.C.R. 423.
[9]R.S.C. 1985, c.3 (2nd Supp.).
[10]In comparison to legislation in a number of U.S.states concerning alimony awards.
[11][1975] 1 S.C.R. at s. 15.2(6).
[2]The unanimous decision of the Supreme Court of Canada in *Moge v. Moge* [1992] 3 S.C.R. 813 authored by Madam Justice Claire l'Heureux Dube was a watershed development in the law of spousal support in Canada. It was written with a strong understanding of the role of gender in the impact of marriage breakdown and attendant economic disadvantages experienced by women.
[13]2004 SCC 22.
[14]See the trial decision at 1999 Carswell BC 2778 (B.C.S.C).
[15]For an excellent analysis of the Supreme Court's degendered analysis of choice, contractual bargaining, and deference to private ordering, see Martha Shaffer, "Developments in Family Law."
[16]There is a growing trend towards using the collaborative family law model in negotiating premarital agreements, arguably resulting in agreements which achieve a better balance between the prospective spouses, an exploration of the interests of both parties, representation, full disclosure, and a review of multiple options for agreement.

WORKS CITED

American Academy of Matrimonial Lawyers, October 16, 2013.

Babcock, Laura and Sarah Laschever *Women Don't Ask: Negotiation and the Gender Divide* Princeton University Press, 2003.

Bedont, Barbara. "Gender Differences in Negotiations and the Doctrine of Unconscionability in Domestic Contracts." *Canadian Family Law Quarterly*, vol. 12, no. 21, 1994, pp. 34-35.

Chang, Mariko. *Shortchanged: Why Women Have Less Wealth and What Can Be Done About It.* Oxford University Press, 2010.

Frommer Brod, Gail. "Premarital Agreements and Gender Justice." *Yale Journal of Law and Feminism*, vol. 6, no. 2, 1993, pp. 229-95.

Gadalla, Tahany. "Gender Differences in Poverty Rates after Marriage Dissolution: A Longitudinal Study." Journal of Divorce and Remarriage, vol. 49, no. 3, 2008, pp. 225-38.

Goodwin, Paula, et al. "Who Marries and When? Age at First Marriage in the United States: 2002." *Centers for Disease Control and Prevention*, 2009, www.cdc.gov/nchs/products/databriefs/db19.htm. Accessed 25 July 2017.

Gordon, Marie. "The Role of Gender in Family Law Negotiations" in *Gender, Sex and the Law in Canada*, edited by Johanne Elizabeth O'Hanlon, Thomson Reuters Canada Ltd., 2015, pp. 1-42.

Guggenheimer, Leah. *A Modest Proposal: The Feminomics of Drafting Premarital Agreements, Women's Rights Law Reporter*, vol. 17, no. 2, 1996, pp. 147-208.

Kane, Libby. "Here's Why Every Couple Should Get a Prenup before Marriage." *Business Insider*, 5 Aug. 2014, www.businessinsider.com/every-couple-needs-a-prenup-2014-8. Accessed 24 July 2017.

Landers, Jeff. "My Best Financial Advice for the Bride-to-Be." *Forbes*, 28 June 2012, www.forbes.com/sites/jefflanders/2012/.../my-best-financial-advice-for-the-bride-to-be. Accessed 24 July 2017.

Leckey, Robert. "Contracting Claims and Family Law Feuds." University of Toronto Law Journal, vol. 57, no. 1, 2007, pp. 1-41.

Lehrer, Evelyne. "Delayed Entry into First Marriage and Marital Stability: Further Evidence on the Becker-Landes-Michael Hypothesis." Demographic Research, vol. 29, no. 20, 2013, pp. 521-533.

Lundberg, Shelly, and Robert Pollak. "The Evolving Role of Marriage: 1950-2010." *Future of Children*, vol. 25, no. 2, 2015, pp. 29-50.

Martin, Wednesday. *Primates of Park Avenue: A Memoir*. Simon & Schuster, 2015.

McCullah, Karen. "Why Every Woman Should Get a Prenup." *Elle*, 9 Jan. 2014, www.elle.com/life-love/sex-relationships/advice/a13998/why-every-woman-should-get-a-prenup/. Accessed 24 July 2017.

Miller, Amalia. "The Effects of Motherhood Timing on Career Path." *Journal of Popular Economics*, vol. 24, no. 3, 2011, pp. 1071-1100.

Moss, Gabrielle. "7 Reasons Getting a Prenup Can Be A Feminist Act." *Bustle*, 5 Jan. 2016, www.bustle.com/articles/133542-7-reasons-getting-a-prenup-can-be-a-feminist-act. Accessed 24 July 2017.

Moyser, Melissa. "Women in Canada: A Gender-Based Statistical Report." *Statistics Canada*, 8 Mar. 2017, www.statcan.gc.ca/pub/89-503-x/2015001/article/14694-eng.pdf. Accessed 24 July 2017.

Philips, Polly. "My Husband Pays Me a Wife Bonus, and I'm Proud of It—It's What Feminists Have Urged for Years." *National Post*, 26 May 2015, nationalpost.com/life/polly-phillips-my-husband-pays-me-a-wife-bonus-and-im-proud-of-it-its-what-feminists-have-urged-for-years. Accessed 24 July 2017.

Shaffer, Martha. "Developments in Family Law: The 2003-2004 Term." *Supreme Court Law Review*, vol. 30, 2005, pp. 359.

Schirle, Tammy. "The Gender Wage Gap in the Canadian Provinces, 1997-2014." Canadian Public Policy, vol. 41, 2015, pp. 309-19.

Traister, Rebecca. *All the Single Ladies: Unmarried Women and the Rise of an Independent Nation*. Simon & Schuster, 2016.

Tolentino, Jia. "'Marriage Changes When You Don't Just Need A Warm Body and a Paycheck': A Talk with Rebecca Traister." *Jezebel*, 3 Mar. 2016, jezebel.com/marriage-changes-when-you-dont-just-need-a-warm-body-an-1762007106. Accessed 24 July 2017.

"Women in the Labor Force: A Databook." *U.S. Bureau of Labour Statistics*, Dec. 2014, www.bls.gov/opub/reports/womens-databook/archive/women-in-the-labor-force-a-databook-2014.pdf.

Accessed 24 July 2017.

Watkin-Hayes, Celeste. "All Women Need Financial Protection." *The New York Times* 1 Oct. 2013, www.nytimes.com/roomfordebate/2013/03/21/the-power-of-the-prenup/all-women-need-financial-protection. Accessed 24 July 2017.

Whitmore, Sarah. "Deconstructing 'Economic Man's Application to Marriage Agreements: An Analysis of the method of Contractual Enforcement in *Hartshorne v. Hartshorne*" Canadian Family Law Quarter, vol. 29, no. 3, 2010, pp. 303-44

11.
"Have Your Cake and Eat It Too"

Challenging and Changing Normative Gender Roles through Partnerships

ANDREA O'REILLY

IN 2012, I WROTE the chapter "'I Should Have Married Another Man: I Couldn't Do What I Do without Him': Intimate Heterosexual Partnerships and Their Impact on Mothers' Success in Academe" for Lynn O'Brien Hallstein's and my edited collection *Academic Motherhood in a Post-Secondary Wave Context*. The chapter—developed from my three-year research project "Being a Mother in Academe" 2006-2009, for which I interviewed sixty plus academic mothers from across Canada and the U.S.—explored the role intimate heterosexual relationships play in determining women's success as academic mothers. The scholarship on academic motherhood has well examined the work and public context of mothers' lives as academics and how such factors as mentoring, childcare, institutional and governmental policy, and workplace practices and attitudes determine women's ability to successfully combine motherhood with an academic career. Little has been said, however, on what impact women's private and intimate lives as partners has on their academic career. Sharing stories of four academic mothers in heterosexual partnerships, the chapter examined how and why traditionally gendered partnerships, particularly as they are manifested in the normative wife role, hinder a mother's success in academe. Conversely, it showed how and why domestic relationships modelled on gender equity work to enhance mothers' success in academe. As the literature on academic motherhood has rightly identified the need to counter and change the normative discourse of the ideal worker, I argue in this chapter that women must likewise defy and deconstruct the normative ideology of the ideal wife in both identity and practice. A successful academic career for mothers is, thus, as contingent upon challenging patriarchal marriage as challenging the masculinist culture of academe. Women must secure gender equity in the home as well as in the workplace.

In this chapter I examine the normative wife role and the wife-work expected and demanded of women in traditional marriage and consider how matrifocal family structures in downplaying the wife role allow for gender fluidity and equity that make possible true partnerships between men and women in heterosexual relationships. I conclude the chapter with a discussion of my own relationship with my partner to show how our lived partnership challenged and changed normative gender roles, which allowed me to succeed in my career.

In the opening of my chapter discussed above, I noted how the beginning of my writing projects is often marked by an uncanny event in my life, one that resonates as I put pen to paper, or in today's world, fingers to keyboard. For this chapter, the commencement of writing was paralleled by a significant event in my own life, which was, in a most uncanny way, thematically linked to the subject matter of the chapter. I learned as I began work on this chapter that after two long years of my file working its way through the labyrinth of my university's bureaucracy that my promotion to full professor was final and complete. And while the official letter from the president on my promotion was itself a cause for celebration, what was equally important to me and of particular relevance to my chapter was a Facebook post from my eldest daughter after she received the news of my promotion. She wrote the following:

> Congratulations to the world-renowned mama scholar and my own mom (yes, I'm a lucky grrrl!) Andrea O'Reilly for her accomplishment of promotion to full professor! So proud of you mom! to all those who say women can't achieve success in both their careers and as mothers, you need to take a look at my mom, her long list of publications, her adoring students and her even more adoring children. She's done it all and then some. Way to go mom.

And although my daughter uses the word mother—because she

is my daughter and views my identity in this context rather than in terms of me being the partner to her father—her comment, nonetheless, signifies the larger argument of this chapter: only by refusing the wife role in name and in practice could I do "it all and then some." In reading my daughter's post as I write this chapter, I realize that my career success was largely attributable to the partnership of our matrifocal family structure, through which I could resist the gendered expectations of the normative wife role. To this discussion, I now turn.

In *Strong Mothers, Weak Wives* Miriam Johnson argues that "It is the wife role and not the mother's role that organizes women's secondary status" (6). Women's secondary status, she maintains, originates not from the maternal core of women's subjectivity but from their heterosexual identity as wives of men. In other words, Johnson maintains that male dominance originates not from the mother-child attachment but from the father-daughter relationship. In contrast to much of motherhood scholarship that locates women's lack of autonomy to the feminine-related sense of self, engendered by the mother-daughter relationship (Chodorow), Johnson argues that women's lack of autonomy originates from the daughters' psychological dependency on her father as a male-orientated "daddy's girl." The relationship between father and daughter, Johnson asserts, "trains daughters to be wives who are expected to be secondary to their husbands" (8). Johnson argues that fathers often romanticize the father-daughter relationship and interact with their daughter as a lover would. Fathers feminize their daughters: daddies teach them to be passive, pleasing, and pretty for men. In Johnson's words," [The father-daughter relationship] reproduce[s] in daughters a disposition to please men in a relationship in which the male dominates" (184). Thus, in most so-called normal, (i.e., male-dominant) families, what is experienced is psychological incest. Johnson explains: "The incest is psychological, not overtly sexual. The father takes his daughter over. She looks up to him because he is her father. He is the king and she is the princess. It is all OK because the male is dominant in 'normal' adult heterosexual relations" (173). In other words, "daddy's girls are in training to be wives" (184). Because "daddy's girls" are trained and rewarded for pleasing and playing up to men, they grow up to be male-defined and male-orientated women.

As Johnson argues it is the wife role, and not the mother's role, that causes women's secondary status in patriarchal culture, in *Wifework: What Marriages Really Mean for Women*, Susan Maushart contends that it is specifically the wifework that women perform that impedes gender equality in marriage. According to Maushart, the tasks and characteristics of wifework include the following:

> Performing a hugely disproportionate share of unpaid household labour.
> Assuming total responsibility for His emotional caretaking.
> Managing His intimacy needs at the expense of Hers.
> Taking full responsibility for child-care drudgework.
> Monitoring His physical well-being.
> Preparing meals tailored specifically to His taste, appetite and schedule.
> Deferring to His agenda.
> Maintaining His extended relationships. (10-11)

Maushart goes on to write that "wife work is a time consuming, energy-draining and emotionally exorbitant enterprise. There is no counterpart to wifework, no reciprocal "husband work" driving males to provide caregiving to their female partners at the expense of their own well-being" (8, 10). Thus there are, in Maushart's words, "two versions of marriage that are fundamentally and perhaps irreconcilably divergent: His marriage versus Her marriage" (3). And as she goes on to argue, "more to the point, we have not yet acknowledged—perhaps not even to ourselves—that His marriage works. And Hers doesn't."(3)

The normative wife role, I argue, assumes and expects that 1) the family will be organized around the career of the husband; 2) the career of the wife, should she have one, will be secondary to her husband's; 3) the wife is to support her husband's career and its advancement; and 4) the woman is responsible for and performs the many and varied tasks of maintaining the household and homemaking. The normative wife role is particularly detrimental to women in demanding professional careers. An academic career, in particular, requires long and intensive years of training, travel for conferences and research, and repeated relocations—all of which are integral to the profession and necessary for advancement in it. Too frequently, motherhood is given as the reason why women leave academe or fail to succeed within it. I suggest, however, that if we look more closely at such stories, tease out the details, we see that traditionally gendered partnerships are often the real reason why mothers "opt out" of careers in academe. It is difficult, if not impossible, for a woman to live up to her career obligations if her career is secondary to that of her husband's and if she is solely responsible for the care and running of the home and household. Traditionally gendered partnerships, organized as they are around the husband's career, prevent the wife from attaining the very things required for a successful academic career: the ability to travel, move, or secure the needed time and focus for her scholarship (and the authority to demand such). Indeed, the findings of my research on academic mothers show that the excessive masculine scripts of academe along with excessive feminine scripts of conventional marriages have created a perfect storm for academic mothers, wherein they find it difficult to achieve academic success—so much so that traditional gendered partnerships become more of a deterrent to academic success than single motherhood.

One possible strategy to address such inequity in marriage is a complete reversal of gender roles: the man becomes the wife (he is the primary at-home parent), whereas the woman becomes the husband (she is the primary breadwinner). An example of this may be found in *Professor Mommy: Finding Work-Family Balance in Academia* by Rachel Connelly and Kristen Ghodsee. Rachel Connelly, a married mother of four, was the first woman to receive tenure in the economics department at her college, the first to be named full professor, and the first to become a chaired professor. Although she does not specifically take up the argument—that the normative wife role is as much a barrier to academic success as that of the ideal worker—I argue that her own lived life experience illustrates just that. Connelly is the sole breadwinner of the family, as her husband is at home full-time with no paid employment. At the conclusion of her biography, she writes the following: "I am well aware that my situation was easier than many since I had a supportive spouse who celebrates what she does and who stays home with the children. Since I had someone else at home, snow days and ear infections were much easier to cope with than they were for most of her women colleagues" (20). I suggest, however, that it was precisely this reversal of gender roles—woman as breadwinner, man as homemaker—that contributed largely to Connelly's success as an academic mother. More specifically I argue that it is precisely because Connelly is not viewed or positioned as a "wife" that affords her the time, space and legitimacy to make her career central to her life and that of her family.

However, given that such a solution is available only to a select few who have the financial means to support a family on one income, gender reversal is not possible for most families and, as importantly, such a solution does not address the larger problem of gender inequity within households. I believe gender equity may be possible without a complete reversal of gender roles through men and women functioning not as husbands and wives but as partners who are equally responsible for what needs to be done to create a home and family: childrearing, housework, and paid employment. A relationship of partnership does not merely reverse gender roles but eliminates them all together. Importantly, models for such partnerships already exist in matrifocal families and cultures.

Matrifocal cultures, as Johnson explains, downplay the wife role and emphasize women's mothering; hence, such cultures are characterized by greater gender equality. In matrifocal societies, Johnson writes, "women play roles of cultural and social significance and define themselves less as wives than as mothers" (226). Johnson goes into further detail:

> Matrifocality, however, does not refer to domestic maternal dominance so much as it does to the relative cultural prestige of the image of mother, a role that is culturally elaborated and valued. Mothers are also structurally central in that mother as a status has some degree of control over the kin unit's economic resources and is critically involved in kin-related decision making processes.... It is not the absence of males (males may be quite present) but the centrality of women as mothers and sisters that

> makes a society matrifocal, and this matrifocal emphasis is accompanied by a minimum of differentiation between women and men. (226)

The wife identity is, thus, less pronounced and prevalent in matrifocal cultures because in these societies, women assume an economic role and experience gender equality in the family unit. Writing on African American women, Patricia Hill Collins argues the following:

> Black mothers have long integrated their activities as economic providers into their mothering relationships. In contrast to the cult of true womanhood, in which work is defined as being in opposition to and incompatible with motherhood, work for black women has been an important and valued dimension of Afrocentric definitions of black motherhood.... Whether they wanted to or not, the majority of African-American women had to work and could not afford the luxury of motherhood as a non-economically productive, female "occupation." (48-9)

Thus, black women, at least among the urban poor, do not assume the wife role that structures women's oppression. Moreover, in African American culture, motherhood, not marriage, emerges as the rite of passage into womanhood. As Joyce Ladner emphasizes in *Tomorrow's Tomorrow*, "If there was one common standard for becoming a woman that was accepted by the majority of the people in the community, it was the time when girls gave birth to their first child. This line of demarcation was extremely clear and separated the girls from the women" (215-16). The matrifocal structure of black families with its emphasis on motherhood over wifedom and black women's role as economic provider means that the wife role is less operative in the African American community.

Matrifocal families, to paraphrase Johnson above, allow women control over the families' economic resources and enable them to be critically involved in decision-making processes. Matrifocal families are also less defined by the gendered spheres of the public and private. Both husbands and wives are engaged in paid employment in the public sphere, and husbands and wives both perform the work of the private sphere. Thus, in matrifocal families there is, to use Johnson's words, "a minimum of differentiation between women and men" (226) and women "define themselves less as wives than as mothers" (226).

When my partner and I began our relationship thirty-five years ago and became first-time parents thirty-three years ago, I was not familiar with the feminist scholarship on matrifocality. But looking back now at how we lived our lives and raised our children, I see that our family structure was indeed matrifocal in the characteristics described above, and it was precisely this matrifocality that allowed my own lived resistance to the gendered expectations of the wife role. My partner and I are of Scottish, English, and Irish ancestry: he was raised in a working-class family, whereas my family was middle class (although I was the first in my family to attend university). We are both from Hamilton, a working-class city in Ontario, and we met at York University in Toronto when my partner, eight years my senior, was in a PhD program, and I had just completed the second year of my honours bachelor's degree. Twenty-one years old, I was happy with my studies and our relationship, and had little thought of the future. However, eighteen months into our dating relationship, I learned that I was pregnant. Motherhood was something I thought I would perhaps do in the very distant future. I was not supposed to be pregnant now and certainly not this way: as an undergraduate student, young, poor, and in a dating relationship. Although I considered having an abortion—and this was the decision most of my friends supported—I knew from the moment the stick tested positive that I would keep the baby and become a mother. My boyfriend, as it turned out, felt the same, so we spent many late nights, talking about how to make this transition to parenthood happen. We agreed that we would move out of our own apartments and move into a family apartment on our university campus. Significantly, we never considered or discussed getting married before or after the birth. When we announced the pregnancy to his family, his mother, though, did start discussing plans for an immediate December wedding. I interrupted politely and simply said we are not getting married. Many couples today, and certainly most in the early

1980s, would marry quickly upon the discovery of an unexpected out-of-wedlock pregnancy. So I wonder looking back now some thirty-five years later why marriage simply did not matter to me and how I remained resolved in my decision not to marry, despite cultural expectations, if not pressure, to do so. I did know my boyfriend would certainly have agreed to marriage if that had been what I wanted. But marriage was simply the furthest thing from my mind. I was not opposed to marriage per se; it simply did not matter to me. What did matter and what did occupy my thoughts was how to become a mother while still being a student. And so my boyfriend and I moved in together at eight-weeks pregnant and began what would later officially be called a common-law relationship. Our son, sharing both our last names in hyphenated format, was born seven months later.

I now realize that my indifference to, or disinterest in, the institution of marriage and my attention to mothering are precisely what characterizes matrifocal families. And in choosing partnership over marriage, I refused, consciously or unconsciously, the normative wife role. Although I do agree that common-law relationships often mimic and enact the gender inequality of marriage described by Maushart above, I still believe that partnerships tend to be more resistant to normative gender roles, precisely because marriage is a patriarchal institution. I say this not to imply that men and women who marry are themselves patriarchal but rather to remind and emphasize that the institution of marriage was created and is maintained to serve the interests of men in a patriarchal culture.

Moreover, law and language do matter: our relationship is not legally sanctioned, and I am not a wife, and he is not a husband. When we speak of, or introduce each other, the word we use is "partner." As partners, we are, to paraphrase Adrienne Rich, outlaws from the institution of marriage. Not defined by the identities of husband or wife or restrained by the history and customs of the institution of marriage, we were able to create and build a family that was matrifocal and one that allowed for greater fluidity and equity in gender roles.

In making this argument, I am not saying that matrifocal families are always characterized by gender equality but rather in such families, gender is not organized hierarchally and what the man and woman do, say, and believe matter equally. Above I argued that the normative wife role assumes and expects that 1) the family will be organized around the career of the husband; 2) the career of the wife, should she have one, will be necessarily secondary to that of her husband; 3) the wife is to support her husband's career and its advancement; and 4) the woman is responsible for and performs the many and varied tasks of maintaining the household and homemaking. In our family, my career mattered as much if not more so, than my partner's, and we were both responsible for the work of household and childcare. Thirty years ago upon the birth of our second child in the first year of my PhD program my partner and I realized that, broke and exhausted as we were with two children, it was impossible for us to both continue in graduate school. My partner made the difficult decision to leave his program and work as contract faculty. I would be the one to finish graduate school and secure the tenure-track job needed for our family's financial stability. Significantly, this decision was determined not by gender but by our own particular circumstances. My partner, as a working-class person and committed more to activism and teaching had become disillusioned with academe, while I was the one keen and determined to have a university career. Traditional gendered scripts would, of course, have dictated otherwise. My partner—eight years older, much further along in his degree than I, and the man in the relationship—should have been the one to continue his career in academe, and I as a "good" woman should have accommodated him by giving up my own career to support his as a devoted wife.

Throughout the very long years of completing my PhD, securing a tenure-track position, and receiving tenure and later full professorship, our family life was organized around my career. When I had chapters to write for my dissertation or had my comprehensive exams to prepare for, he took the kids to his parents' cottage so I could write and study. When a grant deadline occurred the day after Halloween, he bought the candy, got the kids in their costumes, and took them trick or treating. When I was away countless times for a conference or research, he did the shopping and cooking, drove the kids to school and their activities. Although our budget was stretched, money was always found to pay for my education and career. And the many, many times I believed I was not good or smart enough to finish my PhD, get a particular grant, or write an article or book, he told me I was. Though my partner was also employed all those years as an overworked and underpaid adjunct professor, he put my career before his own. In other words, my partner performed what is expected and demanded of women in the normative wife role—to make their career secondary and to support their husband's. Even though our family was organized around my career rather than his, we mutually and equally supported each other in the work we did, both in and outside the home. Our relationship is anything but perfect, yet I do think that in partnership and in our commitment to gender equity and fluidity, we did challenge and change normative gender roles, particularly as they privilege men over women. As well, I believe that it was precisely the so-called unconventionality of our matrifocal partnership that made possible the peculiarity of my public achievement: achieving full professor at a research university at the relatively young age of fifty. And I did it as a first-generation university student, woman, feminist, motherhood scholar, "leftie," activist (or as I am often told, a "troublemaker"), mother of three (who had her children young and close together), and with (until recently) little money.

Most scholarship on academic motherhood contends that as women seek success in the masculine culture of academe, they are still restrained by their identification with normative understandings of good motherhood. I suggest that much of this tension and conflict comes more from the normative wife role than from the actual work of mothering. However, as a society, we are reluctant to acknowledge, let alone analyze how our intimate partnerships shape and influence the public lives we lead and the work we do. After all, we partner for love not for career success. A decade ago, I interviewed my two daughters for a book I was writing on feminist mothering. I share here a comment from my eldest daughter: "I never felt your life was inhibited ... you got what you wanted ... had three kids still and still managed to suck fun out of life.... [The belief] is that a woman is not allowed to be a mother and get a PhD ... and you always did it all. You have your cake and eat it too." If mothers hope to secure success in a career, they must be as attentive to the discriminatory gendered politics and patterns of love as well as work and they must demand true partnership in their relationships so that they, in my daughter's words "may have their cake and eat it too."

WORK CITED

Collins, Patricia Hill. "Shifting the Center: Race, Class, and Feminist Theorizing about Motherhood." *Mothering: Ideology, Experience, and Agency*, edited by Evelyn Nakano Glenn et al., Routledge, 1994, pp. 45-65.

Ladner, Joyce. *Tomorrow's Tomorrow*: Doubleday Press, 1971.

Johnson, Miriam. *Strong Mothers, Weak Wives: The Search for Gender Equality*. University of California Press, 1988.

Maushart, Susan. *Wifework: What Marriage Really Means for Women*. Bloomsbury Press, 2001.

O'Reilly, Andrea. "I Should Have Married Another Man: Heterosexual Partnerships and their Impact on Mothers' Success in Academe." *Academic Motherhood in a Post-Second Wave Context: Challenges, Strategies and Possibilities*, edited by D. Lynn O'Brien Hallstein and Andrea O'Reilly, Demeter Press, 2012, pp. 197-213.

12.
The Fantasy of Capitalism and Romance

Consuming the Self

MELINDA VANDENBELD GILES

IN A WORLD CURRENTLY governed by an ethos of immediacy, expansive options and throw-away culture, construction of "the self" has become the dominating principle of societal and economic functioning. In the article "Love in the Time of Layoffs," Lynn Stuart Parramore writes, "Capitalism gave our fantasy a blank check but it stole our reality." Indeed, I argue that not only has our time of extreme late capitalism promoted a fictitious capitalist world in terms of high finance (Jameson) but that this ephemeral ethos of speculation has also infiltrated beyond Wall Street and into our immediate daily lives and most intimate relationships. Although the romantic fantasy of the "happily ever after" can be traced back historically to modernization and the formation of the nuclear family, this fantasy was fundamentally about creating a dyadic relationship consistent with the needs of industrial capitalist society. Within this chapter, I explore an acceleration in which the extremes of individualism are coinciding with the extremes of neoliberal capitalism to produce a shift in conceptualizations of the "happily ever after."

I argue that this "happily ever after" is increasingly no longer a dyadic romance uniting two individuals but rather a singular romance of the self uniting to one's personal pursuit of happiness. The "other" becomes subsumed and irrelevant as an individual beyond providing the appropriate "fantasy." In other words, if we consider current rates of divorce and alternative marital unions (Gadoua and Larson), increasing singlehood (Traister; Watters), and an expansion of what it means to be intimate beyond monogamy and toward polyamory (Easton and Hardy), we are witnessing not a breakdown of traditional family values, but instead a fundamental shift in the capitalist modes of production creating a corresponding shift in interpersonal relationships and conceptualizations of family and romance.

Theorizing and identifying "love" as a biopolitical and material force has become increasingly prominent (Jónasdóttir and Ferguson 5). Rather than viewing love as something beyond the grasp of political economy, the burgeoning field of "love studies" acknowledges the material and affective dimensions of "love" within a global neoliberal landscape. Within this chapter, I wish to differentiate between what I am calling "singular" versus "communal" love. The fantasy of romantic love has been criticized by feminists as a product of industrial capitalism. The academic theorization of love becomes relegated either to the margins of "domesticity" or placed within a feminist paradigm of patriarchal oppression. Taking the study of love from the margins to the centre, I argue the acceleration of romantic love as an increasingly powerful ideological global force coinciding and colluding with neoliberal capitalism. However, I also wish to acknowledge and push for a greater recognition of "love" beyond this fantastical utopian and/or oppressive vision.

In *All about Love: New Visions,* bell hooks argues for the potential positive power of love as a transformative force (xix). Although it is essential to critique and analyze love within the political-economic structures of society, it is equally necessary to consider how love as a communal rather than singular force can provide potential in offering a powerful counterbalance to the extreme narcissism of late capitalism. How can we understand love beyond the narcissistic self-making project of modernity? How can an expansive vision of love that encompasses community, carework, empathy, and kindness be imagined and considered as an alternative paradigm to the acceleration of the individualistic neoliberal ethos? As Jónasdóttir and Ferguson write in *Love: A Question for Feminism in the Twenty-First Century*, "'love power' like 'labor power' is an alienable and exploitable human social force" (13). However, love "as a specific creative/productive power, can bring about changes and 'make history'" (14). In other words, critiquing singular love does not mean we have to critique the potential positive power of love altogether. By recognizing the fundamental difference between fantastical self-love masked as romance versus love grounded in connection with others, we can open the door to an invigorating and potentially liberating conversation regarding love as a transformative force for social change.

THE ADVENT OF THE "LOVE MARRIAGE"

In *Marriage, A History: How Love Conquered Marriage*, Stephanie Coontz traces the institution of marriage across time revealing the inaccuracy of a mythical past of "good marriages." However, she does write, "The current rearrangement of both married and single life is in fact without historical precedent" (2). Tracing our current conceptualizations of marriage and romance back to the industrial revolution, Coontz defines several historical precedents required for a shift from kin-based to love-based marriage in the Western world. Industrial production moved labour away from the household and into the public sphere creating wage labour divorced from kin obligation. Such a seismic shift in production methods coincided with enlightenment ideals of individual rights and social relations based on reason and justice rather than force (146). Thus a confluence of industrial capitalism and modernity produced what we now identify as the "love marriage." The nuclear family became the primary economic and social unit of society.

In *Modern Loves*, Jennifer Hirsch and Holly Wardlow discuss how "the organization of production and consumption enables or impedes various kinds of conjugal ties" (2). Rather than identifying "romance" as a Western creation, Hirsch and Wardlow link forms of production and consumption to social relationships, identifying which forms are most conducive for societal encouragement of love versus kin-based marriages. Kin-based marriage refers to identifying the institution of marriage as a political or economic alliance rather than an alliance based on the ideology of marital love and emotion. Hirsch and Wardlow write, "Around the world, young people are talking about the importance of affective bonds in creating marital ties, deliberately positioning themselves in contrast to their parents and grandparents" (1). Thus, capitalism and globalization shifted production methods worldwide from subsistence-based agrarian to industrial production effecting corresponding shift in social relationships and marital ideals. Kin obligation may still be a prominent aspect of marriage, but shifting production methods have enabled a global disassociation from familial bonds and toward ideals of individual autonomy. The degree to which these ideals are actualized in particular localities is dependent upon the specific modes of production, consumption, historical precedent, and cultural imperatives.

FROM INDUSTRY TO FINANCE

If we link production methods to marriage ideals, the shift from industrial production to financialization can be seen as an acceleration of existent conceptualizations of the self. Love marriage is intrinsically a self-making project through the concept of choice in partnership. The ascendancy of a finance ethos can be seen as a further extreme of this self-making process in which the physical form of the partner becomes irrelevant as the romantic fantasy is elevated. Instead of "romance" being conceptualized as a dyadic union between two individuals, it becomes a project of self-love masked as "romance." In such an extreme form of the romantic fantasy, the other half of the dyadic union could even be fictional as long as the illusion can be maintained enough to further the individual's self-love project.

In "Financialised Capitalism: Crisis and Financial Expropriation," Costas Lapavitsas describes financialization as the process whereby speculative investment moved from the zone of investment banks, corporations, and states to the everyday zone of personal income (115). Lapavitsas writes, "Financialisation ... has allowed the ethics, morality and mindset of finance to penetrate social and individual life" (116). The ascendancy of speculation as a mediating discourse governing not only economic but also social and political relationships has made assessment and categorization dominant. It is no longer about addressing current need but about speculating over what future needs may arise and how such needs can be identified. Therefore, the speculative process itself becomes prioritized and the "subjects" of speculation become the unfortunate yet "non-essential" by-products.

In other words, the idea of the "other" becomes prioritized over the actualization of the "other." As long as someone can believe they are in a romantic relationship, this is enough to fuel the self-making project. For instance, the popularity of online dating in which the individuals never meet in person or long-distance relationships in which partners are never actually together. It takes the emotional and physical demands of the relationship away and enables the romantic fantasy to continue undisturbed. Speculation is also about always predicting the future and keeping options open, which equally applies to romance. While in these fantasy relationships, another potentially better fantasy is only one click away.

MATERIAL TO EPHEMERAL: PRODUCTION OF GOODS TO PRODUCTION OF EMOTION

How did this movement toward prioritizing the ephemeral over the material become so hegemonic in terms of constructing and defining our current globalized era? To answer this question, we must first explore the neoliberal ethos. Here is where the Marxist paradigm becomes useful. In "Culture and Finance Capital," Fredric Jameson defines Marx's M-C-M (money-capital-money) formula as "the moment in which the focus of the operation is no longer on the *commodity* but on *money*, and in which its impulse now lies in the investment of money in commodity production, not for its own sake, but to increase the return of M, now M'" (my emphasis, 259). In *The Long Twentieth Century*, Giovanni Arrighi defines this capitalist process in terms of a historically contingent cycle in which epochs of material expansion and financial expansion together form two phases that constitute a full systemic cycle of accumulation. Emphasis is ultimately placed on the M and the accumulation of capital increasingly divorced from its productive base as the motivating factor producing crisis and capitalist reorganization (6).

In *The Condition of Postmodernity*, David Harvey consistently advocates the unsustainability of the "fictitious" capital realm, revealing the multiple ways in which the increasing focus on finance capital has resulted in massive polarization, loss of stability, and denigration of resources to a point where "crisis" is inevitable and the need for a completely new governing system has become paramount. There is consensus that "over the last quarter of a century something fundamental seems to have changed in the way in which capitalism works" (Arrighi 1). What has changed is the amplification of finance capital to a state of financialization.

If we consider the fundamental shift from prioritizing use value to almost exclusively prioritizing exchange value, and the manner in which changes in investment practices brought this concept of exchange value to the everyday level, we can begin to understand why such a reputedly irrational economic system such as neoliberalism could create such a hegemonic societal ethos. This is the point where neoliberalism and postmodernism converge. In *The Condition of Postmodernity*, Harvey discusses the shift from Fordism to flexible accumulation. Harvey describes the transition to flexible accumulation as "an entirely new regime of accumulation, coupled with a quite different system of political and social regulation" (145). Harvey's analysis connects the economic with the parallel developments in societal ethos. He associates the more flexible motion of capital with an increasing societal emphasis on the "fleeting, the ephemeral, the fugitive, and the contingent in modern life, rather than the more solid values implanted under Fordism" (171).

The collapse of time and spatial horizons, the embracing of the instantaneous, the deluge of media, film and advertising, the fragment providing the reality—all of these elements, once considered disorienting and disturbing in the modernist world, become elevated and embraced in the realm of the postmodern. The metanarrative is replaced by the fragmented slice-of-life moment. Just as arbitrary value becomes elevated through financial capital in the economic sphere, so, too, does the representation of reality become elevated above the reality it purports to represent in the social sphere. The economic and the social become intertwined and indistinguishable as they enhance and validate the ephemeral. In "Culture and Finance Capital," Jameson discusses how in the financialized ethos, content is suppressed in favour of form: "*the product becomes insignificant*, a mere marketing pretext" (my emphasis, 250). The goal of production is no longer to meet individual need or provide use value, but to produce increasingly greater exchange value. The purpose becomes the movement of goods towards a maximization of profit, not their use. To take this even further, production does not even need to occur and the goods do not even need to exist as long as verification of their movement can be provided to maintain the profit flow. The fantasy of capitalism can be maintained.

It is not difficult to take this convergence of the neoliberal and postmodern in terms of prioritizing the abstract and the speculative, and apply it directly to social relationships. Just as postmodernism prioritizes the representational, and neoliberal economics "fictitious" capital, so, too, does the neoliberal social ethos prioritize the speculative. What unifies these perspectives is a futuristic ethos, wherein the past becomes erased and the present is now defined in terms of the future. The speculative and the ephemeral become prioritized over the present reality. The capacity for future profits becomes the measure of success.

Just as Marx reveals the increasing disconnect of finance capital from its productive base, the material becomes irrelevant, whereas the ephemeral begins to produce its own self-referential and self-justifying paradigm. But this paradigm does inevitably have real effects on the material. In "Finance as Capital's Imagination: Reimagining Value in an Age of Fictitious Capital Crisis," Max Haiven effectively breaks down the segregation between representation and reality. He forces us to recognize how the arbitrary value of money divorced from its productive base, far from being "fictitious," is devastatingly real in its consequences. "Money's value is at once absolutely imaginary ... and terrifyingly material and utterly real in its social effects and its power over social values" (Haiven 10).

LIQUID LOVE

It is at this point where we can begin to directly connect shifting perspectives of the self and marital ideals with the shift from industry to finance. If we identify love marriage as a self-making project of modernity, then reconceptualizations of the "happily-ever-after" can be understood as a further amplification of the self. The primary difference is the amplification of the fantastical. The late modern self-making romantic project no longer requires a dyadic partnership—the illusion of romance is enough to be self-sustaining.

In *Liquid Love*, Zygmunt Bauman discusses the concept of liquid modernity. He identifies liquid modernity in terms of how transience has become a permanent state; there are no longer any rigid rules for determining social roles. Although this flexibility leads to far greater so-called choice, it also means individuals are constantly forced to create themselves. In other words, if no rigidly prescribed social roles exist, individuals must define for themselves what role they wish to take on, leading to the constant process of self-making in late modernity (147). It is a world in which globalization and individualism collude to separate power from politics and capital from production. "The liquid modern world ... abhors everything that is solid and durable, that is unfit for instant use" (29). In other words, if we apply this philosophy to social relationships, Bauman argues that we have moved toward elective affinity based on choice. Since choice is about the individual, should the relation no longer produce its value in terms of social and economic investment, one can choose to move on to more profitable kin networks. As Bauman writes, "It is unimportant which place you are in, who the people are around you and what you are doing in that place filled with those people.... There are always more connections to be used—and so it does not terribly matter how many of them might have proved frail and breakable.... Each connection may be short-lived, but their excess is indestructible" (Bauman 60). The process or idea of connecting become prioritized over actually connecting with another human being.

A key element of the liquid modern world is to have no bindings or dependency. Within a world lacking any reliable career track or stable job, demanding mobility and flexibility, mortgage payments become unsustainable as does having children. Envisioned as self-sufficient, sex is separated from reproduction (Giddens) and has become the fullest incarnation of freedom. Thus having children is constructed as a personal choice: "Having children means accepting such loyalty-dividing dependence for an indefinite time, entering an open-ended and irrevocable commitment with no 'until further notice' clause attached; the kind of obligation that goes against the grain of liquid modern life politics and which most people at most times zealously avoid in other manifestations of their lives" (Bauman 43).

Bauman goes on to discuss *homo consumens*, which is governed by a rationality of consumerism that is not so much about consuming goods but rather using and disposing of them to make room for more goods and their uses. Novelty, variety and speed become virtues. As a result, the by-products of overuse must be managed in global waste-management systems appearing in the forms of refugee camps and displaced populations (49). We can directly apply this concept of speed, efficiency and maximum short-term benefit to flexible relationships, hook-up culture (Heldman and Wade), Internet dating, and contract marriages in which new forms of sociality become as liquid as the world of finance and the throwaway products such maximization of profit engenders. Success is measured by the high turnover—the movement of products (or people) and the process—increasingly detached from the actual product or person. Humans become disposable by-products in the individual self-pursuit of happiness.

Bauman discusses how we always become suspicious of "living a lie" and feeling an obligation to our "authentic self" or potential of future happiness (55). Again, it is a futuristic ethos based on the fantasy of the future rather than the reality of the present. The potential of future relationships and future partners not yet met become prioritized over engagement with actual relationships. Such a self-referential and self-sustaining project of happiness is further endorsed within our narcissistic age by a psychological industry of therapists promoting "self-care," satisfaction, and less dependence on others and their demands for attention and care. The question one must always ask is "What is in it for me?" (Bauman 58). The greatest fallibility in this ethos of self-love is the danger of sacrificing oneself to another. Care for others is not rewarded but seen as weakness. And those who succeed in creating the greatest number of connections become rewarded with endless digital messages verifying their validity. The content and substance of the messages and the identity of the individuals sending them become irrelevant to the form and the execution of receiving and sending them. In other words, we have become a society of consumers and not producers. Value is given through endless consumption. But it is no longer even about consuming goods but consuming emotions. Goods have become part of the waste to be used and discarded as desired. But emotions have become coveted, and the most coveted emotion of all is love.

NARCISSISM AND THE SEARCH FOR SELF IN AN AGE OF LOVE

In *The Culture of Narcissism*, Christopher Lasch writes, "Economic man himself has given way to the psychological man of our times—the final product of bourgeois individualism. The new narcissist is haunted not by guilt but by anxiety. He seeks not to inflict his own certainties on others but to find a meaning in life" (22). Finding meaning and happiness become end goals in themselves, to which all other endeavours are subsumed. Obligation to family, duty, and loyalty become disenfranchised within an ethos of constant flux and obligation to self. The self becomes the only anchor in a sea of instability. Lasch writes about the explosion of therapy and how the need for meaning and love really mean the fulfillment of the patient's emotional requirements: "'Love' as self-sacrifice ... strike[s] the therapeutic sensibility as intolerably oppressive.... To liberate humanity from such outmoded ideas of love and duty has become the mission of the post-Freudian therapies..., for whom mental health means the overthrow of inhibitions and the immediate gratification of every impulse" (43). The ascension of emotion becomes legitimate in its own right. We live in a society where emotion can alter economic destiny. When stocks and bonds are based on the ephemerality of political allegiance and corporate trust, and a "fear index" is a measure of investment possibility and risk (Berezin 335), emotion becomes a powerful economic tool.

The centrality of love in this globalization process cannot be underestimated: "Love—and the practices of affective consumption that surround it—has become a strategy for affective mobility, and a very individually oriented technique for framing oneself as a modern subject" (Padilla et. al. xviii). The reconfiguration of labour and capital flows has produced a corresponding reevaluation of affective bonds. The movement away from kin obligation through industrialism has been advanced through financialization wherein the individual becomes paramount. And in an era governed by emotion, love has become one of the greatest assets. As Eva Illouz writes in *Consuming the Romantic Utopia*, "Romantic love has become an intimate, indispensable part of the democratic ideal of affluence that has accompanied the emergence of the mass market, thereby offering a collective utopia cutting across and transcending social divisions" (2).

In *Technologies of the Self*, Michel Foucault writes, "Technologies of the self ... permit individuals to effect by their own means or with the help of others a certain number of operations on their own bodies and souls, thoughts, conduct, and way of being, so as to transform themselves in order to attain a certain state of happiness, purity, wisdom, perfection, or immortality" (18). Although Foucault effectively reveals how these technologies of the self are not new, what is new in the neoliberal era is the degree to which these technologies of the self have become infiltrated within mainstream paradigms, colluding with the narcissistic elements of the marketplace. Individuals find themselves caught between the obligation to succeed and profit through maximizing self-interest in a competitive globalized space, and the continued desire for human connection. Such extreme individualism magnifies love as the last bastion of hope unsullied by market-driven forces and existing in a fantastical utopia beyond the boundaries of asset maximization. The drive for happiness then becomes the pursuit of love. And yet love, as an intrinsically narcissistic project, only amplifies the neoliberal ethos of self-interest rather than providing a utopian escape.

In *Liquid Love*, Bauman discusses the transition from Ford-Keynes era "community ghettos" to post-Fordist and post-Keynesian "hyperghettos." The primary difference is the movement away from "self-sustaining and self-reproducing social quasi-totalities ... designed to serve the complete inventory of the needs of communal life" and toward "truncated, artificial and blatantly incomplete groupings of people, aggregates but not communities; topographical condensations unable to survive on their own" (145). If we take this analysis and magnify it, one could argue the processes of globalization and neoliberalism have created a hyperghettoization of the world. The drive to become completely self-sustaining and self-sufficient leads to increased dependence. The more we believe in our infallibility, the more vulnerable we become.

Within the mantra of self-maximization, people find themselves searching for what's missing, turning to Buddhism (Gyatso), Yoga, positive affirmations (Hay), minimalistic living (Kondo), and/or mindfulness therapies (Hawn). Despite being constantly encouraged to look after our own self-interests, in the end, there is recognition that something meaningful is lost. But instead of looking to others, the focus becomes even more on turning inward toward the self with the popular slogan: "Learn to love yourself first before you can love others." Within this plethora of heightened self-love, all the more encouraged within our narcissistic age, is there any room for thinking about others?

Kin-based societies fundamentally acknowledge and subsist off human interdependency. In the move toward industrialization, the concept of the individual as separate from society became predominant, only becoming magnified through late capitalism. Yet the less we recognize and acknowledge the interdependency of humanity by isolating ourselves in segregated enclaves, the more desperate we become for human connection, which ironically makes us more rather than less dependent. We cannot exist in isolation. Acknowledging our dependency enables the bridging of connections, the building of community, and the embracing of love as communal rather than singular. It is only through interdependency that any sense of self can be truly achieved. The imperative to maximize self-interest leads to a disassociation from the self and thus loss of the capacity for human connection and community. This insatiable search for connection in turn leads to a greater prioritization of fantastical love as the antidote, only magnifying the pursuit of self-interest. Thus romantic love becomes one of the primary drivers of the globalized neoliberal economy.

It is important to distinguish communal from singular love. Communal love is a transformative force. It embodies strength, vision, empathy, and an understanding of the self as being enmeshed with others. Communal love and kindness can provide an alternative paradigm to neoliberalism. Singular love is fantastical and narcissistic, encompassing only the self and the desire for meeting individual need. Yet singular love has become a dominating economic force. In *Love and Globalization,* the editors discuss how love connects conceptually to work, family, and gender relations (Padilla et al. ix). Given our neoliberal context in which the domain of work and family have merged, the desire for love, far from being a domesticated emotion, is now at the heart of the neoliberal economy. Going beyond the selling of sex through mass media and sex tourism (Padilla 40-41), love itself is now the most prized commodity to be bought and sold. Whether directly through the "girl-friend experience" (Bernstein 192), transnational romances (Brennan 204), or "love games" (Cheng 226-227), the selling of love involves just as much an emotional investment as a physical one. Indeed, the very concept of romantic love has become enmeshed with modernity symbolizing "progress," affecting how intimate relationships are conceptualized across the globe. The very shift from kin-based to choice marriages is emblematic of this altering paradigm of love. From Mexico to Brazil and from Nigeria to Papua New Guinea, this love imperative is creating both emotional and economic change. As the editors write in *Modern Loves*, the shift toward the romantic love ideal, far from creating greater gender equality, often masks and exacerbates female subordination and derides other forms of relationality and kinship. For example, matrifocal families and communal forms of parenting become pathologized, as individuals believe the key to happiness and success is through the romantic partnership ideal (Hirsch and Wardlow 24).

In *Distant Love*, Ulrich Beck and Elisabeth Beck-Gernsheim write, "Today, at the beginning of the twenty-first century, the model of individualized love has become universal. Wherever it assumes a radical form, everything is related to 'me'—and that includes the 'us.' It is an 'us' that is one thing above all else, namely a space for self-presentation and self-dramatization.... the futility of the desire for a happiness that knows no bounds" (61). Love becomes the ultimate wasteland of justification for the extreme pursuit of self-interest. And in this fantastical world of boundless love, the eradication of the alterity of the "other" is almost complete. Yet the ephemeral "other" remains essential: "The primary concern is how the person with whom I am living, or whom I am marrying, enriches and glorifies me and succeeds in disclosing my self to me ... the decisive factor that identifies me for all the world to see is my choice of partner—for the time being" (62).

COMMUNAL LOVE

In Michael Hardt's "About Love" lecture, he discusses the potential for love as a political concept if we can move beyond the nuclear family or identitarian enclosure of love. An identitarian perspective of love only acknowledges love for those who are the "same" or who are the closest to you. He discusses the possibility for an open and a social concept of love that encompasses a love of difference and an ethics of alterity. Such an expansive and political view of love enables greater possibility and hope. However, the concept of communal love is not a utopian vision of global harmony to replace the romantic love utopia. Communal love as a political and revolutionary force must be grounded in the capacity and celebration of universalism while still acknowledging fundamental difference. Within a world segregated by increasing protectionism, division and exclusionary politics, an expansive conceptualization of love is needed. But this expansive view cannot obscure the very real and everyday material and affective consequences of structural inequalities. The specifics of identity, difference, and historicity are crucial but do not need to be divisionary. Any politics of love is also a personal politics of identity. The potential for love as a communal globalizing force countering the narcissistic neoliberal ethos can only exist if it is grounded within the daily realities of individual lives.

CONCLUSION

The current late modern era is one in which contradiction, flux, and instability have become normalized. Global precarity alongside transnationalism has produced immediate and local effects. Examining the direct connection between such globalized economic and political forces intersecting with shifting social conceptualizations has been the purpose of this chapter. Far from interpreting the "happily ever after" as a quaint romantic conceptualization no longer in vogue, I argue its increasing centrality in our current era of emotion, finance, and individualized self-gratification. In our age of narcissism, the romantic love and "happily ever after" ideal has become a utopian anchor in a time of isolation, anxiety, and disillusionment. Yet such an anchor is as ephemeral and unstable as a financialized world in which fear can bring down a global banking system.

What we are witnessing is a large-scale global shift away from kin-based obligation and toward individual desire. As an emotion, desire becomes a powerful marketing tool. The pursuing of love becomes paramount while the maintaining of human connection is lost. People become subsumed by their own self-referential ideologies, too busy constructing their own identities to be reflexive of who they are. Love requires the alterity of another human being. Alterity involves the recognition of the "other" as an individual rather than another object of consumption. As long as the fantasy of love predominates, the potentiality for deep human connection becomes lost. However, love does have the enormous potential to be transformative. It is precisely within the grounded and powerful politics of communal love where social change can happen.

WORKS CITED

Arrighi, Giovanni. *The Long Twentieth Century: Money, Power, and the Origins of Our Times*. Verso, 1994.

Bauman, Zygmunt. *Liquid Love: On the Frailty of Human Bonds*. Polity Press, 2003.

Beck, Ulrich, and Elisabeth Beck-Gernsheim. *Distant Love: Personal Life in the Global Age*. Polity Press, 2014.

Berezin, Mabel. "Exploring Emotions and the Economy: New Contributions from Sociological Theory." *Theory and Society*, vol. 38, no. 4, 2009, pp. 335-46.

Bernstein, Elizabeth. "Buying and Selling the Girlfriend Experience: The Social and Subjective Contours of Market Intimacy." *Love and Globalization: Transformations of Intimacy in the Contemporary World*, edited by Mark Padilla et al., Vanderbilt University Press, 2007, pp. 186-202.

Brennan, Denise. "Love Work in a Tourist Town: Dominican Sex

Workers Perform at Love." *Love and Globalization: Transformations of Intimacy in the Contemporary World*, edited by Mark Padilla, et al., Vanderbilt University Press, 2007, pp. 203-25.

Cheng, Sealing. "Romancing the Club: Love Dynamics between Filipina Entertainers and GIs in U.S. Military Camp Towns in South Korea." *Love and Globalization: Transformations of Intimacy in the Contemporary World*, edited by Mark Padilla et al., Vanderbilt University Press, 2007, pp. 226-51.

Coontz, Stephanie. *Marriage, A History: How Love Conquered Marriage*. Penguin Books, 2005.

Easton, Dossie, and Janet W. Hardy. *The Ethical Slut: A Practical Guide to Polyamory, Open Relationships and Other Adventures*. Celestial Arts, 2009.

Foucault, Michel. *Technologies of the Self: A Seminar with Michel Foucault*. Edited by Luther Martin et al. The University of Massachusetts Press, 1988.

Gadoua, Susan Pease, and Vicki Larson. *The New "I Do": Reshaping Marriage for Skeptics, Realists and Rebels*. Seal Press, 2014.

Giddens, Anthony. *The Transformation of Intimacy: Sexuality, Love and Eroticism in Modern Societies*. Polity Press, 1992.

Gyatso, Geshe Kelsang. *Understanding the Mind. The Nature and Power of the Mind*. Tharpa Publications, 2010.

Haiven, Max. "Finance as Capital's Imagination: Reimagining Value in an Age of Fictitious Capital Crisis." *Social Text 108* vol. 29, no. 3, 2011, pp. 93-124.

Hardt, Michael. "About Love." *The European Graduate School*, 2007, egs.edu/faculty/michael-hardt/lectures. Accessed 25 July 2016.

Harvey, David. *The Condition of Postmodernity: An Enquiry into the Origins of Cultural Change*. Blackwell Publishing, 1990.

Hawn, Goldie. *10 Mindful Minutes: Giving Our Children—and Ourselves—the Social and Emotional Skills to Reduce Stress and Anxiety for Healthier, Happier Lives*. Perigee, 2011.

Hay, Louise. *You Can Heal Your Life*. Hay House, 1984.

Heldman, Caroline, and Lisa Wade. "Hook-Up Culture: Setting a New Research Agenda." *Sexuality Research and Social Policy*, vol.7, no. 4, 2010, 323-33.

Hirsch, Jennifer, and Holly Wardlow, editors. *Modern Loves:*

The Anthropology of Romantic Courtship and Companionate Marriage. University of Michigan Press, 2006.

hooks, bell. *All about Love: New Visions*. William Morrow and Company, Inc., 2000.

Illouz, Eva. *Consuming the Romantic Utopia: Love and the Cultural Contradictions of Capitalism*. University of California Press, 1997.

Jameson, Fredric. "Culture and Finance Capital." *Critical Inquiry*, vol. 24, no. 2, 1997, pp. 246-65.

Jónasdóttir, Anna G. and Ann Ferguson. "Introduction." *Love: A Question for Feminism in the Twenty-First Century*, edited by Anna G. Jónasdóttir and Ann Ferguson, Routledge, 2014, pp. 1-10.

Kondo, Marie. *The Life-Changing Magic of Tidying Up: The Japanese Art of Decluttering and Organizing*. Ten Speed Press, 2014.

Lasch, Christopher. *The Culture of Narcissism: American Life in an Age of Diminishing Expectations*. W.W. Norton & Company, Inc., 1979.

Lapavitsas, Costas. "Financialised Capitalism: Crisis and Financial Expropriation." *Historical Materialism*, vol. 17 (2009): 114-48. Print.

Padilla, Mark, et al, editors. *Love and Globalization: Transformations of Intimacy in the Contemporary World*. Vanderbilt University Press, 2007.

Padilla, Mark. "Tourism and Tigueraje: The Structures of Love and Silence among Dominican Male Sex Workers." *Love and Globalization: Transformations of Intimacy in the Contemporary World*, edited by Mark Padilla et al., Vanderbilt University Press, 2007, pp. 38-69.

Parramore, Lynn Stuart. "Love in the Time of Layoffs." *Alternet*, 13 Feb. 2013, www.alternet.org/comments/sex-amp-relationships/love-time-layoffs. Accessed 23 July 2017.

Traister, Rebecca. *All the Single Ladies: Unmarried Women and the Rise of an Independent Nation*. Simon & Schuster, 2016.

Watters, Ethan. *Urban Tribes: Are Friends the New Family?* Bloomsbury Publishing, 2003.

Epilogue

Separateness and Connectedness in the Happily Ever After

LINDA ROSE ENNIS

As I GLANCE OUT of my window at the double helix mobile hanging outside, I realize it is like two hands clapping, apart and then clasped together. I understand, then, that the mobile, a DNA model, may be an external reflection of what essentially is going on internally—a mirror of the internal world played out in our experience of life as a balance of hopeful expectations and realistic outcomes in a state of interactiveness between separateness and connectedness. As Anthony Storr has said, "Two opposing drives operate throughout life: the drive for companionship, love and everything else which brings us close to our fellow men and the drive toward being independent, separate and autonomous" (Storr xi). Perhaps with the decrease of connectedness within the nuclear family as well as to the extended family, there is even more of an imbalance between the two states of separateness and connectedness.

If marriage is a milestone in our adult lives because it is an expected "right of passage," a developmental stage, there may be an interaction between states of independence and dependence that is being played out in this developmental crisis, as it is in other major events along the continuum of life (Ennis, *Intensive Mothering*, "Motherhood"). If this is so, there needs to be a balance between separateness and connectedness in the "happily ever after," and a recognition of the struggle between autonomy and connection. In our search for empowerment in marriage and cohabitation, this model, like two sides of a coin, may prove an effective place to start for the purpose of understanding the "happily ever after."

Both parties in a marriage want independence and connection, which is often quite different for each partner. Where there is imbalance, fantasy is implemented because idealization in marriage, the roots of the "perfect mother," is an attempt to balance the imbalance in marriage. Fantasy is a transitional space between separateness and connectedness, a place to work through inequity and a lack of equilibrium. In addition, the bridging of separateness and connectedness may entail parents transitioning into parenthood and bringing the uninvolved parent into an "equitable parenting arrangement," both in marriage and in divorce (Ennis, The Best Interests"). The split is clearly seen in the autonomy versus connection model of paternal involvement (Gerson), as it does in the traditionalist and modernist models of marriage. In the traditionalist model of marriage, there are two contradictory lines of thinking or narratives, which operate simultaneously. They are the optional caring parent along with the sole responsible caregiver, who is usually the mother. This occurs even though we strive to embrace "the full human complexity of each caregiving parent regardless of gender" (Frye 29). Although traditionalism in marriage may offer, for some, feelings of security, worthiness, and consistency and for others a sense of oppression, it also entails a less fluid definition of each party's roles.

The journey and ultimate goal in marriage involve moving from individualism towards cooperativeness, taking into account personal differences and changes in criteria over the lifespan. Just as every personality is different, so is the style of marriage. As Stephanie Coontz says, "The answers that men and women come up with vary from individual to individual, as do the consequences of the choices they make" (Coontz 301). In order to make these choices in a balanced marriage, it is critical to discuss expectations going into marriage to encourage realistic outcomes (O'Brien Hallstein, in volume).

The tension between separateness and connectedness is also apparent in the individualism versus collectivism that neoliberalism promotes. In a marriage, the individual, usually the mother, is left with all the responsibility of managing the family's needs with very little government support, especially in countries that do not offer maternity leave, social support, such as daycare, or socialized health care. As a result, intensive mothering becomes encouraged, whereby the needs of children become mostly the responsibility of mothers, despite the conflict between the need for mothers to both work and mother full time (Ennis, *Intensive*). In our attempt to more effectively integrate fathers into parenting, perhaps a definition of "intensive mothering" will expand to include "intensive parenting," which may affect marital success, hopefully because of a less patriarchal and more empowered form of mothering within marriage.

In closing, this volume has examined the issue of the "happily ever after" through three lenses: thoughts about marriage; living within marriage; and marriage: looking out and forward. In the first section, the first chapter looked at the conversations women need to have with their future parenting partners to resist adopting a neotraditional family formation, and to engage in empowered mothering. The next chapter analyzed commonly held stereotypes of lesbian relationships and questioned whether mainstreaming lesbianism, through the advent of marriage, only legitimizes the power dynamics that many lesbians have inherited from their socialization or whether they will challenge them. The third chapter deconstructed the framework of the "grandmother hypothesis" and outlined the importance of grandmothering to families. The final chapter of the section described the adult attachment theory and explained how both partners embark on marriage with their own attachment insecurities, which can then lead them to experience either conflict or harmony, disconnection or intimacy, despair or happiness.

The second section began with a chapter examining how heterosexual couples with children reproduce or challenge a gendered division of labour, revealing the diverse ways couples negotiate the division of labor and push toward a more egalitarian division of labour. The next chapter analyzed parenting relationships of Polish women, who maintain an intimate relationship with a female partner and together raise a child from a previous, heterosexual relationship. The following chapter explored how young mothers build various effective and creative family formation models, which was followed by a chapter examining how social media posts may affect both the spousal pair and those who read the posts. The section concluded with a chapter examining the problematic effects in-laws can have on a relationship.

The last section started with looking at the ways in which contractual sanctity and the pressure to enter into prenuptial agreements conflict with the lived reality of women's lives, followed by a chapter highlighting how matrifocal family structures allow for gender equity that make possible true partnerships between men and women in heterosexual relationships. And the final chapter of the section advocated for a movement away from fantastical and romantic conceptualization of love toward "communal love," which counters the individualistic narcissism of the neoliberal age.

Further work is needed in the following areas: analyzing how the nuclear and extended family can be constructively integrated into marriage; looking at how "intensive parenting" affects marriage; measuring the role of both financial security and love as contributing factors in choosing marriage; examining marriage throughout the lifespan; exploring cross-cultural differences in the definitions and approaches to marriage; comparing socioeconomic classes, cultures, and immigrants' experiences of marriage; and understanding better alternatives to marriage, such as nontransitory and permanent cohabitation.

In particular, I would like to see more qualitative research in this field, exploring why both parties enter into the decision of marriage, which will help us further understand their motivations for pursuing the relationship—whether it is for love, financial gain or maintaining one's financial status, a sense of security, or a sense of belonging and purpose. In addition, it would be important to better understand the emotional component of what the experience of marriage entails, such as the feelings of boredom that many describe. Certainly, the discomfort with talking about marriage was clearly observed in compiling this collection, and this needs to be more fully understood. Perhaps the uneasiness is reflective of the difficulty reconciling what we hear marriage is like with what we hope it will be.

The practical and theoretical implications of marriage need to be further addressed and bridged, whereby the needs of individuals, couples, and families have to be taken into account in a more holistic way. These needs may be met in the form of government policy changes, socialized childcare, change in gender ideology roles, and flexible work schedules (Ennis, *Intensive*). Although support systems move us beyond individualistic decisions, reliance on government support should not preclude the responsibility and cooperation of the couple and extended family. As always, there is the hope that there will be a respectful acknowledgment of couples' choices whether to marry and how they wish to achieve this goal. Many may choose a more traditionalist approach to marriage, and there needs to be an understanding as to why they choose to do so.

We may start thinking about the importance of a sense of co-operativeness (Coontz), moving from individualism towards co-operativeness, as well as reclaiming the extended family, not as a means to displace responsibility but to embrace parenting within the context of the family. This can be possible if we, potentially, apply Vygoysky's sociocultural theory of the "zone of proximal development" (qtd. in DeHart et al, 16), where one's current performance and potential performance can be bridged if given guidance by someone more skilled. This would entail moving from "intensive mothering" to "intensive parenting" through education and more paternal involvement, and where appropriate, a comfortable "transitioning into an equitable parenting arrangement," not necessarily an equal parenting one, as introduced above (Ennis, "The Best Interests"). Additionally, in applying the mindfulness philosophy, through attending to experiences in the moment, one may create a space where a new idea may grow, in this case, "intensive and equitable parenting." As Gerson has said, "to combine the traditional values of forging a lifelong commitment with the contemporary values of living a balanced life and creating a flexible, egalitarian partnership" (213) is the key to our understanding of marriage. Subsequently, respecting the individual, as well as the couple relationship, in an intricate balance may be the start of a successful "happily ever after."

WORKS CITED

Coontz, Stephanie. *Marriage, a History: How Love Conquered Marriage*. Penguin Books, 2006.

DeHart, G., et al. *Child Development: Its Nature and Course*. 4th ed. McGraw Hill, 2000.
Ennis, Linda Rose. *Intensive Mothering: The Cultural Contradictions of Modern Motherhood*. Demeter Press, 2014.
Ennis, Linda. Rose. "Motherhood and Employment". *Encyclopedia of Motherhood*, edited by Andrea O'Reilly, Sage, 2010, pp. 343-46.
Ennis, Linda Rose. "The Best Interests of the Child." Unpublished paper, 2016.
Frye, Joanne. "Parental Thinking." *Essential Breakthroughs*, edited by Fiona Green and Gary Pelletier, Demeter Press, 2015, pp. 14-31.
Gerson, Kathleen. *The Unfinished Revolution*. Oxford University Press, 2010.
Storr, Anthony. *Solitude*. Wm. Collins Sons, 1988.

About the Contributors

Lorin Basden Arnold is a family communication and gender scholar. Her recent scholarly work has primarily related to understandings and enactments of motherhood. She is a co-editor of the Demeter volume *Taking the Village Online: Mothers, Motherhood, and Social Media*. Her work has appeared in additional Demeter texts, including *Intensive Mothering: The Cultural Contradictions of Modern Motherhood* and *What's Cooking Mom? Narratives about Food and Family*. She is the provost and vice president for academic affairs at the State University of New York, New Paltz.

Sarah Bekaert, RN, MSc, is a children's nurse specializing in teenage health and a lecturer in child health at City University London, UK. Her research interests are the social contexts for teenage pregnancy decision making, intimate partner violence, and the experience of pregnancy loss on teenage fertility decisions. In her work, she also challenges deficit models of adolescence.

Audrey Brassard, PhD, completed her doctorate in clinical psychology at the Université du Québec à Trois-Rivières in 2006. She is a professor in the department of psychology at the Université de Sherbrooke, Québec, where she teaches couple therapy. Her research interests include romantic relationships, attachment, sexuality, and intimate partner violence.

Solveig Brown, PhD, is an anthropologist who has done extensive research on American mothers. She is the author of *All on One*

Plate: Cultural Expectations on American Mothers, and has contributed to the collections *Stay at Home Mothers: Dialogues and Debates*, and *Intensive Mothering: The Cultural Contradictions of Modern Motherhood.*

Alys Einion is a senior lecturer in midwifery, programme leader for the innovative HE certificate in maternity care, lifelong feminist, writer, blogger, mother, and midwife. Her research interests include midwifery education; feminism and reproduction; motherhood; lesbian and queer families; women's life writing and narratives; and narrative construction. She is also a novelist, an avid and unashamed bibliophile, and an advocate for LGBT+ rights within the workplace.

Linda Rose Ennis, PhD, is a psychoanalytic therapist in private practice, a family mediator, an author, a lecturer, and is affiliated with York University. She has a PhD in psychology and education. She has written extensively on the topic of motherhood and work, including "On Combining Motherhood with Employment," which was the first qualitative piece done in this area. She has, more recently, written contributions in the *Encyclopedia of Motherhood*, and has contributed a chapter to *Academic Motherhood in a Post-Second Wave Context* (Demeter Press 2012). Most recently, she has published her edited collection, *Intensive Mothering: The Cultural Contradictions of Modern* Motherhood (Demeter Press 2014).

Marie L. Gordon, Q.C., has been a family lawyer in Edmonton since 1980. She also teaches family law at the University of Alberta, Faculty of Law, and has written and presented papers for many years to a variety of audiences including the National Judicial Institute and the National Family Law Programme. Marie is currently the president of the Canadian Research Institute for Law and the Family, and is an active volunteer and board member with the Edmonton Community Legal Centre.

Lynn O'Brien Hallstein is an associate professor of rhetoric in the College of General Studies at Boston University. She is the author of *White Feminists and Contemporary Maternity: Purging Matrophobia*; *Bikini-Ready Moms: Celebrity Profiles, Motherhood, and the Body*. She is co-editor of *Academic Motherhood in a Post-Second Wave Context: Challenges, Strategies, and Possibilities*, and *Contemporary Maternity in an Era of Choice: Explorations into Discourses of Reproduction*, which won the Organization for the Study of Communication, Language, and Gender's 2011 Outstanding Book Award for an Edited Volume. She has been published in variety of feminist, communication, and motherhood journals.

Sue Johnson, EdD is the leading developer of emotionally focused therapy (or EFT). She is a professor emeritus of clinical psychology at the University of Ottawa, distinguished research professor in the Marital and Family Therapy Program at Alliant University in San Diego, director of the International Centre for Excellence in Emotionally Focused Therapy (ICEEFT), and director of the Ottawa Couple and Family Institute Inc. Sue is the author of *Love Sense: The Revolutionary New Science in Romantic Relationships*, and is also the author of the bestseller *Hold Me Tight: Seven Conversations for a Lifetime of Love*.

Małgorzata Kot is a PhD candidate in sociology in the Graduate School for Social Research of the Institute of Philosophy and Sociology at the Polish Academy of Sciences. Her PhD regards queer mothering and the process of becoming a mother in non-heteronormative women relationships in Poland.

Kristen M. Norwood, PhD, University of Iowa, serves as assistant professor of communication, Fontbonne University, in St. Louis, Missouri. Dr. Norwood's research examines how meaning is constructed for identities and relationships, particularly in stress, contradiction, or struggle. She writes primarily in the areas of interpersonal, family, and gendered communication as well as about research methods. She has published numerous research reports and overview essays. Her work has appeared in numerous national journalsm including the *Communication Monographs*, *Journal of Family Communication*, and *Human Relations* as well as in prestigious edited volumes, including the *Handbook of Family Communication* (Sage 2014) and *Transgender Communication Studies: Histories, Trends, and Trajectories* (Lexington 2015).

Andrea O'Reilly, PhD, is professor in the School of Gender, Sexuality and Women's Studies at York University. O'Reilly is founder and director of the Motherhood Initiative for Research and Community Involvement, founder and editor-in-chief of the Journal of the Motherhood Initiative, and founder and publisher of Demeter Press. She is the co-editor or editor of twenty books, including *Mothers, Mothering and Motherhood Across Cultural Differences: A Reader* (2014) and *Academic Motherhood in a Post Second Wave Context: Challenges, Strategies, Possibilities* (2012).O'Reilly is author of *Toni Morrison and Motherhood: A Politics of the Heart* (2004) and *Rocking the Cradle: Thoughts on Motherhood, Feminism, and the Possibility of Empowered Mothering* (2006), and *Matricentric Feminism: Theory, Activism, and Practice* (2016). She is editor of the first encyclopedia on motherhood, with three volumes and over seven hundred entries (2010). She is a recipient of the CAUT Sarah Shorten Award for outstanding achievements in the promotion of the advancement of women in Canadian universities and colleges. She is twice the recipient of York University's "Professor of the Year Award" for teaching excellence, and in 2014, she was the first inductee into the Museum of Motherhood Hall of Fame.

Tiffany Stokes has a bachelor of arts from Meredith College in Raleigh, North Carolina and a juris doctor from the University of Alberta Faculty of Law in Edmonton, Alberta. She is an associate at Gordon Zwaenepoel where she practices exclusively in the area of family law.

Melinda Vandenbeld Giles is a writer, editor, and lecturer in social anthropology and women's, gender, and sexuality studies, and a PhD candidate at the University of Toronto. She has an edited collection titled *Mothering in the Age of Neoliberalism* published by Demeter Press in 2014, and she is co-editing the Routledge *Companion to Motherhood* to be released in 2018. Her debut feminist fiction novel titled *Clara Awake* was published by Inanna in June 2017. Melinda's work also appears in many journals, including *JMI* (Journal of the Motherhood Initiative), *Development* (Journal of the Society for International Development), and several Demeter Press edited collections.

Lynne M. Webb, 1980, serves as professor in communication arts, Florida International University, Miami, Florida. She previously held tenured appointments at the Universities of Florida, Memphis, and most recently Arkansas where she was named a J. William Fulbright Master Researcher. Dr. Webb's research examines three objects of study: social media, family communication, and romantic communication. She has published three scholarly readers and over eighty essays, including multiple theories, research reports, pedagogical essays, and methods pieces. Her work has appeared in numerous national and international journals including the *Journal of Family Communication, Journal of Applied Communication, Health Communication, Computers in Human Behavior,* and the *International Journal of Social Research and Methodology* as well as in prestigious edited volumes including the *Handbook of Family Communication* (Sage, 2014) and *Handbook of Research on the Social Impact of Digital Media* (IGI Global, 2015).

Ann Reed Wilder is an assistant professor at Stephen F. Austin State University School of Social Work. She is the mother of two equally fabulous and uniquely talented children. Ann's ethnic heritage is Syrian-Lebanese, and growing up in a family where having strong ties between women was the cultural norm.